BLOOM

Olympiad ACE

A Comprehensive Practice Book

for School Olympiads & Talent Search Exams

REASONING

Class 8

by

Pallavi Sharma

Olympiad ACE

BLOOM

Bloom Cap Edu Ventures Pvt. Ltd.

Administrative & Production Office

'Ramchhaya' 4577/15, Agarwal Road, Darya Ganj, New Delhi -110002
Tele: 011- 47630600, 43518550

PRICE ₹125.00

Published by Arihant Publications (I) Ltd.

For further information about the books log on to
www.bloomcap.org

Follow us on

Preface

"Future belongs to those Who prepares for it today"

School Olympiads are National & International level competitions conducted by different Government, Non-Government & Educational Organisations with the purpose of making the children ready to face competitive exams.

The challenging Questions asked in Olympiads motivate them to learn more & more and bring out the best result with improved academic performance. The Awards & Scholarship offered by Olympiads motivate children to aspire & strive for doing better and emerge out to be the best.

Science Olympiads

Being a Scientist or Engineer or Doctor has always been a dream of each school going child. A good command over Science is a must for any of these. Questions of Science Olympiads are structured to help students to develop scientific temperament & motivate them to understand the concepts of science. They also focuses on improving existing knowledge of a student by adding more information.

'Bloom Science Olympiad Study Book Class 8' is a perfect resource to Study & Practice for Olympiad Exams and other National & State Level Talent Search Exams & Other Competitions.

Some Special Features of Bloom Science Olympiad Study Books are;

- Chapterwise Exercises having different types of Objective Questions; Analytical, Applications, Remembering etc, at par with the Olympiad Level.
- Detailed Explanation for each question.
- Olympiad Pattern Practice Sets at the end.

This book is prepared by Expert Panel with the utmost care, still if you have any suggestions regarding its improvement then feel free to contact us at support@bloomcap.org. We will try to inculcate your suggestions in the further editions.

Contents

Chapter 01

Analogy

"Analogy" means "Similarity of Pairs". When an element of a pair is related to the other element in a certain way and if the same relation exists between the elements of a other pair, then this is called Analogy.

There are following five types of Analogies.

1. Number based
2. Alphabet based
3. Word based
4. Mixed
5. Picture/Figure based

1. Number Based Analogy

In this type of Analogy, numbers in one pair possess certain relation which is also possessed by the numbers in other pair.

Example 1 Which number will come in place of question mark?

45 : 20 : : 51 : ?

(a) 22 (b) 27 (c) 23 (d) 19

Sol. *(a)* Here, the relation can be represented as

$$45 \div 3 + 5 = 15 + 5 - 20$$

In the same way,

$$51 \div 3 + 5 = 17 + 5 = 22$$

Hence, option (a) correct.

2. Alphabet Based Analogy

In this type of analogy, letters/alphabet in one pair possess certain relation which is also possessed by the letters/alphabet in the other pair.

Example 2 Choose the set of letters that best represents a similar relationship to the one expressed in original pair of letters' group.

PW : QX :: AF : ?

(a) BG (b) BC

(c) GH (d) FG

Sol. *(a)* Here, the relation can be represented as

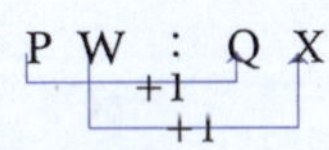

In the same way,

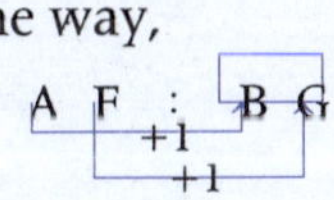

Hence, option (a) is correct.

3. Word Based Analogy

In this type of analogy words in one pair possess some relation which is also possessed by the words in the other pair.

Example 3 MOUNTAIN is related to VALLEY in the same way as ENEMY is related to

(a) CRUEL (b) FRIEND
(c) COUNTRY (d) STRANGER

Sol. *(b)* MOUNTAIN is the antonym of VALLEY. Similarly, FRIEND is the antonym of ENEMY.

Hence, option (b) is correct.

4. Mixed Analogy

In this type of analogy, the elements of the pairs can be the combination of alphabets and numbers which possess some relation which is also possessed by elements of the other pair.

Example 4 What will come at the place of '?'

D 5 F : G 25 I : : M 6 P : ?

(a) P 36 S
(b) S 36 P
(c) P 16 S
(d) Q 16 P

Sol. *(a)* As, in the first pair,

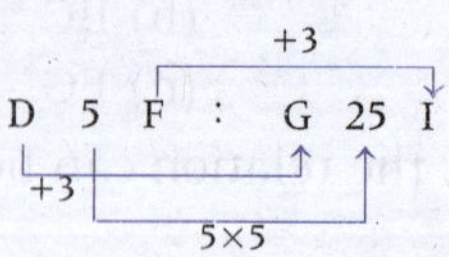

[∵ 5×5=25]

Similarly in the second pair,

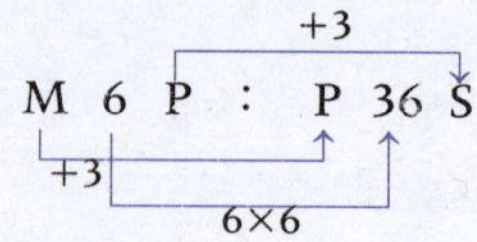

[∵ 6×6=36]

5. Picture/Figure Based Analogy

In this type of analogy a picture in one pair possess some relation which is also possessed by the pictures in the other pair.

Example 5 Identify the correct matching pair?

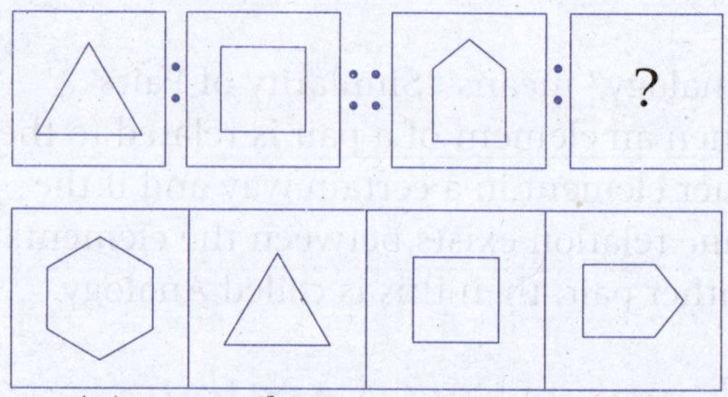

(a) (b) (c) (d)

Sol. *(a)* In the first pair, the first figure is a triangle with 3 sides and the second figure is a square with 4 sides, which means the side is increasing by one. Therefore in the second pair, the first figure has 5 sides so, the figure which will come at the place of '?' will be a hexagon with six sides.

Let's Practice

1 Mark Questions

Directions (Q. Nos. 1-5) Which number completes the second pair in the same way as the first pair?

1. 11 is to 12 as 15 is to '?'
(a) 20 (b) 16
(c) 19 (d) None of these

2. 13 is to 39 as 15 is to '?'
(a) 30 (b) 45
(c) 35 (d) None of these

3. 350 is to 175 as '?' is to 121
(a) 242 (b) 444
(c) 222 (d) None of these

4. 12 is to 18 as 20 is to '?'
(a) 25 (b) 30
(c) 40 (d) None of these

5. 14 : 30 : : 13 : '?'
(a) 28 (b) 30
(c) 26 (d) None of these

6. 600 is related to 575 in the same way 450 is related to
(a) 475 (b) 400
(c) 500 (d) 425

7. 5 is related to 24 in the same way 8 is related to
(a) 65 (b) 63 (c) 62 (d) 64

8. 65 is related to 13 in the same way 180 is related to
(a) 93 (b) 36 (c) 133 (d) 102

9. 11 is related to 101 in the same way 73 is related to
(a) 153 (b) 330
(c) 543 (d) 703

Directions (Q. Nos. 10-13) Choose the letters' group that completes the second pair in the same way as the first pair.

10. AP : BQ :: WM : ?
(a) WX (b) NX
(c) XN (d) NW

11. ADE : CFG :: PLK : ?
(a) RNM (b) RMN
(c) MRN (d) NRM

12. ADE : FIJ :: PQS : ?
(a) UVY (b) VUY (c) UVX (d) VUX

13. abc : bdf :: pqr : ?
(a) qst (b) qrt (c) qsu (d) psu

14. HIJK is related to FGHI in the same way ZYXW is related to
(a) XWVU (b) WVUT
(c) YXWU (d) MNOP

15. HIRO is related to JKTQ in the same way LJFP Is related to
(a) MKGQ (b) NLHR
(c) RHNL (d) OMIS

16. ODRS is related to OSRD in the same way PAGJ is related to
(a) PJGA (b) PJAG
(c) PGJA (d) PGAJ

17. NEEDLE is related to SEWING in the same way as SCISSORS is related to
(a) EATING (b) TAILORING
(c) CUTTING (d) SLICING

18. LINE is related to SQUARE in the same way as ARC is related to
(a) RING (b) BALL
(c) CIRCLE (d) SPHERE

19. DRAMA is related to DIRECTOR in the same way as MAGAZINE is related to
(a) SPONSOR (b) PLAYWRIGHT
(c) EDITOR (d) OWNER

20. TREE is related to FOREST in the same way as SOLDIER is related to
(a) BATTLE (b) ARMY
(c) GUN (d) GENERAL

Directions (Q. Nos. 21-23) In each of the following questions, a pair of related words followed by four pair of words (a), (b), (c) and (d) is given. Select a word pair that expresses a relationship which is most similar to the one expressed in the given pair.

21. Rain : Drizzle :: ____ : ____
(a) Swim : Dive (b) Juggle : Bounce
(c) Walk : Run (d) Run : Jog

22. Jaundice : Liver :: ____ : ____
(a) Imagination : Brain
(b) Rash : Skin
(c) Dialysis : Kidney
(d) Valentine : Heart

23. Writer : Pen :: ____ : ____
(a) Needle : Tailor
(b) Artist : Brush
(c) Paint : Painter
(d) Teacher : Class

Directions (Q. Nos. 24-26) Find what will come at the place of question mark in the following questions.

24. M 5 : : P 10 : : T 20 : ?
(a) W 40 (b) V 10
(c) W 30 (d) S 40

25. J 24 : G 12 : : L 18 : ?
(a) J 22 (b) I 20
(c) J 9 (d) I 9

26. H : 64 : : E : ?
(a) 8 (b) 36 (c) 25 (d) 16

Directions (Q. Nos. 27-30) There is a definite relationship between the pair given on the either side of : : . Identify the relationship between the pair and the missing figure.

27. **Problem Figures**

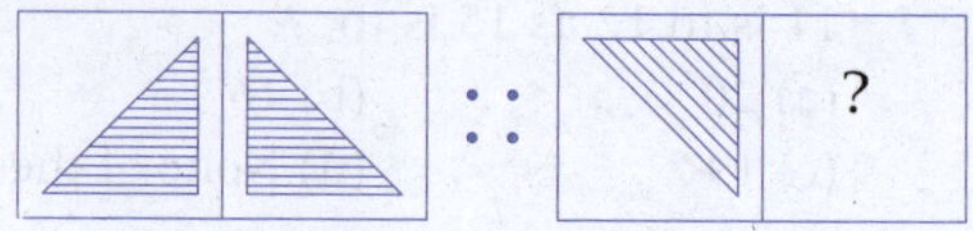

Answer Figures

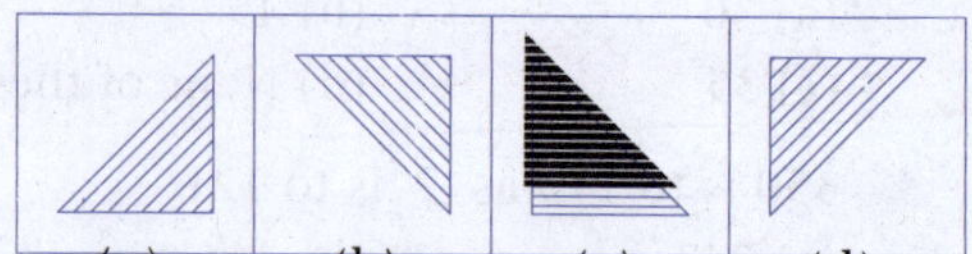

(a) (b) (c) (d)

28. **Problem Figures**

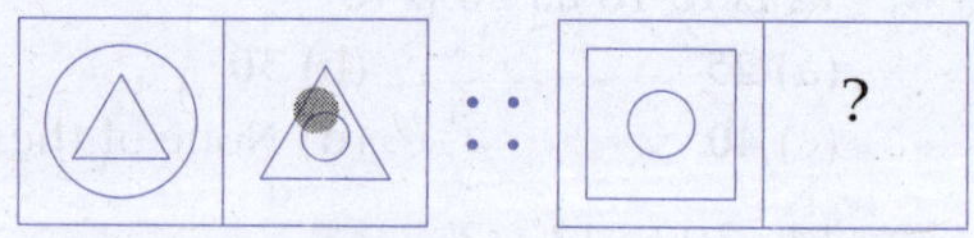

Answer Figures

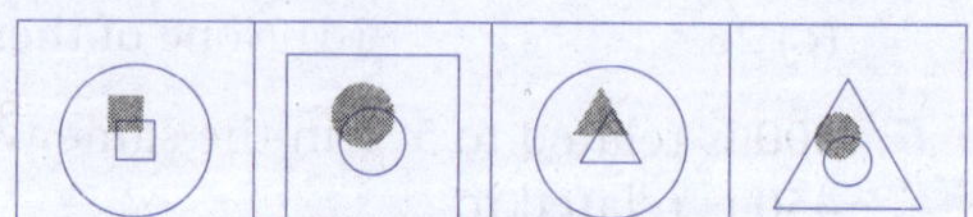

(a) (b) (c) (d)

29. **Problem Figures**

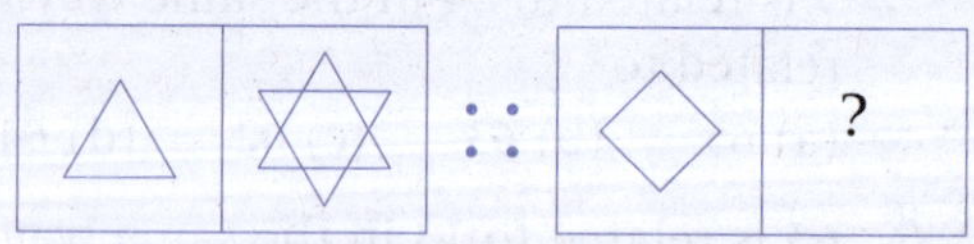

Answer Figures

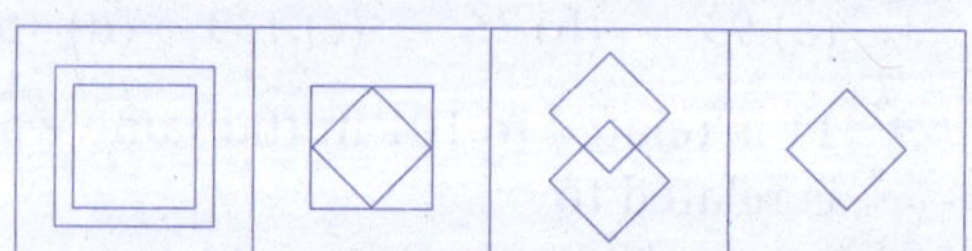

(a) (b) (c) (d)

30. **Problem Figures**

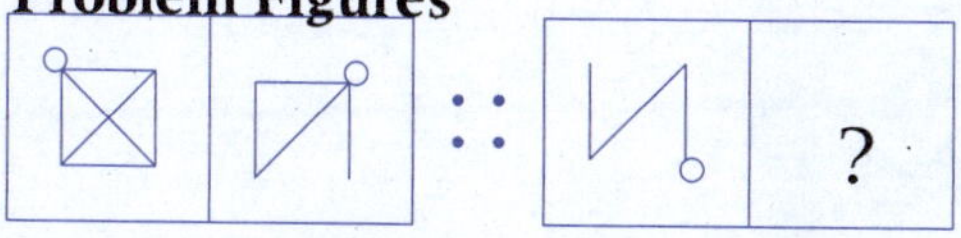

Answer Figures

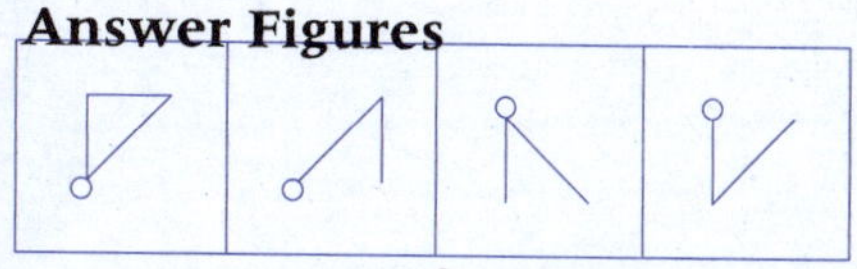

(a) (b) (c) (d)

2 Marks Questions

31. 16 : 30 :: 17 : '?'

(a) 30 (b) 34
(c) 32 (d) None of these

32. Choose the set of numbers which is similar to the given set.
Given set (6, 24, 96)

(a) (2, 6, 18) (b) (7, 28, 56)
(c) (5, 20, 30) (d) (2, 8, 32)

33. ABILITY is related to IBALYTI in the same way as SOLVING is related to

(a) GNIVLOS (b) GNIVSOL
(c) LOSVGNI (d) LOSVING

34. SODIUM is related to SALT in the same way as OXYGEN is related to

(a) HYDROGEN (b) CHEMISTRY
(c) SUGAR (d) WATER

35. GREAT : 25 : : NUMBER : ?

(a) 36 (b) 38
(c) 27 (d) 24

Directions (Q. Nos. 36-38) There is a definite relationship between the pair given on the either side of (: :). Identify the relationship between the pair and the missing figure.

36. **Problem Figures**

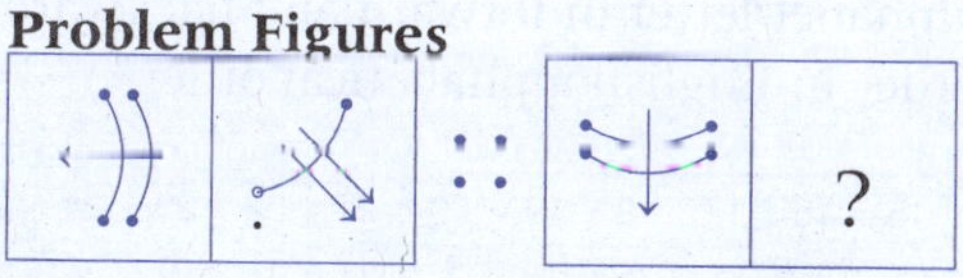

Answer Figures

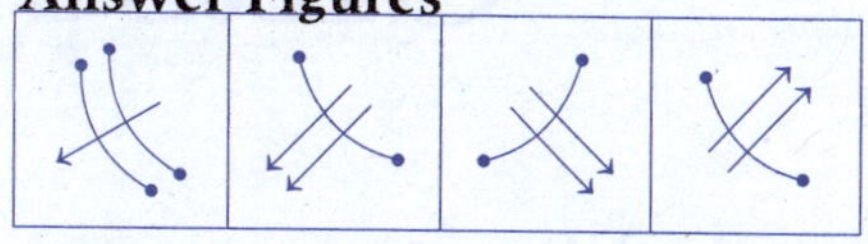

(a) (b) (c) (d)

37. **Problem Figures**

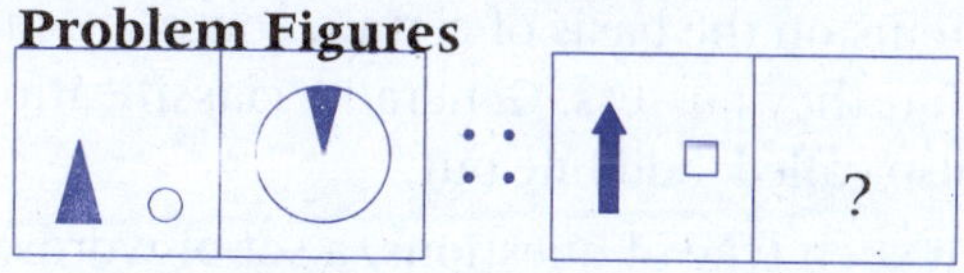

Answer Figures

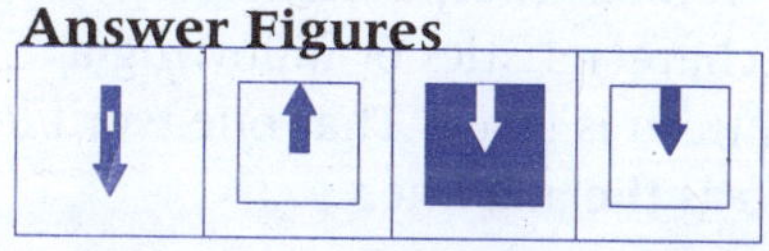

(a) (b) (c) (d)

38. **Problem Figures**

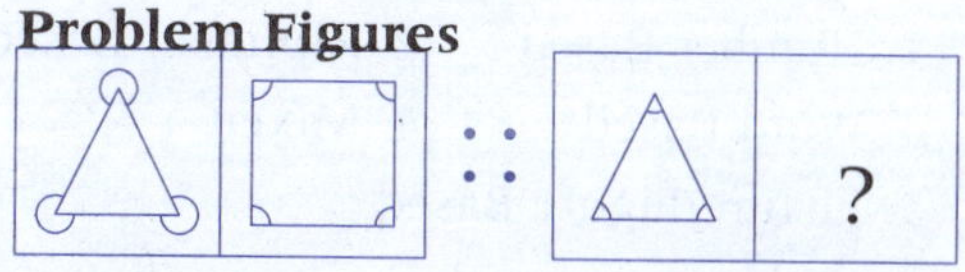

Answer Figures

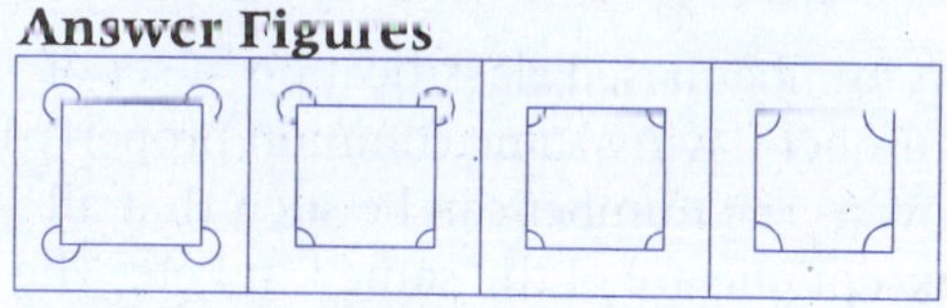

(a) (b) (c) (d)

39. AKU is related to AJS in the same way CRD is related to

(a) BQE (b) CQB
(c) DSB (d) APC

Chapter 02

Classification

Classification

Classification means to group the given items on the basis of certain common quality that they possess. Generally 'classification' is also called 'odd one out'.

In such type of questions, a set of words, letters or number except one having a common characteristics or following a certain pattern is given. That one word/letter or number is the add one.

Questions based on classification are of following five types

1. Number Based
2. Alphabet Based
3. Word Based
4. Mixed
5. Picture/Figure Based

1. Number Based Classification

In number based classification, a set of number having some common property is given. The number can be such that all except one are of the same kind etc. The number which is different from the rest of number is to be identified. This number is called odd number.

Example 1 Choose the pair of numbers which is different from others.

(a) (58, 42) (b) (94, 84)
(c) (63, 37) (d) (49, 51)

Sol. *(b)* Here, the sum of numbers in each pair equals to 100 but (94, 84) does not follow this pattern, as shown

$58+42=100, 94+84=178 \neq 100,$

$63+37=100$

and $49+51=100.$

So, $(94, 84)$ is odd one out.

Hence, option (b) is correct.

2. Alphabet based Classification

In alphabet/letter classification, a set of alphabet/letter (or alphabets'/letters groups) having some common property is given and the letter (or letters' group) which is different from the rest is to be identified. This letter or group of letters is called the odd letter (or letters' group).

The following table shows the position of alphabet/letter in forward and backward order in English alphabetical order.

Forward	1	2	3	4	5	6	7	8	9	10	11	12	13	14	15	16	17	18	19	20	21	22	23	24	25	26
Alphabet	A	B	C	D	E	F	G	H	I	J	K	L	M	N	O	P	Q	R	S	T	U	V	W	X	Y	Z
Backward	26	25	24	23	22	21	20	19	18	17	16	15	14	13	12	11	10	9	8	7	6	5	4	3	2	1

Example 2 Choose the group of letters which is different from others.

(a) JTR (b) HPN
(c) MZX (d) KVS

Sol. *(d)* The relation between the letters is shown as

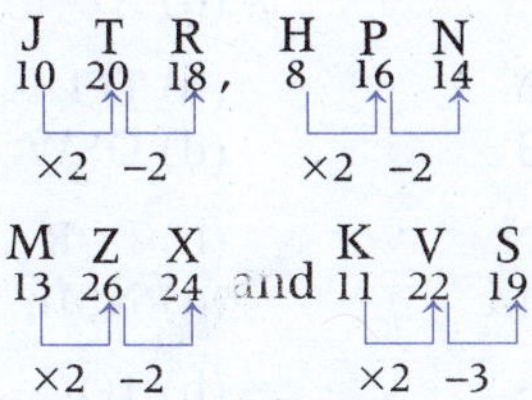

Here, we see that letters' groups JTR, HPN and MZX follow a similar pattern but letters' group KVS does not follow this pattern.

So, KVS is odd one out.

Hence, option (d) is correct.

3. Word Classification

In word classification, a set of words having a common property or meaning is given and the word having different property or different meaning from the rest is to be identified. This different word is the odd word.

In word classification, following types of questions are generally asked

Example 3 Choose the word which is different from others.

(a) Ring (b) Tyre (c) Plate (d) Bangle

Sol. *(c)* Ring, tyre and bangle have a hole but the plate does not have hole.

So, plate is odd one out.

Hence, option (c) is correct.

4. Mixed Classification

In mixed classification, a set of combination of letters and numbers having some common property is given and the combination which is different from the rest is to be identified. This different combination is called the odd term. In mixed classification, following types of questions are generally asked

Example 4 Choose the term which is different from the other

(a) OE3 (b) XD6 (c) JB5 (d) PH3

Sol. (d) Here putting the positional values of letters according to English alphabetical series, and solving the options, we have

$$OE3 \Rightarrow OE = O \div E = 15 \div 5 = 3$$

$$XD6 \Rightarrow XD = X \div D = 24 \div 4 = 6$$

$$JB5 \Rightarrow JB - J \div B = 10 \div 2 = 5$$

But $PH3 \Rightarrow PH = P \div H = 16 \div 8 = 2 \neq 3$

In PH3, the number should be 2 instead of 3 because $16 \div 8 = 2$,

Hence, PH3 is different from the others.

5. Picture Based Classification

In this type of classification a set of geometrical figures or pictures having a common property or features is given. One figure will have a different property from the rest. This figure will be the odd figure.

Example 5 Choose the figure which is different from the others.

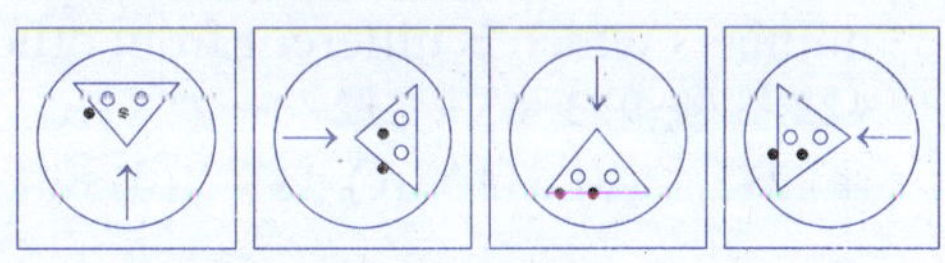

(a) (b) (c) (d)

Sol. *(d)* In all the figures the '• •' is at the corners of the triangles except in option (d).

So, option (d) is the odd one out.

Let's Practice

1 Mark Questions

Directions (Q. Nos. 1-8) Choose the number/pair of numbers.

1. (a) 4 (b) 20 (c) 25 (d) 40

2. (a) 7 (b) 21 (c) 27 (d) 35

3. (a) 15-45 (b) 12-72
(c) 13-169 (d) 11-90

4. (a) (24, 30) (b) (30, 44)
(c) (45, 53) (d) (34, 46)

5. (a) (4, 16, 64) (b) (3, 27 36)
(c) (5, 25, 53) (d) (7, 21, 35)

Directions (Q. Nos. 6-8) Find the number from the given sequence which does not belong to the sequence.

6.

1	9	25	36	81	121	169

(a) 1 (b) 25 (c) 81 (d) 36

7. 98, 108, 123, 148, 168
(a) 108 (b) 123
(c) 148 (d) 168

8. 5, 7, 9, 11, 13
(a) 7 (b) 9
(c) 11 (d) 13

9. Find the number from the given set of numbers which is different from others.
422, 824, 933, 633, 212
(a) 212 (b) 633 (c) 933 (d) 824

Directions (Q. Nos. 10-16) Choose the letter/group of letters which is different from others.

10. (a) OD (b) IK
(c) EA (d) UP

11. (a) LM (b) PQ
(c) RS (d) XZ

12. (a) NJF (b) TPL
(c) RNJ (d) OSW

13. (a) PON (b) PQR
(c) ONM (d) NML

14. (a) TOS (b) TOU
(c) DEF (d) NID

15. (a) DA (b) FC
(c) KU (d) ME

16. (a) QRWX (b) MNTU
(c) LMRS (d) CDIJ

Directions (Q. Nos. 17-21) Choose the word which is different from others.

17. (a) Swimming (b) Boating
(c) Driving (d) Diving

18. (a) Kilogram (b) Crores
(c) Thousands (d) Hundreds

19. (a) Rickshaw (b) Cart
(c) Cycle (d) Taxi

20. (a) Goal
(b) Red card
(c) Penalty shoot
(d) No ball

21. (a) Know
(b) Recognise
(c) Identify
(d) Unaware

Directions (Q. Nos. 22 and 23) Choose the term which is different from others.

22. (a) 13M (b) 9I
(c) 26Z (d) 19T

23. (a) 4H2 (b) 5J2 (c) 5N3 (d) 4P4

Directions (Q. Nos. 24-30) In the following questions, choose the odd figure.

24.

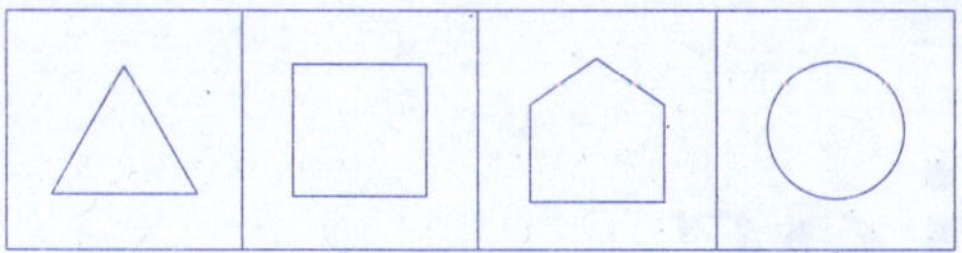

(a) (b) (c) (d)

25.

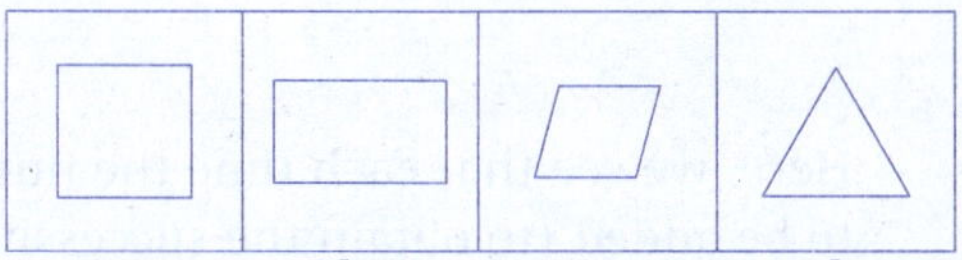

(a) (b) (c) (d)

26.

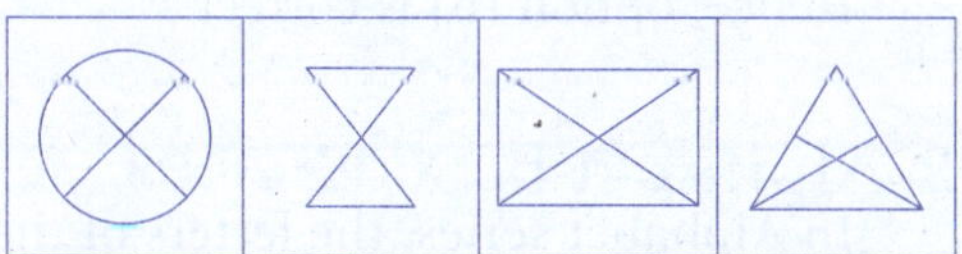

(a) (b) (c) (d)

27.

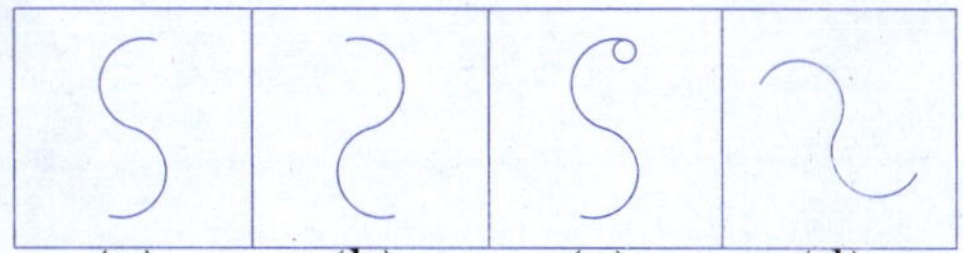

(a) (b) (c) (d)

28.

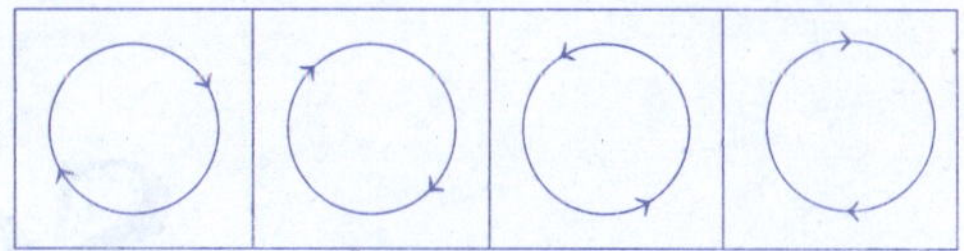

(a) (b) (c) (d)

29.

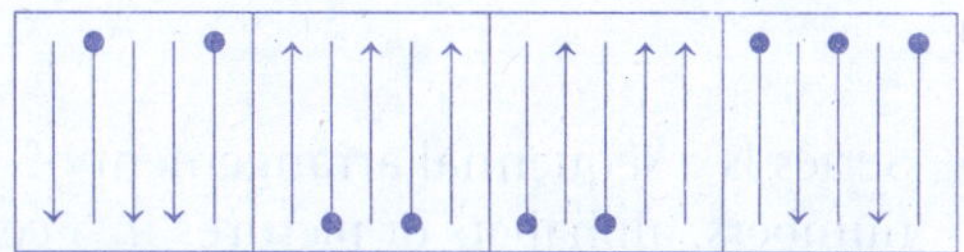

(a) (b) (c) (d)

30.

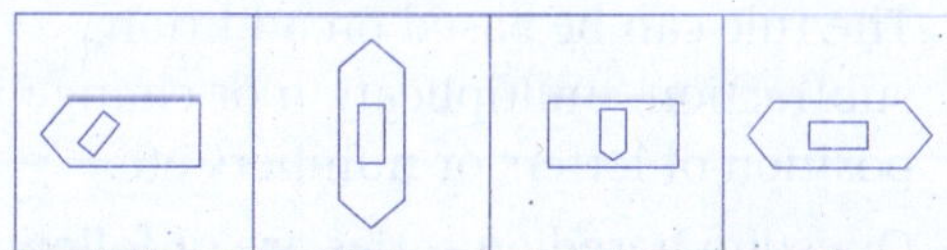

(a) (b) (c) (d)

2 Marks Questions

31. Choose the number which is different from others.

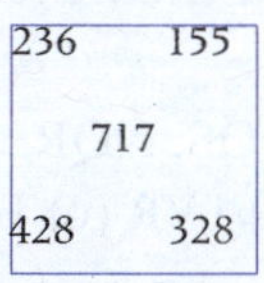

(a) 428 (b) 155 (c) 328 (d) 236

32. Choose the number which is different from others.

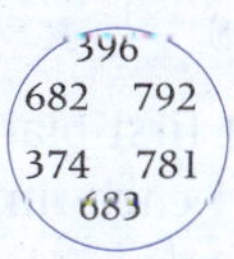

(a) 683 (b) 781 (c) 374 (d) 236

33. Find the number from the given set of numbers which is different from others.
(24-6), (48-12), (60-15), (100-20), (80-20)

(a) 48-12 (b) 60-15
(c) 100-20 (d) 80-20

34. Choose the term which is different from others.
(a) KQ14 (b) AY13 (c) MR11 (d) GW15

Directions (Q. Nos. 35 and 36) In the following questions, choose the odd figure.

35.

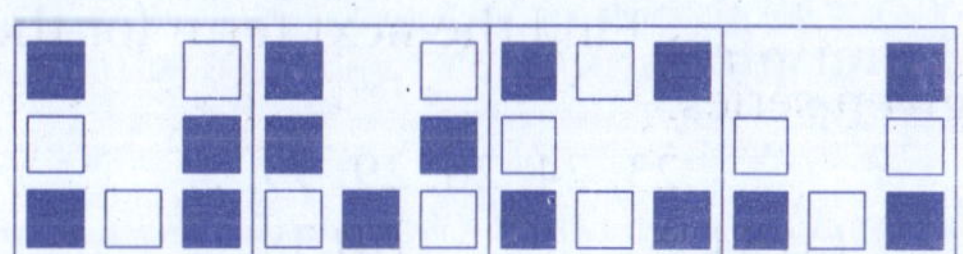

(a) (b) (c) (d)

36.

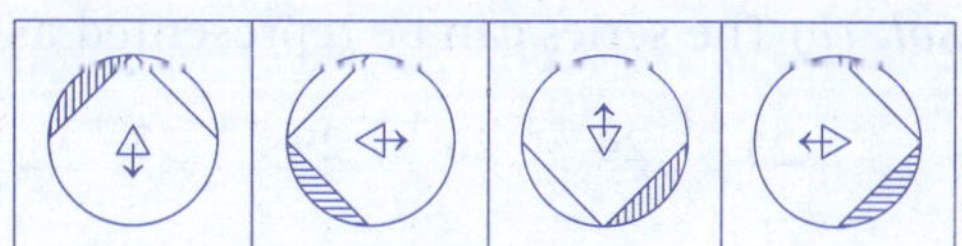

(a) (b) (c) (d)

Chapter
03

Series

- Series is a sequential arrangement of numbers, alphabets or pictures in a certain fixed rule.
- The rule can be based on addition, subtraction, multiplication or change in position of letters or numbers etc.
- Question based on series are of following types

  1. Number Based 2. Alphabet Based
  3. Mixed 4. Picture Based

1. Number Based Series

In number series, various numbers are arranged in an order by following certain mathematical rules based on addition, subtraction, division, multiplication or a combination of these, square root, cube root etc.

Example 1 Find the next term for the given series.

23, 24, 26, 29, 33, ?

(a) 34 (b) 38
(c) 39 (d) 37

Sol. *(b)* The series can be represented as

$$23 \xrightarrow{+1} 24 \xrightarrow{+2} 26 \xrightarrow{+3} 29 \xrightarrow{+4} 33 \xrightarrow{+5} \boxed{38}$$

Here, we see that each time the number to be added (to obtain the successive term) is increased by 1.

Hence, option (b) is correct.

2. Alphabet Based Series

In Alphabet series, the letters of the English alphabet are arranged in a certain order by following some rule based on their positions in the alphabetical series.

Example 2 Find the next term in the given series.

PMT, OOS, NQR, MSQ, ?

(a) LWP (b) LVR (c) LVP (d) LUP

Sol. *(d)* The series can be represented as

$$\begin{array}{l} P \xrightarrow{-1} O \xrightarrow{-1} N \xrightarrow{-1} M \xrightarrow{-1} L \\ M \xrightarrow{+2} O \xrightarrow{+2} Q \xrightarrow{+2} S \xrightarrow{+2} U \\ T \xrightarrow{-1} S \xrightarrow{-1} R \xrightarrow{-1} Q \xrightarrow{-1} P \end{array}$$

Here, letter at first place in each term is decreased by 1 each time, letter at second place in each term is increased by 2 each time and letter at third place is decreased by 1 each time to get the next term.

Hence, option (d) is correct.

3. Mixed Series

This series is based on the combination of both the letters and numbers.

Each term in the series follows a certain rule based on either the alphabetical position of the letters or the numbers in different correlation.

Example 3 Replace the question mark (?) in the following series with suitable option. C-3, E-5, G-7, I-9, ?, ?

(a) M-18, K-14
(b) K-11, M-13
(c) X-24, M-21
(d) O-15, X-24

Sol. (*b*) Pattern of the series is as shown below

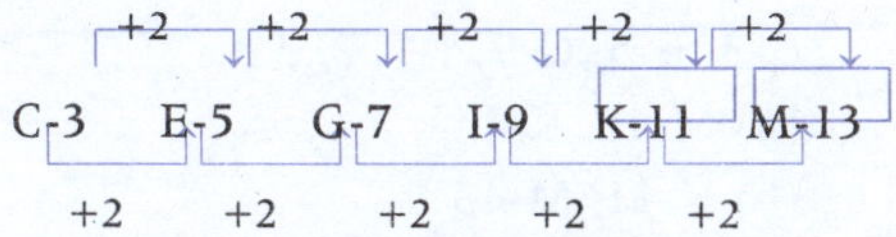

In this series, every letter is given its alphabetical position and one letter is skipped in between each term.

Hence, the missing terms are K-11 and M-13.

4. Picture Based Series

In picture based series a sequence of figures or shapes, following a certain pattern is given. The students are required to find out the next/missing term of the given sequence.

Example 4 What comes next in the series given below?

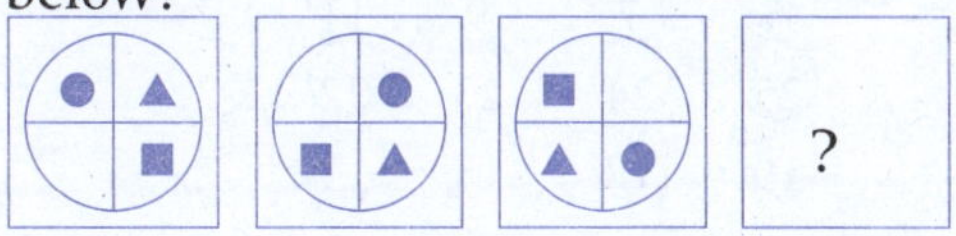

(1) (2) (3) (4)

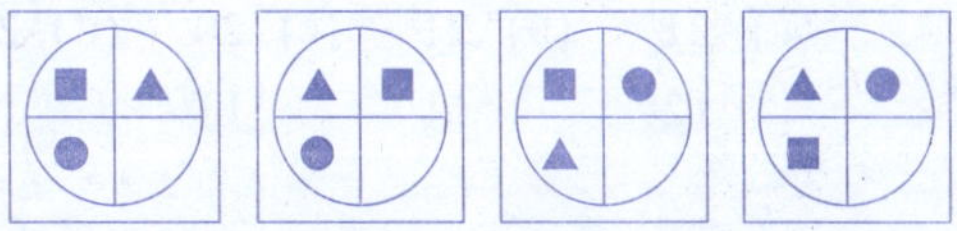

(a) (b) (c) (d)

Sol. (*b*) Here, the circle, triangle and square all are rotating in clockwise direction as shown

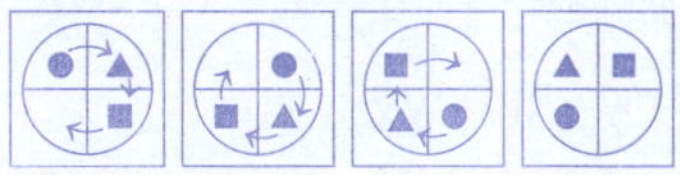

(1) (2) (3) (4)

The next term is similar to the figure given in option (b).

Hence, option (b) is correct.

Let's Practice

1 Mark Questions

Directions (Q. Nos. 1-6) Find the next/missing term(s) for the given series.

1. 4 , 7 , 10 , 13 , 16 , ?

(a) 15 (b) 16
(c) 17 (d) 19

2. 49 , 45 , 41 , 37 , 33 , ?

(a) 29 (b) 27 (c) 25 (d) 31

3. 567, 189, 63 , 21 , ?

(a) 7 (b) 15 (c) 3 (d) 1

4. (1), (2), (6), (24), ?, ?

(a) 120, 620 (b) 110, 620
(c) 120, 720 (d) 100, 700

5. (358), (467), ?, (685), (794)

(a) 585 (b) 576 (c) 575 (d) 565

6.

5	7	9	11	?
25	24	23	22	?
19	17	15	13	?

(a) 10, 21, 12 (b) 13, 21, 11 (c) 13, 20, 11 (d) 12, 20, 10

Directions (Q. Nos. 7-11) Find the next/missing term(s) for the given series.

7. PF RE TD VC ?

(a) XA (b) XB (c) WB (d) WA

8. (Pr), (Su), (Vx), (Ya), ?

(a) Bc (b) Bd (c) Ac (d) Ab

9. (BPL), (CQM), (DRN), (ESO), ?

(a) TTP (b) QBT (c) TFP (d) FTP

10.

J	K	M	P	?
Z	Y	X	W	?

(a) T/V (b) R/V (c) V/R (d) Q/X

11.

O	Q	S	U	?
J	I	H	G	?

(a) W/F (b) T/E (c) X/H (d) F/W

Directions (Q.Nos. 12 and 13) Find the next/missing term in the following series.

12. DKY, FJW, HIU, JHS, ?

(a) LFQ (b) LGQ (c) KGR (d) KFR

13. YVP, WTN, URL, ?

(a) VSP (b) SRJ
(c) SPJ (d) TQL

Directions (Q.Nos. 14 and 15) Find the next/missing term in the following series.

14. (C8W), (E11V), (G14U), (I17T), ?

(a) R 18 K (b) J 20 U
(c) K 20 S (d) K 20 R

15.

J	K	?	M	N
6	5	?	3	2

(a) L/4 (b) M/5 (c) P/5 (d) N/5

16. Replace the question mark (?) in the following series with suitable option.

C-3, E-5, G-7, I-9, ?, ?

(a) M-18, K-14
(b) K-11, M-13
(c) X-24, M-21
(d) O-15, X-24

Directions (Q. Nos. 17-21) Find the next term in the series given below.

17.

(1) (2) (3) (4) (5) (6)

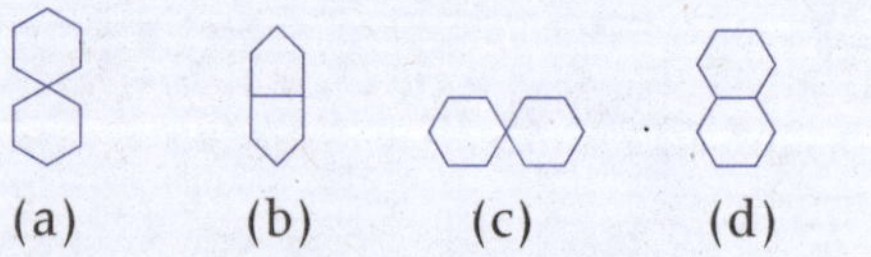

(a) (b) (c) (d)

18.

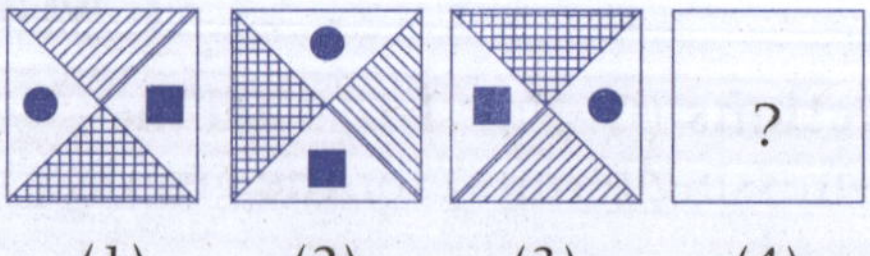

(1) (2) (3) (4)

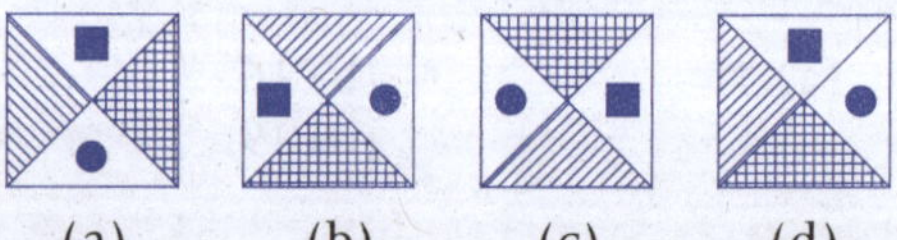

(a) (b) (c) (d)

19. 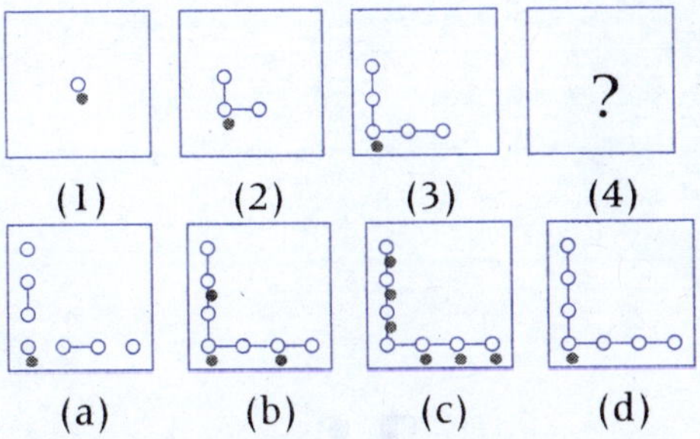

20. 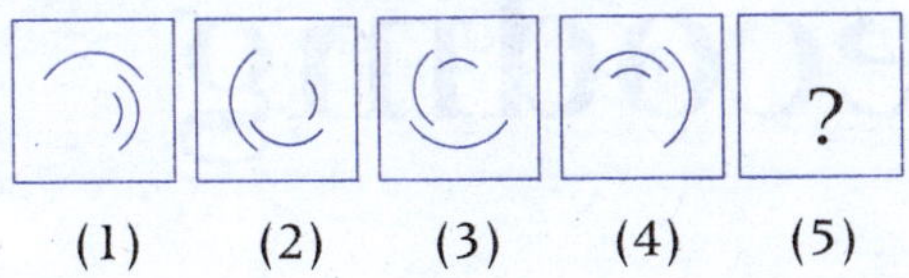

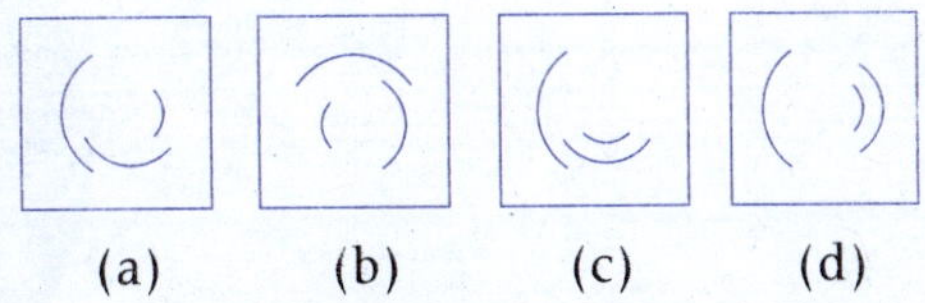

21. 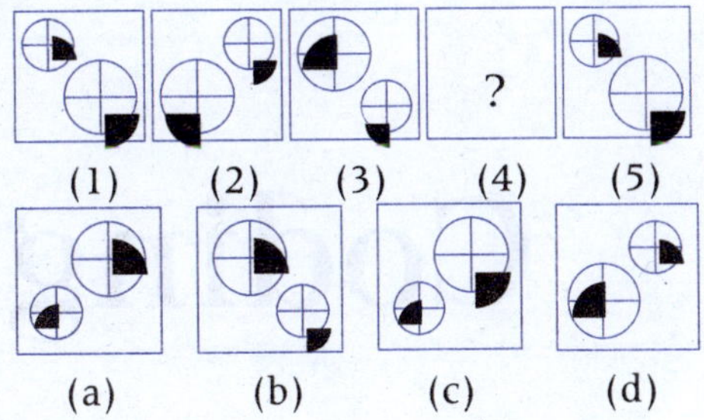

2 Marks Questions

Directions (Q. Nos. 22-27) Find the next/missing term(s) in the series given below.

22. 1, 2.25, 4.5, 7.75, ?

(a) 10 (b) 12
(c) 12.75 (d) 15

23. 216, 125, 64, 27, ?

(a) 16 (b) 1
(c) 4 (d) 8

24. 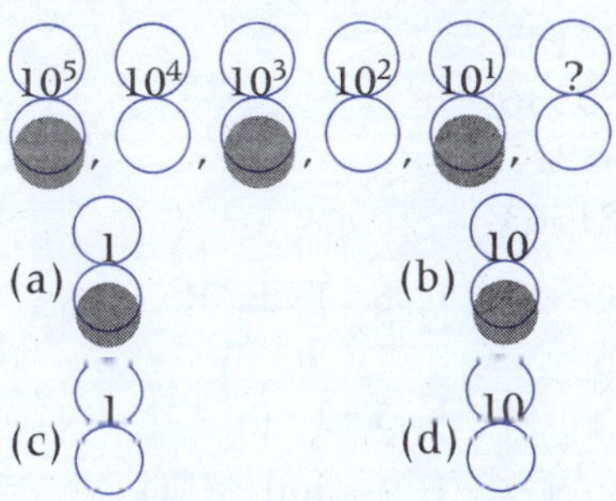

25. 12/77/3, 17/70/11, 22/63/19, 27/56/27, ?/?/?

(a) 32/49/35 (b) 30/50/34 (c) 32/50/30 (d) 29/49/35

26. YXW, UTSR, PONML, JIHGFE, ?

(a) CDEFGHI (b) CBAZYXW
(c) BAZYX (d) DCBAZYX

27. 15, Q, 10, L, 6, H, ?, E, 1,
C, O, B

(a) 3 (b) 1 (c) –1 (d) –2

Directions (Q.Nos. 28 and 29) Find the missing figure in the series given below.

28. 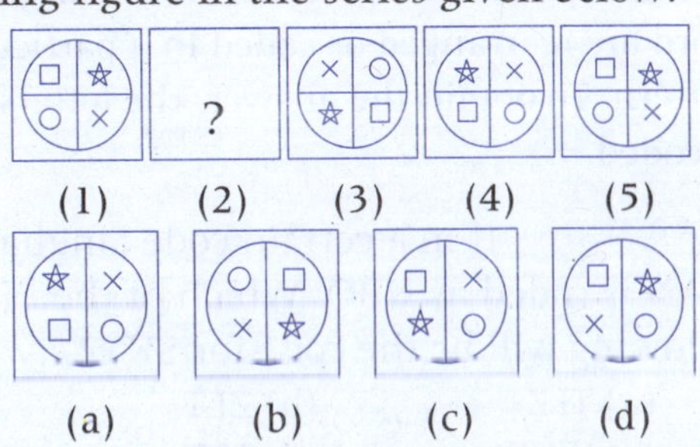

29. 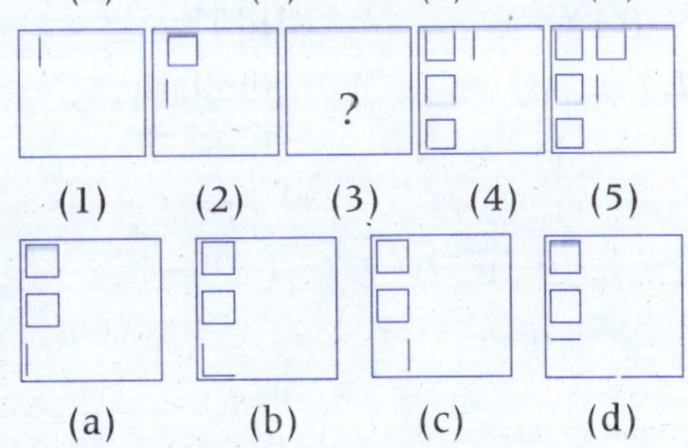

Chapter 04

Coding-Decoding

Coding means to hide the meaning of any message and decoding means to understand the actual meaning of that message.

In this topic, a word or sentence is coded in a particular way and the candidates are asked to code the other word or sentence in the same way or to decode the word or sentence.

Questions based on Coding-Decoding are of following/types

1. Letter Coding

In this type of coding, letters of the original word are rearranged or coded in a particular pattern. To obtain the answer, the letters are decoded.

Example 1 If in a certain code language MAN is coded as NBO. Which of the following will be the code for SKY?

(a) TLZ (b) ZLT

(c) YKS (d) LTZ

Sol. *(a)* As,

M A N → (+1 +1 +1) → N B O

Similarly,

S K Y → (+1 +1 +1) → T L Z

2. Number Coding

In this type of coding, the letters of a word are replaced by certain other letters or numbers according to a specific pattern/rule to form a code students are required to detect the coding pattern/rule and answer the question.

Example 2 In a given code, SISTER is coded as 535301. UNCLE as 84670 and BOY as 129. How is RUSTIC written in that code?

(a) 633185

(b) 185336

(c) 363815

(d) 581363

Sol. *(b)* As,

S I S T E R → 5 3 5 3 0 1

U N C L E → 8 4 6 7 0 and B O Y → 1 2 9

Therefore,

R U S T I C → 1 8 5 3 3 6

3. Symbol Coding

In symbol coding, various symbols are assigned to the letters of a word and based upon their correlation or similarity, the candidates are required to find the rules or pattern which is being followed and answer the question.

Example 3 In a certain code language 'GONE' is written as '5%2#' and 'MEDAL' is written as '4#3$@', then how will 'GOLD' be written in the code language ?

(a) 5@%3 (b) 5%@3
(c) 5#@3 (d) 5%#3

Sol. *(b)* As,

G O N E and M E D A L
5 % 2 # 4 # 3 $ @

Similarly, G O L D
5 % @ 3

∴ GOLD ⇒ 5%@3

4. Substitution Coding

In this type of coding, some particular words are coded with certain substituted word, and on the basis of the substituted word, the code of given word is derived.

Example 4 If 'white' is called 'blue', 'blue' is called 'red', 'red' is called 'yellow', 'yellow' is called 'green', 'green' is called 'black', 'black' is called 'violet' and 'violet' is called 'orange', then what would be the colour of human blood?

(a) Red (b) Green
(c) Yellow (d) Violet

Sol. *(c)* We know that, the colour of human blood is 'red' but here 'red' is called 'yellow'. So, the colour of human blood will be 'yellow'.

5. Sentence Coding

In this type of coding, some sentence are provided in the code language and some codes are assigned to each word of the message.

Example 5 In a certain code lauguage 'he is great' is written as 'ka pa ra' and 'is ram hungry' is written as 'na sa ka'. Find the code for 'is'.

(a) na (b) sa
(c) ka (d) ra

Sol. *(c)* he (is) great → (ka) pa ra
(is) ram hungry → na sa (ka)
Clearly, the code for 'is' is 'ka'.

6. Mixed Coding

In this type of coding, students deal with the coding related to letters, numbers and symbols or their combination.

Example 6 In a certain code, the following numbers are coded by assigning signs

1	2	3	4	5	6	7	8	9
<	+	=	@	↑	→	>	#	–

Which number can be decoded from the given symbols?

→ # > = <

(a) 63181 (b) 68731
(c) 62781 (d) 63118

Sol. *(b)* According to the given sign's table,

→ # > = <
6 8 7 3 1

Hence, option (b) is correct.

Let's Practice

1 Mark Questions

1. If in a certain code, TELEVISION is written as ANCNLBZBTD, then how will SEVEN be written in the same code?
(a) ZNLND (b) BNLNZ
(c) ZNLNT (d) BNLNT

2. If MISIRAL is the code for SIMILAR, then which word is coded as NIWDSWO?
(a) WILLOWS (b) WINDOWS
(c) WIDOWS (d) WONDERS

3. If RIDER is written as QHCDQ, then how will HONDA be written in that code?
(a) GMNCZ (b) GNMDY
(c) GNMCZ (d) GNMDZ

4. In a code A is denoted by C, B by D, C by E and so on till W, then PILATES is denoted in the same code by
(a) RKNCVGU (b) RJNBVGT
(c) RJNBVFU (d) RKNCWGU

5. If 'WATER' is written as 'YCVGT', then what is written as 'HKTG'?
(a) IRFJ (b) JMVI (c) REJI (d) JRIF

6. In a certain code, REASON is written as 621754 and TRUTH as 86983. Find out the codes for TREASON.
(a) 7548261 (b) 8621754
(c) 7452861 (d) 2865614

7. If in a certain code language 'RAMAN' is coded as '18113114', then how will 'KAPILA' be coded in that language?
(a) 11196112 (b) 111169112
(c) 111169121 (d) 116116121

8. If in a certain code language 'HIGH' is written as '8978', then how will 'DEAF' be written in that language?
(a) 5416 (b) 4516
(c) 4561 (d) 4156

9. If in a certain code language 'HACB' is written as '8132', then how will 'DEFA' be written in that language?
(a) 4651 (b) 4561 (c) 4156 (d) 5641

10. If in a certain code language 'STAR' is written as '5$*2', 'TORE' is written as '$ 3 2 @', then how will 'OATS' be written in that language?
(a) 3 * 5 $ (b) 3 * $ 5
(c) 3 $ * 5 (d) 3 5 * $

11. If in a certain code language 'ROPE' is written as '% 5 7 $', 'DOUBT' is written as '3 5 # 8 *' and 'LIVE' is written as '@ 2 4 $', then how will 'TROUBLE' be written in that language?
(a) * % 5 $ 8 @ $ (b) *%#58@$
(c) *%5#8@4 (d) *%5#8@$

12. In a certain code, 'BASKET' is written as '5$3%#1' and 'TRIED' is written as '14 * # 2'. How is 'SKIRT' written in that code?
(a) 3%*41 (b) 3*%41
(c) 3%#41 (d) 3#4%1

13. If in a certain language 'RAT' is written as '*Δ%', 'CAT' is written as '#Δ%' and 'FAT' is written as '$Δ%', then how will 'CAR' be written in that language?
(a) $%Δ (b) #%$
(c) #HΔ (d) #Δ*

14. If 'RED' is called 'GREEN', 'GREEN' is called 'YELLOW', 'YELLOW' is called 'VIOLET', 'VIOLET' is called 'BLUE', BLUE' is called 'ORANGE', then what is the colour of 'LADY FINGER'?
(a) GREEN (b) BLUE
(c) VIOLET (d) YELLOW

15. If 'DOG' is called 'COW',COW is called 'LION', 'LION' is called 'BUFFALO', 'BUFFALO' is called 'OX', 'OX' is called 'CAT', then which of the following animals is wild one?
(a) DOG (b) BUFFALO
(c) LION (d) OX

16. If 'CAR' is called 'BIKE, 'BIKE' is called 'BICYCLE', 'BICYCLE' is called 'SCOOTER', 'SCOOTER' is called 'TRAIN', 'TRAIN' is called 'AEROPLANE', then which one of the following options is associated with railways?
(a) BIKE (b) TRAIN
(c) AEROPLANE (d) SCOOTER

17. If in a certain code language 'Sachin is great' is written as 'ga ma ra', 'is he poor' is written as' 'ta sa ga', then find the code for 'is'?
(a) ta (b) ma
(c) ga (d) ra

18. If in a certain code language 'pick and choose' is written as 'ko ho po' and 'pick up and come' is written as 'to no ko po', then how will 'pick' be written in that language?
(a) ko
(b) po
(c) ko or po
(d) Cannot be determined

19. If in a certain code language 'open the door' is written as 'ka te jo', 'door is closed' is written as 'jo pa ma' and 'this is good' is written as 'la ra pa', then how will 'closed' be written in that language?
(a) ma (b) pa (c) ja (d) ka

20. If in a certain code language 'where are you' is written as 'pit ka ta' and 'are they there' is written as 'sa da ka' and 'they may come' is written as 'da na ja', then how will 'there' be written in that language?
(a) da (b) sa
(c) ka (d) Data inadequate

21. In a certain code language, the following alphabets are coded in a certain way given below.

Alphabet	Y	P	M	Q	O	R	N	S	K	E
Code	@	#	α	β	γ	Δ	θ	2	8	7

How is 'MONKEY' be written in that code language?
(a) α γ θ 8 7 @ (b) @ # β γ Δ
(c) θ Δ γ β α @ (d) 7 8 θ Δ γ β

22. In a certain code, the following alphabets are coded in a certain way by assigning numbers as follows.

A	D	I	L	M	N	O	R	W
1	2	3	4	5	6	7	8	9

Which word can be decoded from the following?
1 6 3 5 1 4 9 7 8 4 2
(a) Animal world
(b) Animal less world
(c) World of animals
(d) Animals world

2 Marks Questions

23. In a certain code, MINGLE is written as EIGNLM, then how will BRAZIL be written in the same code?

(a) LIZARB (b) LRAZIB
(c) LIAZRB (d) LRZAIB

24. In a certain code, 'CERTAIN' is coded as 'XVIGZRM', 'SEQUENCE' is coded as 'HVJFVMXV'. How would 'REQUIRED' be coded?

(a) FJIVWVIR (b) VJIFWTRV
(c) WVJRIFVI (d) IVJFRIVW

25. If in a certain language 'HEART' is written as '@8531', 'FEAST' us written as '#8541', then how will 'FARTHEST' be written in that language?

(a) @8543#18 (b) #5314@81
(c) #531@841 (d) 4531@845

26. In a certain code language, 'Sue Re Nik' means 'She is brave', 'Pi Sor Re Nik' means 'She is always smiling' and 'Sor Re Zhi' means 'Is always cheerful'. What is the code used for the word 'smiling'?

(a) Sor (b) Nik
(c) Re (d) Pi

27. If in a certain code language 'nik ma de' is written as 'he has come', 'de lit pa' is written as 'come here fast' and 'ma la se' is written as 'she has gone' then how will 'he' be written in that language?

(a) nik
(b) ma
(c) de
(d) Cannot be determined

28. Given below are capital letters in the first line and symbols in the second line, symbols and letters are codes for each other. Choose the correct code for the given letters.

<table>
<tr><td>A</td><td>C</td><td>E</td><td>G</td><td>H</td><td>I</td><td>O</td><td>N</td><td>P</td><td>R</td><td>T</td><td>S</td><td>B</td><td>D</td><td>M</td></tr>
<tr><td>+</td><td>−</td><td>÷</td><td>×</td><td>=</td><td>(</td><td>)</td><td>[</td><td>]</td><td>≠</td><td>||</td><td>#</td><td>|</td><td>></td><td><</td></tr>
</table>

BEAST

(a) |++≠| (b) | + × # |
(c) ÷ + # | | (d) | ++ ≠

29. If each of the letters in the English alphabet is assinged odd numerical value beginning A = 1, B = 3 and so on, what will be the total value of the letters of word DICE

(a) 33 (b) 35
(c) 38 (d) 41

30. In a certain code,, '786' means 'Study very nice', '958' 'nice work pays' and '645' means 'study and work' which of the following is the code for 'work'

(a) 8 (b) 5
(c) 9 (d) 4

Chapter 05

Alphabet and Number Sequence Test

Alphabet and number sequence test has questions based on letters of English alphabet and numbers. These questions are generally based on arrangement of alphabets or letters according to their position in English alphabetical series.

Sometimes questions are based on numbers, alphabets, symbols or their combination. There are following four types of questions asked from alphabet and number sequence test.

1. Alphabet Based Test
2. Number Based Test
3. Alphanumeric Based Test
4. Symbolic Sequence

1. Alphabet Based Test

These types of questions are based on letters of English alphabet. These questions require the understanding of the positions of letters in English alphabet.

1. Positional Values of letters in English alphabet.

Forward	1	2	3	4	5	6	7	8	9	10	11	12	13	14	15	16	17	18	19	20	21	22	23	24	25	26
Alphabet	A	B	C	D	E	F	G	H	I	J	K	L	M	N	O	P	Q	R	S	T	U	V	W	X	Y	Z
Backward	26	25	24	23	22	21	20	19	10	17	16	15	14	13	12	11	10	9	8	7	6	5	4	3	2	1

Example 1 If each vowel in the word 'GLADIOLUS' is substituted with the next letter of the English alphabetical series and each consonant is substituted with the letter preceding it. How many vowels are present in the new arrangement?

(a) None (b) One (c) Two (d) Three

Sol. *(a)* According to the question,

Given word G L A D I O L U S

↓ ↓ ↓ ↓ ↓ ↓ ↓ ↓ ↓

New word F K B C J P K V R

So, no vowel is present in the new arrangement.

Example 2 In the following letter series, how many times do PQR occur in such a way that Q is in the middle of P and R?

QMPNPQRROPQNOPPQRPMQROPQRPPR RPQRP

(a) 5 (b) 6
(c) 4 (d) 3

Sol. *(c)* Here, Q M P N P Q R R O P Q N O P P Q R P M Q R O P Q R P P R R P Q R P

So, in the above arrangement, PQR occur 4 times in such a way that Q is in the middle of P and R.

2. Number Based Test

These types of questions are generally based on arrangement of numbers, their sequence and their operations.

Example 3 The position of how many digits in the number 53269718 will remain unchanged. If the digits within the number are rearranged in ascending order?

(a) None (b) One (c) Two (d) three

Sol. *(b)* Let us see

The given number 5 3 2 6 9 7 1 8
Ascending order arrangement 1 2 3 5 6 7 8 9

So, position of only one digit i.e. 7 remains unchanged.

3. Alpha Numeric Based Test

In this type of questions, a jumbled sequence of some letters and numbers are given.

Example 4 How many letters are there in the given alpha-numeric sequence which are immediately preceded by an odd digit but not immediately followed by an odd digit?

A 2 B 7 C 5 D 4 E 4 F 9 G 2 H 1 I 8 J 3 K 6

(a) Two (b) Three
(c) One (d) Four

Sol. *(d)* The given sequence contains four such letters.

A 2 B 7 C 5 D 4 E 4 F 9 G 2 H 1 I 8 J 3 K 6

Hence, option (d) is correct.

4. Symbolic Sequence

In this type of questions a sequence of symbols or sequence of symbols along with letter and numbers are given.

Example 5 How many consonants are there in the given arrangement, which are preceded by a number and not followed by a letter?

F @ 3 9 H © A D I % 4 E ★ $ M K 2 U R P 5 W δ 8 1 T J V 7

(a) None (b) One
(c) Two (d) Three

Sol. *(c)* Here, F @ 3 9 H © A D I % 4 E ★ $ M K 2 U R P 5 W δ 8 1 T J V 7

In the given arrangement, 2 such consonants are there *viz.* 9 H © and 5 W δ which are preceded by a number and not followed by a letter.

Let's Practice

1 Mark Questions

1. Which letter is 8th to the right of 7th letter from the left in the English alphabet?
(a) Q (b) O
(c) R (d) S

2. If English alphabet is written in the backward order, then which letter is 7th to the right of K?
(a) A (b) B
(c) C (d) D

3. Which letter is between midway of 8th letter from left and 7th letter from right in the English alphabet?
(a) N (b) M (c) P (d) O

4. How many such letters are there in the word 'MONKEY' which remain the same in its position, if the letters are arranged in descending order alphabetically?
(a) None (b) One
(c) Two (d) Three

5. How many M's occur in the following series such that it is preceded by W and following by V?
X U V M R S T M W N V M W O P M W U V M W A C W M V H P N V W M W T U N
(a) 3 (b) 2
(c) 1 (d) 5

6. If the 1st half of the alphabets is written in the reverse order, which letter will be exactly middle between the 9th letter from the left and the 10th letter from the right end?
(a) B (b) A
(c) D (d) None of these

7. If in the word 'DISTURBANCE', the first letter is interchanged with the last letter, the second letter is interchanged with the tenth letter and so on, which letter would come after the letter 'T' in the newly formed word?
(a) I (b) N
(c) N (d) S

8. The position of how many digits in the number 8247531 will remain unchanged after the digits are rearranged in ascending order within the number?
(a) None (b) One
(c) Two (d) Three

9. The position of the first and fifth digits in the number 83146759 are interchanged. Similarly, the second and the sixth digits are interchanged and so on. Which of the following will be the third digit from the right end after the rearrangement?
(a) 3 (b) 1
(c) 6 (d) 2

10. How many 7's immediately preceded by 6 but not immediately followed by 4 are there in the following series?
7 4 2 7 6 4 3 6 7 5 3 5 7 8 4 3 7 6 7 2 4 0 6 7 4 3
(a) One (b) Two
(c) Four (d) Six

11. Which number has come maximum time in the following number series?
5 4 3 3 5 4 8 8 3 2 5 3 6 5 5
(a) 5 (b) 4
(c) 3 (d) 2

12. Which number comes least in the given series?

8 4 6 7 3 4 3 7 8 3 4 4 5 6 3 4 6 4 3 4 8

(a) 8 (b) 7
(c) 5 (d) 4

13. How many letters are there in the given alpha-numeric sequence which are immediately preceded by an even number and immediately succeeded by an odd number.

2 X 4 Y 3 A B D 7 F 2 M 9 Z

(a) Two (b) Three
(c) Five (d) One

14. How many numbers are there in the given alphanumeric series, which are immediately preceded by a consonant and immediately followed by a vowel.

X Y A 2 E P I 8 O P 7 U 9 E X E 5 O

(a) Two (b) One
(c) Three (d) None

15. In the following alpha numeric sequence, if all the vowels and even numbers are dropped (removed), then which element will be fourth from the left.

a 8 t e 4 3 i 9 2 r 0 6 q p u 7

(a) 9 (b) 7
(c) p (d) r

16. How many elements are there in the given sequence which are immediately preceded by a small case letter and immediately followed by an even digit?

$ A o 5 # 6 b C 1 d m 6 M $ d = 8

(a) 3 (b) 1
(c) 4 (d) 2

17. How many consonants are there in the below sequence which are immediately preceded by a symbol and immediately followed by a digit

E G 4 B H 7 5 @ K 8 D N £ Q Z $ W 3 C 1 9 * L B 2 S 6

(a) One (b) Two
(c) Three (d) None of these

Directions (Q. Nos. 18 and 19) Study the following arrangement carefully and answer the questions given below.

F 4 © J 2 E % M P 5 W 9 @ I Q R 6 U H 3 Z 7 * A T B 8 V # G $ Y D

18. How many such consonants are there in the above arrangement, each of which is immediately preceded by a number but not immediately followed by a number?

(a) None (b) One
(c) Two (d) Three

19. Which of the following is the 10th to the right of the 19th from the right end of the above arrangement?

(a) M (b) T
(c) # (d) 2

2 Marks Questions

20. If the first and second letters in the word 'COMMUNICATIONS' were interchanged, also the third and the fourth letters, the fifth and sixth letters, and so on. Which letter would be the tenth letter counting from your right?

(a) U (b) A
(c) T (d) N

21. If each consonant in the word 'TOLERANT' is replaced the previous letters in the English alphabet and each vowel in the word is replaced by the next letter in the English alphabet and a new set of letters is arranged alphabetically, which of the following will be the 4th from the right end after the replacement?

(a) M (b) P
(c) Q (d) K

22. In the number 3856490271, positions of the first and second digits are interchanged, positions of the third and fourth digits are interchanged and so on till the positions of 9th and 10th digits are interchanged, then which digit will be fifth from the left end?

(a) 6 (b) 4
(c) 9 (d) 0

Direction (Q. No. 23) Following questions are based on the five three-digit numbers given below.

528 739 846 492 375

23. Which of the following represents the sum of the first two digits of the highest number?

(a) 7 (b) 10 (c) 12 (d) 13

Directions (Q. Nos. 24 and 25) Study the following arrangement of combinations of English letters numerals and symbols carefully and answer the questions given below it.

8 C L M @ N £ T 2 Y 6 S £ Q $ 7 * W # Z 3 U E % A 4

24. If we dropped all the numbers and symbols then which of the following letter will be 7th from the left end?

(a) S (b) Q (c) W (d) A

25. How many symbols are there in the above series each of which is immediately preceded and also immediately followed by a vowel?

(a) One (b) Two
(c) Three (d) None of these

Chapter 06

Direction and Distance Sense Test

'Direction Sense Test' assesses a student's ability to determine the direction (and distance) when an object or a person moves from one place to another.

Directions can be classified as, primary directions and secondary directions. Primary directions include North, South, East and West and secondary directions include North-East, South-East, North-West and South-West, as shown in the figure below.

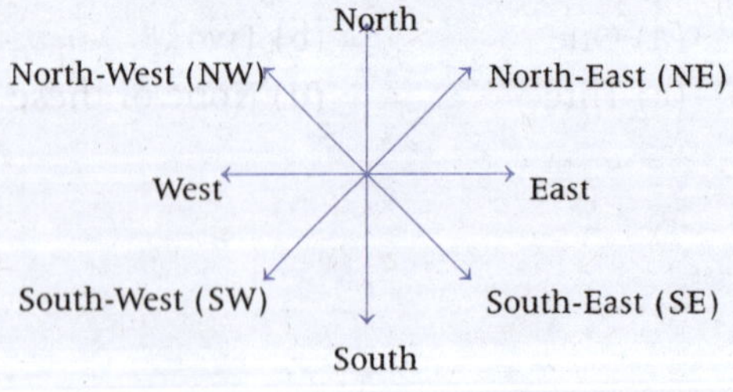

Questions based on direction and distance test are of following types

1. Statement based direction
2. Calculation of distance
3. Shadow based
4. Based on clockwise and anti-clockwise rotation

1. **Statement based direction** In this type of question, the path travelled by a person is given and the students are required to find out the final direction.

Example 1 Ram starts from his house facing towards East and moves 5 m, then he turns right and again moves 5 m. Towards which direction is he facing now?

(a) East (b) West
(c) North (d) South

Sol. *(d)* It is given that, Ram is facing towards East and moves 5 m.

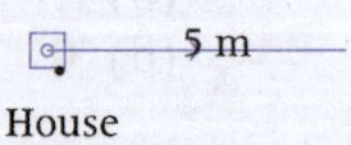

Now, he takes right turn and moves another 5 m. Then,

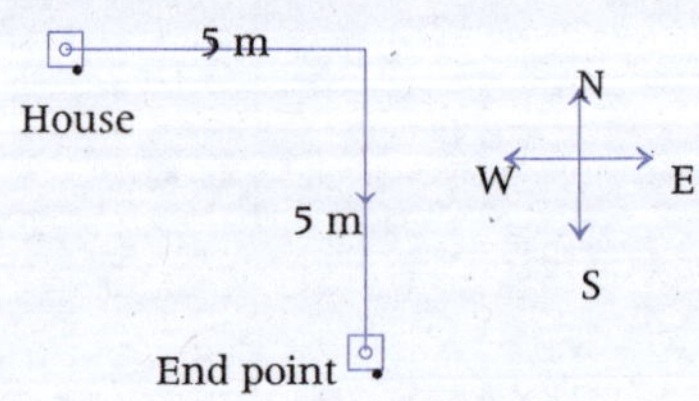

As seen above, Ram is facing towards the South direction.

Hence, option (d) is correct.

Example 2 If point Q is to the South-West of point P. Point R is to the East of point Q and also South-East of point P. Point S is to the North of point R in line with point QP, then in which direction of P is S located?

(a) North (b) South
(c) North-East (d) South-East

Sol. *(c)* According to the question

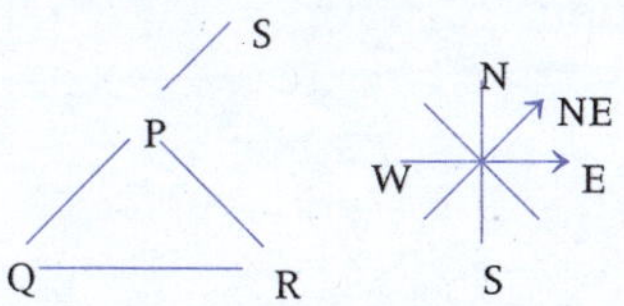

Clearly, point S is in North-East of point P.

Hence, option (c) is correct.

2. **Calculation of distance** In this type of questions, total distance travelled by a person from his starting point to end point is calculated. Sometimes students are also asked shortest distance between initial and final point.

Example 3 Shivam starts from point A towards North. After covering 20 km, he turns to his right and covers 10 km, then again he turns to his left and covers 10 km. Find the total distance covered by Shivam.

(a) 30 km (b) 40 km
(c) 50 km (d) 45 km

Sol. *(b)* According to the question,

Total distance covered by Shivam

$= AB + BC + CD$

$= 20 + 10 + 10 = 40$ km

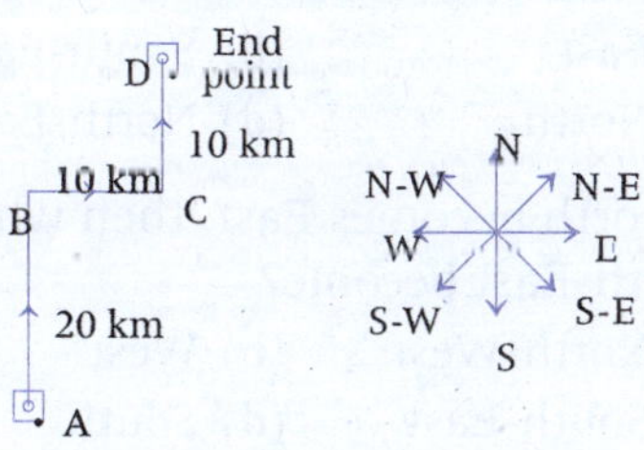

Hence, option (b) is correct.

3. **Shadow Based** These type of questions are based on formation of shadow during sunrise or sunset.

Shadows at the Time of Sunrise

In the morning, sun rises in the East, the shadow of any person or object falls in the West

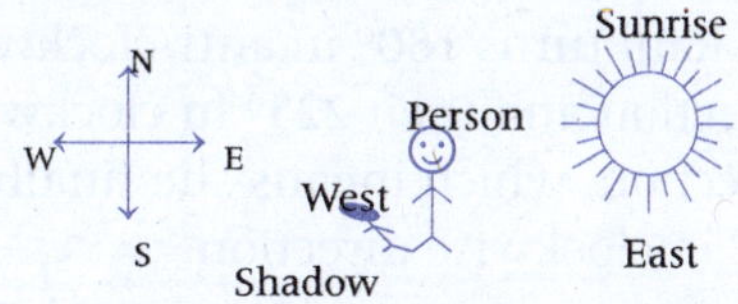

Shadow at the Time of Sunset

In the evening, when the sun sets in the West the shadow of a person or an object falls in the East

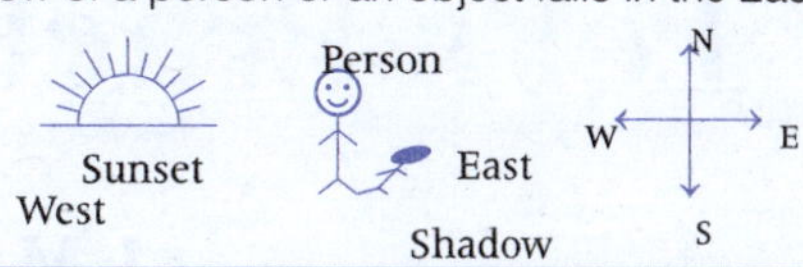

Example 4 At sunrise, Piyush and Gaurav are having a conversation standing in front of each other. The shadow of Gaurav is formed towards the right hand of Piyush. What direction is Gaurav facing?

(a) North
(b) East
(c) South
(d) North-East

Sol. *(a)* According to the direction,

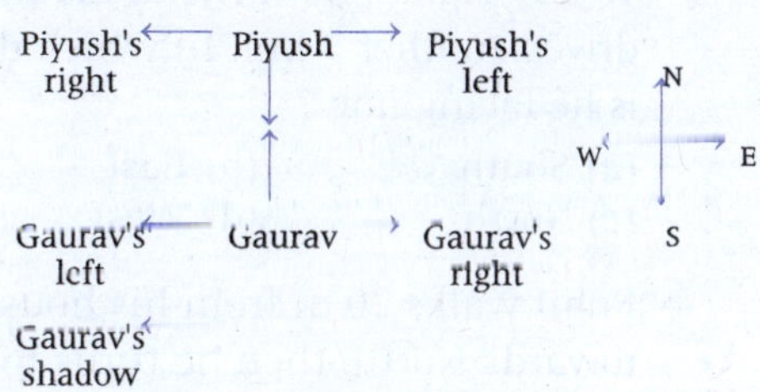

Clearly, Gaurav is facing North.

4. **Based on clockwise and anti-clockwise direction** In this type of questions, students are asked to find the final direction when, the person rotates by a certain angle in clockwise or in anti-clockwise direction.

Example 5 Rani is facing North. She turns 180° in anti-clockwise direction and then 225° in the clockwise direction. Which direction is she facing now?

(a) West (b) North-East

(c) South-East (d) East

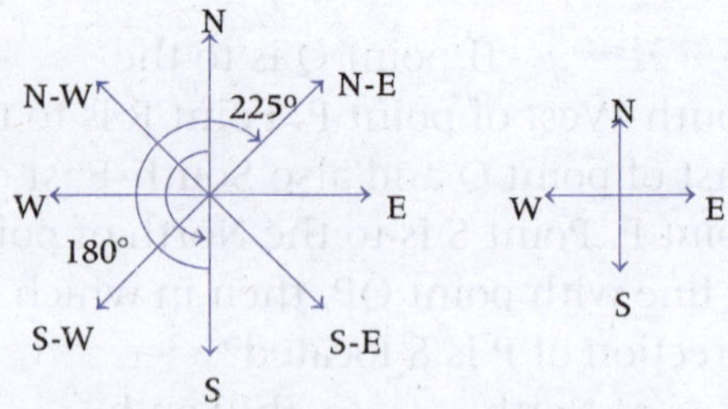

Sol. *(b)* Rani turns 180° in anti-clockwise direction and then 225° in clockwise direction, which means she finally turns 45° in clockwise direction.

Initially she was facing North. So, now she is facing North-East direction.

Let's Practice

1 Mark Questions

1. Raju after finishing his work in his office moves 500 m towards West and then turns to his right and walks 200 m. In which direction is he facing now?

(a) East (b) North

(c) South (d) North-West

2. A person drives 20 km towards South, he then turns to his left and moves 10 km. Again, he turns to his right and drives another 5 km. In which direction is he facing now?

(a) South (b) East

(c) North (d) West

3. Rohit walks 20 m from his house towards North, then he turns to his left and walks 15 m and again he turns to his left and walks another 20 m. In which direction is he now from his starting point?

(a) West (b) South

(c) North (d) East

4. If Mohit stands facing towards East, then his left hand is towards which direction?

(a) South (b) West

(c) North (d) South-East

5. Jitesh starts from his office and walks 25 m towards West, he then turns to his right and then walks 50 m and again he turns to his left and walks 30 m. In which direction is he now from his office?

(a) North-West (b) North-East

(c) South-West (d) West

6. Ramesh walks 15 m towards North, then he turns to his right and walks another 10 m and again turns to his left and walks 10 m. Now, in which direction is he from his starting point?

(a) East (b) South-East

(c) North (d) North-East

7. If North becomes East, then what will North-East become?

(a) North-West (b) West

(c) South-East (d) South

8. Rajesh starts from point A and moves 400 m towards East. He then turns towards North and walking for 300 m before finally turning towards South and walking 500 m. Find the total path covered by Rajesh.

(a) 1300 m (b) 1.2 km
(c) 1.5 km (d) 900 m

9. Shivam walks 50 m towards East, then takes a semi-circular path of 150 m length directing Southwards and then turns towards South and covers 50 m. Find the total distance travelled by Shivam.

(a) 150 m (b) 250 m
(c) 300 m (d) 200 m

10. A tourist drives 10 km towards East and turns to right hand and drives 3 km. Then, he drives towards West for 3 km. He then turns to his left and drives 2 km. Finally, he turns to his right and travels 7 km. How far is he from his starting point?

(a) 10 km (b) 5 km
(c) 8 km (d) 6 km

11. The given figure shows the map of interconnected cities.

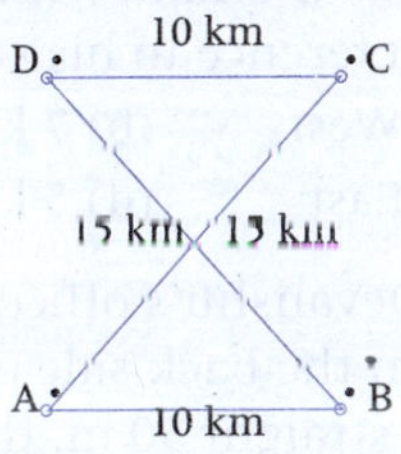

Calculate the distance travelled by Ramesh from A to B via D.

(a) 50 km
(b) 30 km
(c) 40 km
(d) 25 km

12. Sudiksha walked 12 m towards West, then turns to her right and walked 8 m and then turns to her left and walked 6 m. Finally she turns around and walked 12 m straight. What is the shortest distance between her starting point and the present position?

(a) 40 m (b) 30 m
(c) 20 m (d) 10 m

13. Rakesh walks towards his house at 8:00 am and observe his shadow to his right. In which direction is he walking?

(a) North (b) South
(c) East (d) West

14. One evening before sunset two friends Gaurav and Rahul were talking to each other face to face. If Rahul's shadow was exactly to his right side. Which direction was Gaurav facing?

(a) North (b) West
(c) South (d) None of these

15. One evening before sunset, two friends Tina and Aanchal were talking to each other face to face. If Tina's shadow was exactly to her left side, which direction was Aanchal facing?

(a) West (b) East (c) North (d) South

16. Reena is facing North-West. She turns in clockwise direction by 90°, then 180° in the anti-clockwise direction and then another 90° in the same direction. Which direction is facing she now?

(a) South West (b) West
(c) South (d) South-East

17. Raj kumar is facing South. He turns 135° anti-clockwise direction and then 180° clockwise. Which direction he is facing now?

(a) North-East (b) West
(c) South-East (d) South-West

18. Aditya is facing West. He turns 45° in the clockwise direction and then another 180° in the same direction and then 270° in the anti-clockwise direction. Which direction is he facing now?
(a) South (b) North-West
(c) West (d) South-West

19. A man is facing North-West. He turns 90° in the clockwise direction and then 135° in the anti-clockwise direction, which direction is he facing now?
(a) East
(b) West
(c) North
(d) South

2 Marks Questions

20. Deepti moved a distance 80 m towards north. She then turned to the left and walking about 30 m, turned left again and walked 85 m. Finally, she turned to the right at an angle of 45°. In which direction is she finally moving?
(a) North-East (b) North-West
(c) South (d) South-West

21. Lakshman leaves from his house. He first walks 30 m in North-West direction and then 30 m in South-West direction.
Next, he walks 30 m in South-East direction. Finally she turns towards her house. In which direction is he moving?
(a) North-East (b) North-West
(c) South-East (d) South-West

22. Rashi moves towards South-East a distance of 7 km then she moves towards West and travels a distance 14 m. From here, she moves towards North-West a distance of 7 m and finally she moves a distance of 4 m towards East and stood at that point. How far is the starting point from where she stood?
(a) 3 m (b) 4 m (c) 10 m (d) 11m

23. Joy walks 10 m in front and 10 m to the right. Then every time turning to his left he walks 5 m, 15 m and 15 m respectively. How far is he from the starting point?
(a) 5 m (b) 10 m
(c) 20 m (d) 23 m

24. Nayan walks 20 m North. Then he turns right and walks 30m. Then he turn right and walks 35 m. Then he turns left and walks 15 m. Then he again turns left and walks 15 m. In which direction and how many metres away is he from his original position?
(a) 15 m, West (b) 30 m, East
(c) 30 m, West (d) 45 m, East

25. Ranbir walks 10 km towards North. From there he walks 6 km towards South. Then, he walks 3 km towards East. How far and in which direction is he with reference to his starting point?
(a) 5 km West (b) 7 km West
(c) 7 km East (d) 5 km North-East

26. Door of Devanshu's office faces the East, from the back side of his house, he walks straight 50 m, then turns to the right and walks 50 m again. Finally, he turns towards left and stops after walking 25 m. Now, Devanshu is in which direction from the starting point?
(a) South-East (b) North-East
(c) South-West (d) North-West

Chapter 07

Blood Relations

In this type of test, the information about the blood relations of a group of persons is given in jumbled form. On the basis of those information candidates are required to answer the questions.

Some of the relations in the society has been given as below.

1.	Grandfather's son	Father or uncle
2.	Grandmother's son	Father or uncle
3.	Grandfather's only son	Father
4.	Grandmother's only son	Father
5.	Mother's or father's mother	Grandmother
6.	Mother's or father's father	Grandfather
7.	Grandfather's only daughter-in-law	Mother
8.	Grandmother's only daughter-in-law	Mother
9.	Mother's or father's son	Brother
10.	Mother's or father's daughter	Sister
11.	Mother's or father's brother	Uncle
12.	Mother's or father's sister	Aunt
13.	Husband's or wife's sister	Sister-in-law
14.	Husband's or wife's brother	Brother-in-law
15.	Son's wife	Daughter-in-law
16.	Daughter's husband	Son-in-law
17.	Brother's son	Nephew
18.	Brother's daughter	Niece
19.	Uncle's or Aunt's son or daughter	Cousin
20.	Sister's husband	Brother-in-law
21.	Brother's wife	Sister-in-law

- There are following two types of questions based on blood relations

1. Statement based 2. Symbol based

1. Statement Based Blood Relations

In this type of questions, a person gives information to the another person either about particular person in a photograph or a person present in front of him. The information is given in the form of a statement.

Example 1 Anuj is the friend of Ram. Pointing to an old man Anuj asked Ram who is he? Ram said "His son is my son's uncle". The old man is related to Ram as

(a) Father-in-law (b) Father
(c) Uncle (d) Grand-father

Sol. *(b)* According to the question,

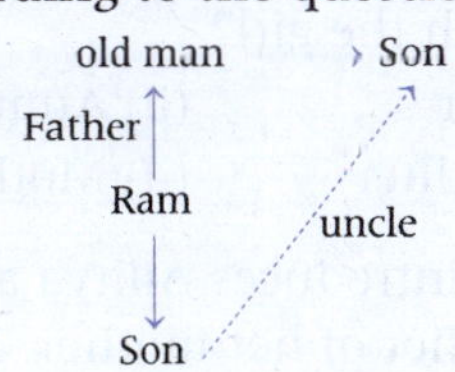

Hence, old man is the father of Ram.

2. Symbol Based Blood Relation

In this type of questions certain symbols are used to represent the relationship.

Example 2 If 'A + Q' means 'A is the father of B'. 'A – B' means 'A is the wife of B'. 'A × B' means 'A is the brother of B' and 'A ÷ B' means 'A is the daughter of B'. If P – Q + R, then which of the following statement is true?

(a) P is the daughter of R
(b) R is the aunt of P
(c) P is the mother of R
(d) P is the aunt of R

Sol. *(c)* From the given information,

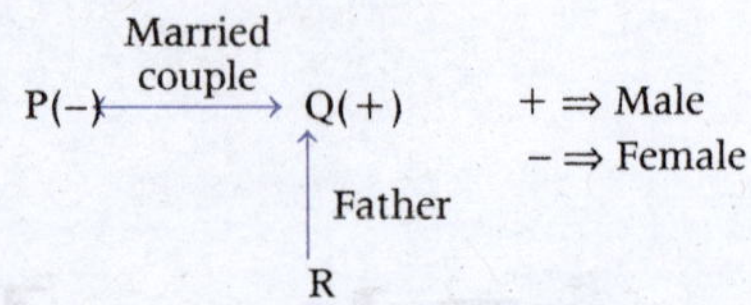

Now, it is clear that 'P is the mother of R'.

Let's Practice

1 Mark Questions

1. Akash said to Mohit, "That boy in blue shirt is younger of the two brothers of the daughter of my father's wife". How is the boy in blue shirt related to Akash?

(a) Father (b) Uncle
(c) Brother (d) Nephew

2. Pointing to a man on the stage. Reena said, "He is the brother of daughter of the wife of my husband". How is the man on the stage related to Reena?

(a) Son (b) Husband
(c) Cousin (d) Nephew

3. Pointing to a girl Rohan says, "This girl is the daughter of the only child of my father". What is the relation of Rohan's wife with the girl?

(a) Sister (b) Aunt
(c) Daughter (d) Mother

4. Madhu introduces Aditya as the son of the brother of her mother. How is Aditya related to Madhu?

(a) Nephew (b) Son
(c) Cousin (d) Uncle

5. A is the brother of B, B is the brother of C, C is the husband of D and E is the father of A. D is related to E as

(a) Daughter (b) Daughter-in-law
(c) Sister-in-law (d) Sister

6. A's mother is the sister of B and daughter of C. D is the daughter of B and sister of E. How is C related to E?

(a) Sister
(b) Mother
(c) Father
(d) Grandmother or grandfather

7. Ayush told Vijay, "Yesterday I defeated the only brother of the daughter of my grandmother". Whom did Ayush defeated?

(a) Father
(b) Son
(c) Brother
(d) Father-in-law

8. Q's mother is the sister of P and daughter of M. S is the daughter of P and sister of T.
How is M related to T?
(a) Grandmother
(b) Father
(c) Grandfather
(d) Grandfather/Grandmother

9. If 'A + B' means 'A is the daughter of B', 'A × B' means 'A is the son of B', and 'A – B' means 'A is the wife of B'.
If 'P × Q – S', which of the following is true?
(a) S is the wife of Q
(b) S is the father of P
(c) P is the daughter of Q
(d) Q is the father of P

10. If 'P × Q' means 'P is the sister of Q', 'P + Q' means 'Q is the daughter of P' and 'P ÷ Q' means 'P is the mother of Q', then how will 'N is the aunt of M' be denoted?
(a) M + L × N (b) M ÷ L + N
(c) L × N ÷ M (d) N × L ÷ M

11. If 'A $ B' means that 'A is the father of B', 'A * B' means that 'A is the mother of B', and 'A @ B' means that 'A is the wife of B', then which of the following means 'M is the grandmother of N'?
(a) A * R $ T @ N (b) M * R @ T @ N
(c) M * T $ N @ R (d) M * T $ N @ R

Directions (Q. Nos. 12 and 13) Read the following information carefully and answer the questions given below.

I. 'M × N' means 'M is the father of N'.
II. 'M – N' means 'M is the sister of N'.
III. 'M + N' means 'M is the mother of N'.
IV. 'M ÷ N' means 'M is the brother of N'.

12. In the expression B + D × M ÷ N, how M related to B?
(a) Grandmother
(b) Son
(c) Grandson
(d) Granddaughter or grandson

13. Which of the following represents 'R is the neice of M'?
(a) M ÷ K × T – R
(b) M – J + R – N
(c) R – M × T ÷ W
(d) None of the above

Directions (Q. Nos. 14 and 15) Read the following information carefully and answer the questions which follow.

- 'P * Q' means 'P is the mother of Q'.
- 'P × Q' means 'P is the father of Q'.
- 'P + Q' means 'P is the sister of Q'.
- 'P – Q' means 'P is the brother of Q'.
- 'P > Q' means 'P is the son of Q'.
- 'P < Q' means 'P is the daughter of Q'.

14. In the expression 'A × B + R > S', how is S related to A?
(a) Daughter-in-law
(b) Daughter
(c) Wife
(d) Sister

15. Which of the following means P is the father of S?
(a) P × Q < R * S
(b) R × P < Q – S
(c) R + S > Q + P
(d) S + Q – R * P

2 Marks Questions

16. P and Q are brothers. R and S are sisters. The son of P is the brother of S. Q is related to R as

(a) father (b) son (c) brother (d) uncle

17. Raghu and Shyam are twins. Shyam's sister is Reema. Reema's husband is Rajan. Raghu's mother is Lalita. Lalita's husband is Rajesh. How is Rajesh related to Rajan?

(a) Son (b) Father-in-law
(c) Brother (d) Brother-in-law

18. P is the father of R and S is the son of Q and T is the brother of P. If R is the sister of S, how is Q related to T?

(a) Wife
(b) Sister-in-law
(c) Brother-in-law
(d) Daughter-in-law

19. If M3N means M is the mother of N. M4N, means M is the brother of N. M9N, means M is the husband of N. M5N means M is the daughter of N. Which of the following means 'C is the husband of B'?

(a) B 9 N 3 A 4 C
(b) B 9 N 5 A 3 C
(c) A 5 C 9 B 3 N
(d) None of the above

Directions (Q. Nos. 20 and 21) Study the following information and answer the question.

- 'P % Q' means 'P is the daughter of Q'.
- 'P @ Q' means 'P is the husband of Q'.
- 'P # Q' means 'P is the father of Q'.
- 'P $ Q' means 'P is the mother of Q.

20. What is the relation between P and T, if P @ Q $ M # T?

(a) Maternal grandfather
(b) Paternal grandfather
(c) Maternal grandmother
(d) Cannot be determined

21. If F @ D % K # M, then how is F related to M?

(a) Brother-in-law
(b) Sister
(c) Sister-in-law
(d) Cannot be determined

22. If 'A $\times$ B' means 'A is the son of B', 'A + B' means 'A is the father of B', 'A $>$ B' means 'A is the daughter of B' and 'A $<$ B' means 'A is the wife of B'. What will come in the place of '?', if it is given that M is the grandmother of F in the expression 'F $\times$ R $<$ S ? M'?

(a) $>$ (b) $<$
(c) + (d) $\times$

Chapter 08

Puzzles

A 'Puzzle' is a question in which the information or data is given in a confusing/jumbled manner and the students are required to proceed systematically by interrelating all the given information in order to arrive at the correct answer.

e.g. Ashok is younger than Prabir and Gopal. Sohan is younger than Prabir but older than Gopal. Who is the eldest?

Here, on the basis of age the descending order will be Prabir > Sohan > Gopal > Ashok.

Hence, Prabir is the eldest.

In puzzle test, questions are based on following types

- Determining the sequential order of persons/things in a row or in a circular arrangement.
- Ranking the persons as per their ages/heights/weights etc.

In puzzle test, following types of questions are generally asked.

Example 1 Four friends Anubhav, Gautam, Narendra and Varun are standing in a row. Gautam and Anubhav are standing to the left of Narendra and there are two persons standing between Gautam and Varun. Who is standing at the extreme right position?

(a) Narendra
(b) Varun
(c) Anubhav
(d) Gautam

Sol. *(b)* Let us mark the positions from left to right as 1, 2, 3 and 4.

$\overline{1}\ \overline{2}\ \overline{3}\ \overline{4}$

Narendra cannot be either at position 1 or 2 because there are two persons standing to the left of Narendra. He also cannot be at position 4 because, in that case, there will be no way left to accommodate two persons between Gautam and Varun. So, Narendra stands at position 3.

The only possible case is

Gautam	Anubhav	Narendra	Varun
1	2	3	4

From the above arrangement, it is clear that Varun is standing at the extreme right position.

Hence, option (b) is correct.

Example 2 Shaan and Kunal are good in cricket and football. Sonu and Shaan are good in cricket and hockey. Abhishek is good in hockey. Who is good in all the three games?

(a) Shaan (b) Kunal
(c) Sonu (d) Abhishek

Sol. (a) Information given in the question can be arranged as

	Cricket	Football	Hockey
Shaan	✓	✓	✓
Kunal	✓	✓	×
Sonu	✓	×	✓
Abhishek	×	×	✓

It is clear from the above table that, Shaan is good in all the three games.
Hence, option (a) is correct.

Directions (Ex. Nos. 3-5) Read the following information and answer the question given below.

There are four friends Ravi, Hari, Manu and Jatin. One of them lives at Kanpur and his hobbies are reading and writing. Hari and Jatin live at Lucknow. Hari's hobby is stamp collection. Common hobby of two friends staying at Lucknow is coin collection. Ravi lives at Allahabad. One boy staying at Lucknow also loves to hear music. The boy staying at Allahabad loves to travel and read comics. All the boys have two hobbies.

3. Who lives in Kanpur?

(a) Jatin (b) Manu (c) Ravi (d) Hari

4. Coin collection and listening to music are the hobbies of

(a) Manu (b) Ravi
(c) Hari (d) Jatin

5. Which of the following is not the hobby of Ravi?

(a) Reading comics
(b) Writing
(c) Travelling
(d) Cannot be said

Sol. (Q. Nos. 3-5) Information given in the question can be arranged as

Name	Staying at	Hobbies
Ravi	Allahabad	Travelling, Reading comics
Hari	Lucknow	Stamp and Coin collection
Manu	Kanpur	Reading, Writing
Jatin	Lucknow	Music, Coin collection

3. *(b)* Manu lives in Kanpur.
Hence, option (b) is correct.

4. *(d)* Coin collection and listening to music are hobbies of Jatin.
Hence, option (d) is correct.

5. *(b)* Ravi's hobbies are travelling and reading comics.
So, from the given options writing is not the hobby of Ravi.
Hence, option (b) is correct.

Let's Practice

1 Mark Questions

1. Priya scored more than Raj. Yash scored as much as Divya. Lucky scored less than Manav. Raj scored more than Divya. Who scored the lowest?
(a) Priya (b) Raj
(c) Lucky (d) Manav

2. Radhika and Sonam are good in English and Mathematics. Preeti and Radhika are good in English and Science. Anita is good in Science. Who is good in all the three subjects?
(a) Radhika (b) Sonam
(c) Preeti (d) Anita

Directions (Q. Nos. 3 and 4) Read the information given below carefully and answer the questions that follow.

A group of girls is standing in a row. Chandni is standing exactly in the middle. Rekha who is standing three positions to the right of Chandni. Chandni is fourth from the right end.

3. The group comprises of .... girls.
(a) 10 (b) 11
(c) 7 (d) 5

4. If the number of girls standing between Roshni and Chandni is same as that between Rekha and Chandni, then Rekha is .... to the .... of Roshni.
(a) 5 th, left
(b) 6th, right
(c) 7th, left
(d) 6th, left

Directions (Q. Nos. 5-7) Read the following information and answer the questions based on it.

There are four persons A, B, C and D. One of them is a lecturer and plays football and cricket. A and B are accountants. A plays badminton. Both the accountants are swimmers. D is a bank clerk. One accountant also plays tennis. The bank clerk plays carrom and is a swimmer. All the four persons play two games each and follow one profession.

5. Who is a lecturer?
(a) A (b) B (c) C (d) D

6. Who plays tennis?
(a) A (b) B (c) C (d) D

7. Who plays badminton and is an accountant?
(a) A (b) B (c) C (d) D

Directions (Q. Nos. 8-10) Read the following information carefully and answer the questions.

1. Madhav and Sheena are good in Drama and Science
2. Anju and Madhav are good in Science and Polity.
3. Anju, Pavitra and Neena are good in Polity and History.
4. Neena and Anju are good in Polity and Mythology.
5. Pavitra and Sheena are good in History and Drama.

8. Who is good in Polity, History and Mythology but not in Science?
(a) Madhav (b) Pavitra
(c) Neena (d) Anju

9. Who is good in Polity, History and Drama?
(a) Pavitra (b) Sheena
(c) Madhav (d) Anju

10. Who is good in History, Polity, Science and Mythology?
(a) Pavitra (b) Sheena
(c) Madhav (d) Anju

Directions (Q. Nos. 11-13) Read the following information and answer the questions given below.

Five cities Agra, Bengaluru, Chennai, Delhi and Ernakulum are famous for garden, jewellery, education, pottery and scents but not in the same order.

(i) Agra and Chennai are neither famous for education nor for garden.
(ii) Bengaluru and Ernakulum are not famous for jewellery or pottery.
(iii) Scents and jewellery have nothing to do with Agra.
(iv) Delhi and Ernakulum are not famous for garden and jewellery.
(v) Delhi is not famous for education.

11. Which of the following cities are famous for gardens?
(a) Agra (b) Chennai
(c) Delhi (d) Bengaluru

12. Pottery is available in which of the following cities?
(a) Agra (b) Chennai
(c) Ernakulum (d) Bengaluru

13. Ernakulum is famous for which of the following?
(a) Jewellery
(b) Education
(c) Pottery
(d) Scents

Directions (Q. Nos. 14-16) Read the information given below and answer the questions.

Out of four persons Anamika, Bablu, Chandni and Dabbu, two are interested in handball, two in cricket, two are painters, one is a singer and one is dancer. Each person has one outdoor interest and one hobby concerned with fine arts.

(i) Anamika is neither a painter nor she plays handball.
(ii) Bablu does not dance.
(iii) Dancer plays handball.
(iv) Bablu and Dabbu do not play cricket.

14. Who among the following plays cricket and is interested in painting?
(a) Anamika
(b) Bablu
(c) Chandni
(d) Anamika and Chandni

15. Who among the following is a singer?
(a) Dabbu (b) Anamika
(c) Chandni (d) Bablu

16. Which pair shows the correct relationship of the game and hobby of Dabbu?
(a) Cricket, Singing
(b) Cricket, Painting
(c) Cricket, Dancing
(d) Handball, Dancing

Example 2 If $12 \star 4 = 3$, $27 \star 9 = 3$ and $36 \star 12 = 3$, then $\star$ stands for

(a) + (b) –

(c) ÷ (d) ×

Sol. *(c)* On finding the relation, we get

$$12 \star 4 = 3 = 12 \div 4$$

$$27 \star 9 = 3 = 27 \div 9$$

$$36 \star 12 = 3 = 36 \div 12$$

So, the symbol '★' represents '÷'.

Hence, option (c) is correct.

3. Statement based

In this type of questions information in the form of statements are given. Students have to analyse the information and answer the given questions.

Example 3 If the cost of 11 books is ₹ 1331, what is the cost of $3\frac{1}{2}$ dozen of books?

(a) ₹ 5082 (b) ₹ 8052

(c) ₹ 5041 (d) ₹ 5042

Sol. (a) Cost of 1 book $= \frac{1331}{11} =$ ₹ 121

Number of books in $3\frac{1}{2}$ dozen

$$= 3\frac{1}{2} \times 12$$

$$= \frac{7}{2} \times 12 = 42 \text{ books}$$

Total cost = ₹ 121×42

= ₹ 5082

Let's Practice

1 Mark Questions

1. Find the value of expression

$18 \text{ of } \frac{1}{3} + 2 - 8 \div 2(3 + 1)$

(a) 6 (b) 7 (c) 9 (d) 4

2. Find the value of expression

$15 \div 5 \times 3 + 6 - 2$

(a) 13 (b) 8 (c) 7 (d) 9

3. Select the correct set of operators that will fit in the blank spaces of 8_4_10_2 = 22.

(a) ÷, ×, + (b) ×, ÷, +

(c) –, +, × (d) ÷, +, –

4. Select the correct set of operators that will fit in the blank spaces of

2 ... 4 ... 8 ... 5 = 11.

(a) ÷, ×, + (b) +, –, +

(c) ×, –, + (d) ×, +, –

5. If '÷' means '×', '×' means '$<$', '$<$' means '÷' and '+' means '$>$', then which of the following equations is correct?

(a) $25 < 5 \div 2 \times 20$ (b) $25 \times 5 \div 2 < 20$

(c) $20 < 5 \div 2 + 25$ (d) $5 \div 2 \times 20 < 25$

6. If '÷' stands for 'multiplication', '–' stands for 'addition', '+' stands for 'subtraction' and '×' stands for 'division', then which of the following equations is correct?

(a) $8 - 5 + 10 \times 2 \div 3 = 20$

(b) $8 \div 5 - 10 \times 2 + 3 = 42$

(c) $10 \times 2 \div 5 + 3 - 8 = 84$

(d) $2 \times 3 - 10 \div 5 + 8 = 13$

7. If 's' stands for '+', 'r' stands for '–', stands for '×', and 'p' stands for '÷', then find the value of

1000 p 10 q 5 r 250 s 50.

(a) 380 (b) 450 (c) 300 (d) 350

8. If '–' denotes '+', '×' denotes '–', '+' denotes '÷', '÷' denotes '×', then what is the value of given expression?

$$25 \div 4 + 2 \times 10 - 35$$

(a) 37 (b) 90 (c) 0 (d) 75

9. If the interchanges '+' and '÷', as well as '2' and '4' are made, then which one of the following alternatives will become correct?

(a) $4 \div 2 + 3 = 5$ (b) $2 + 4 \div 6 = 8$
(c) $4 + 2 \div 6 = 1.5$ (d) $2 + 4 \div 3 = 3$

10. Which one of the four interchanges in signs and numbers would make the given equation correct?

$$4 \times 6 - 2 = 14$$

(a) × to ÷, 2 and 4 (b) – to ÷, 2 and 6
(c) – to +, 2 and 6 (d) × to +, 4 and 6

11. If 'you' stands for '÷', 'are' stands for '+' and 'great' stands for '×', then what will be the value of

'50 you 2 are 3 great 4'?

(a) 32 (b) 37 (c) 47 (d) 73

12. If 22⊕ = 88, 16 ⊕ = 64 and 9 ⊕ = 36, then symbol '⊕' represents

(a) +4 (b) ×4 (c) ×8 (d) +66

13. If 5 @ 9 = 45, 6 @ 12 = 72 and 8 @ 6 = 48, then '@' stands for

(a) + (b) – (c) × (d) ÷

14. If 94★14 = 80, 68★9 = 59 and 52★12 = 40, then '★' stands for

(a) + (b) – (c) × (d) ÷

15. There were total 17 tigers in a forest. All but eight died. How many was left in the forest?

(a) 11 (b) 10
(c) 9 (d) 8

16. If a number is multiplied by itself two times, then the value obtained is 8000, what is that number?

(a) 18 (b) 19
(c) 20 (d) 21

17. Ramanujan divides 92 by half and adds one-fourth of 12 to the result. What number he gets at the end?

(a) 178 (b) 187
(c) 188 (d) 189

18. A is greater than B by 50% and greater than C by 20%. The ratio of B and C is

(a) 4:5 (b) 7:8
(c) 3:1 (d) 5:4

2 Marks Questions

Directions (Q. Nos. 19-21) If '★' means '+', '■' means '–', '●' means '×' and '▲' means '÷', then find the value of question mark '?'.

19. 5 ■ 3 ● 6 ▲ 3 = ?

(a) –1 (b) +1
(c) 0 (d) None of these

20. 8 ★ 4 ▲ ? ■ 3 = 9

(a) 1 (b) 3 (c) 1/2 (d) 2

21. 5 ? 3 ● 12 ▲ 6 = 11

(a) ★ (b) ■ (c) ▲ (d) ●

22. The ratio of present ages of Ayush and Amit is 3 : 4. If the age of Ayush 20 yr hence will be 62 yr, then what is the present age of Amit?

(a) 56 yr (b) 64 yr
(c) 60 yr (d) 52 yr

23. Which one of the four interchanges in signs and numbers would make the given equation correct?

$$3 \times 6 \div 2 + 1 = 5$$

(a) 3 and 2, ÷ and + (b) 3 and 6, × and ÷
(c) 3 and 1, × and + (d) 1 and 6, ÷ and ×

Chapter 10

Venn-Diagram

Venn diagrams are diagrams which are used to represent logical relationship among given group of elements.

Different geometrical figures like circles, triangles, squares and rectangles are used to represent these diagrams.

Question based on venn-diagrams are of generally following two types.

1. Identification of Venn-Diagram.
2. Analysis of venn diagram.

1. Identification of Venn-Diagram

In this type of questions, some elements are given which have certain relationship among them. Students have to analyse that relationship and identify the diagram which logically define them.

Example 1 Which of the following best represents the relation between

Earth, Moon, Planet

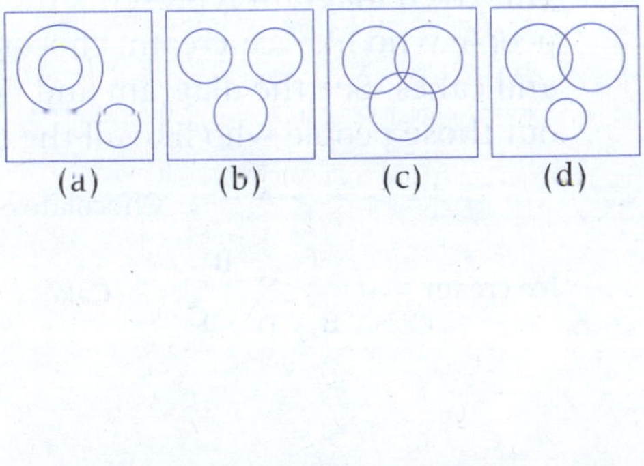

Sol. *(a)*

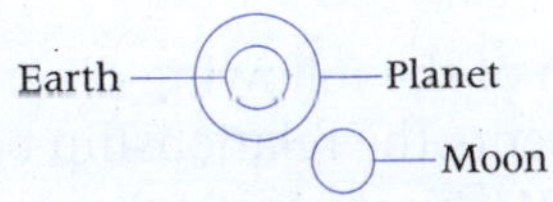

Earth is a planet, whereas moon is a satellite, which is different.

2. Analysis of Venn-Diagram

In this type of questions, generally a Venn diagram comprising of different geometrical figures is given. Each geometrical figure in the diagram represents certain class. The candidate is required to study and analyse the figure carefully and then answer the given questions based on it.

Example 2 In the given figure, how many automobiles are petrol based?

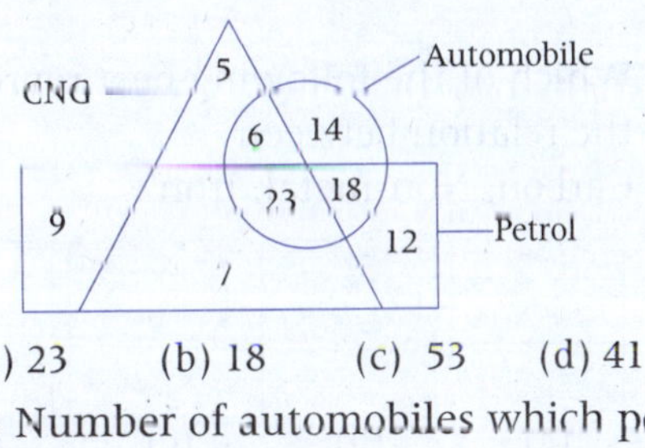

(a) 23 (b) 18 (c) 53 (d) 41

Sol. *(d)* Number of automobiles which petrol based $= 23 + 18 = 41$

Let's Practice

1 Mark Questions

1. Which of the following figures correctly represents the relationship between Woman, Teacher, Pilot?

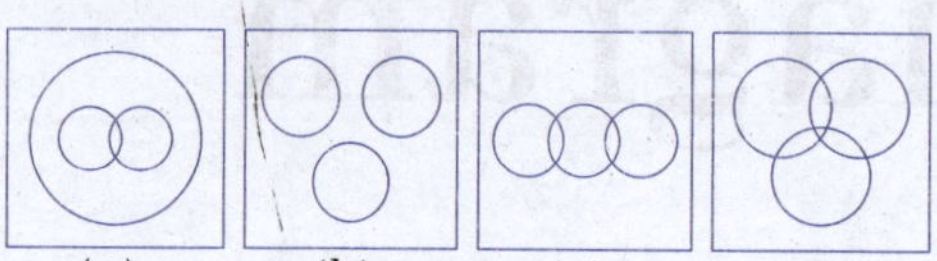

(a) (b) (c) (d)

2. Which of the following diagram best represents the relationship between Deer, Herbivorous, Dog?

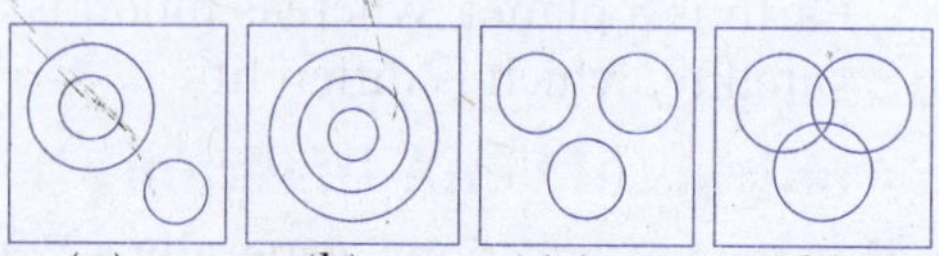

(a) (b) (c) (d)

3. Which of the following best represents the relation between Necklace, Earings, Bangles?

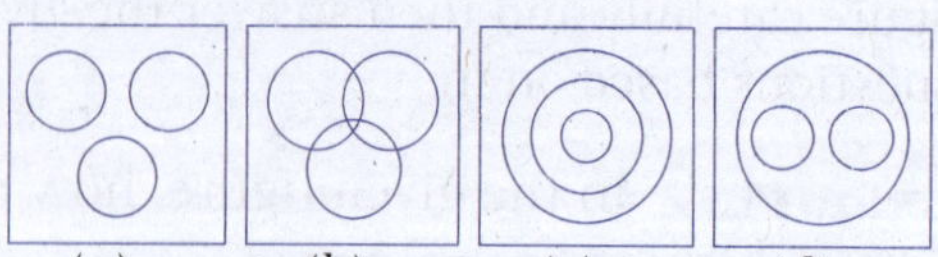

(a) (b) (c) (d)

4. Which of the following best represents the relation between Carbon, Non-metal, Iron?

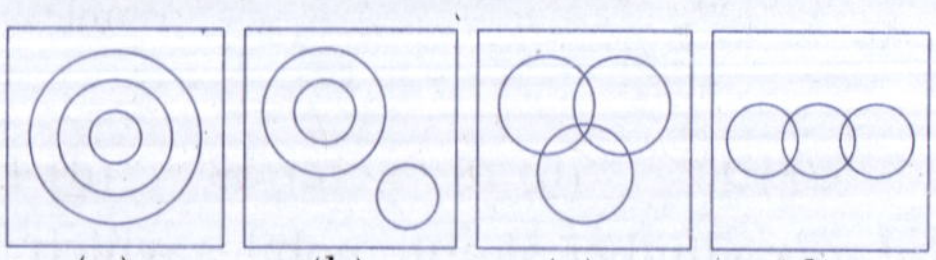

(a) (b) (c) (d)

5. Which of the following diagram best represents the relation between Mammals, Tiger, Peacock?

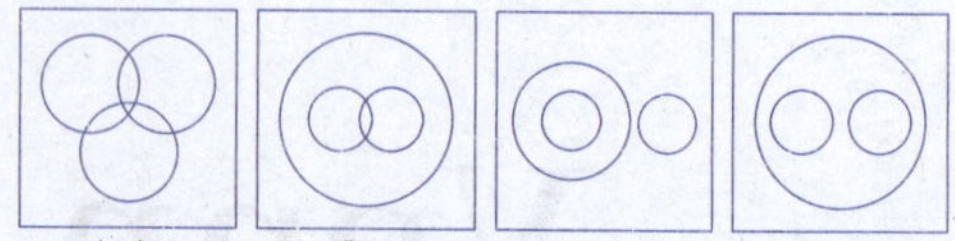

(a) (b) (c) (d)

6. Which of the following diagram best represents the relation between. Woman, Teacher, Prime Minister?

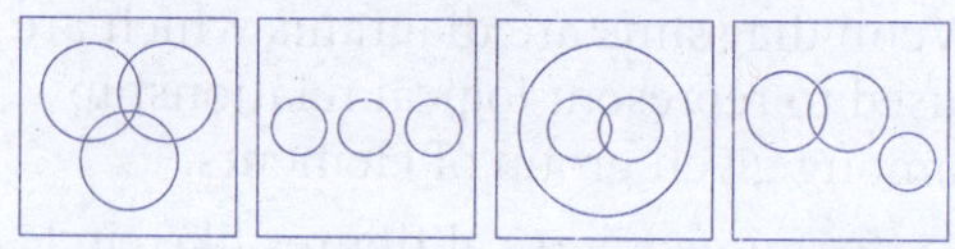

(a) (b) (c) (d)

7. Which of the following diagram best represents the relation between Tajmahal, Charminar, Monuments?

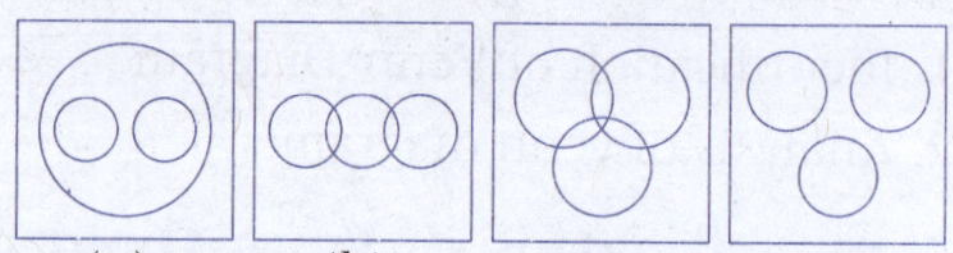

(a) (b) (c) (d)

8. Which of the following diagram best represents the relationship between. Oxygen, Neon, Mercury?

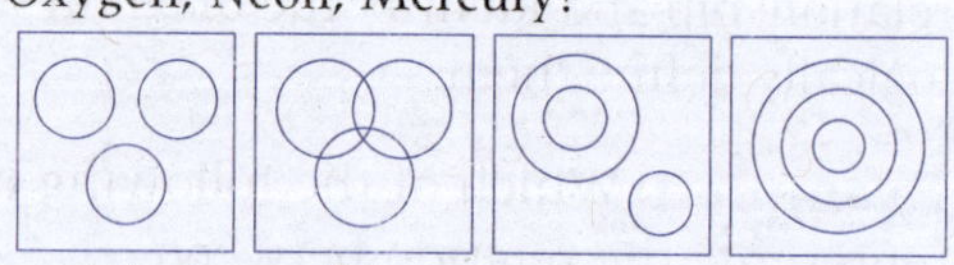

(a) (b) (c) (d)

9. The given diagram represents those people who like ice-cream, chocolates and cakes. See the diagram and find out those people who like all the three.

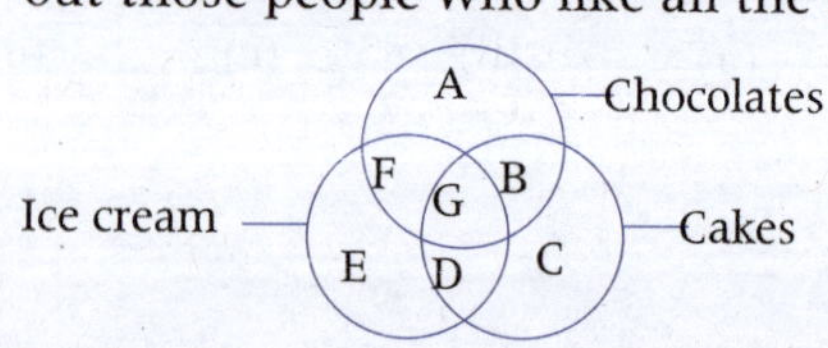

(a) G
(b) A + B + C
(c) B + G
(d) G + D + B

10. In the following figure, square represents lawyers, triangle represents cyclists, circle represents men and rectangle represents post-graduates, which set of letters represents men who are not cyclists?

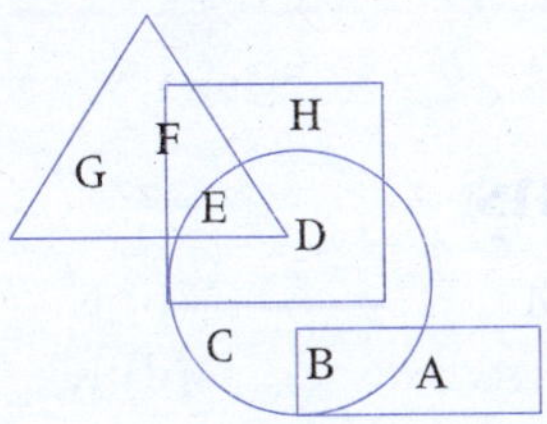

(a) B, C, D (b) E
(c) G, F (d) G, F, H, A

11. In the following figure, square represents policeman, triangle represents salesmen, circle represents therapists and rectangle represents american.
Which set of letters represents american, who are not policeman?

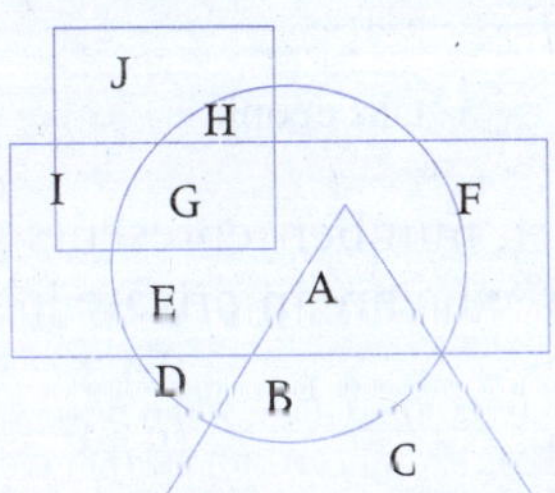

(a) E, F
(b) I, G
(c) E, A, F
(d) G, E, A

12. In the following figure, square represents Rangers, triangle represents socialists, circle represents australian and rectangle represents fathers. Which set of letters represents australian who are rangers?

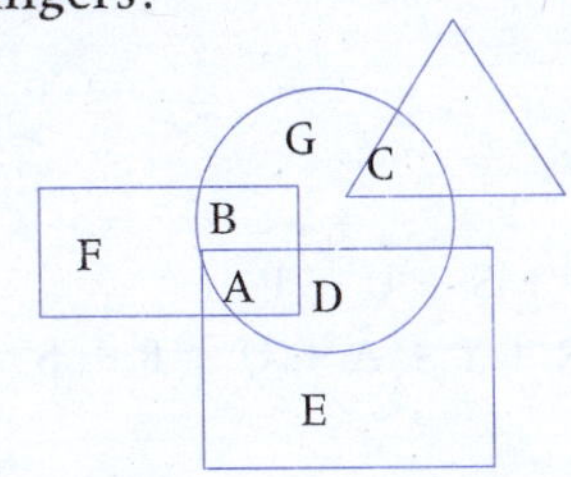

(a) F, B, D,E (b) A, D
(c) G, C, D (d) B, C, G, F

13. In the following figure, number of people studying different subjects are given.

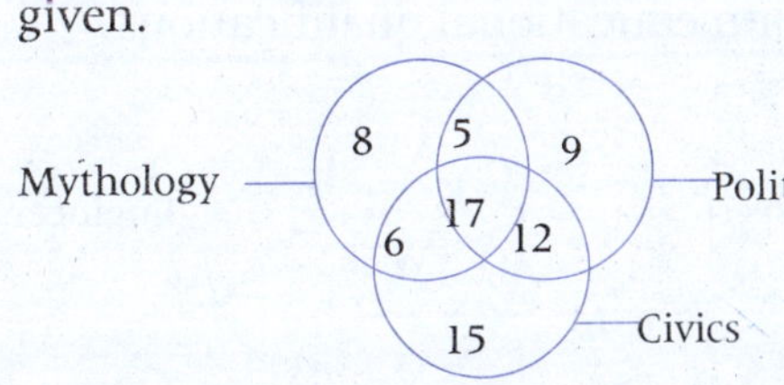

How many people study only 2 subjects?
(a) 11 (b) 23 (c) 12 (d) 40

14. In the following figure how many women are scientist?

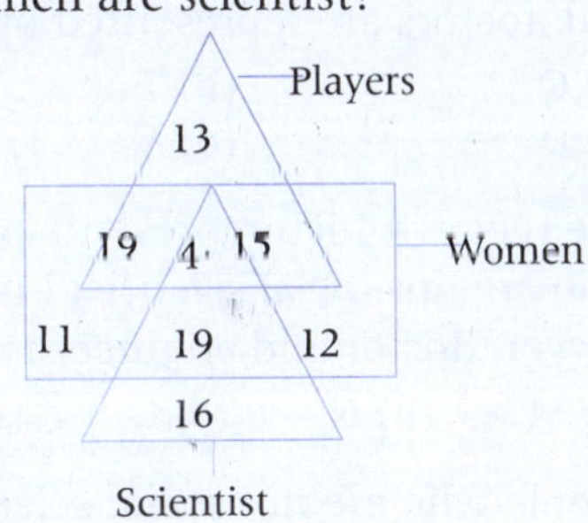

(a) 23 (b) 19
(c) 12 (d) 15

15. The diagram below represents the students who study Physics, Chemistry and Mathematics. Study the diagram and identify the region which represents students who study both Physics and Chemistry but not Mathematics?

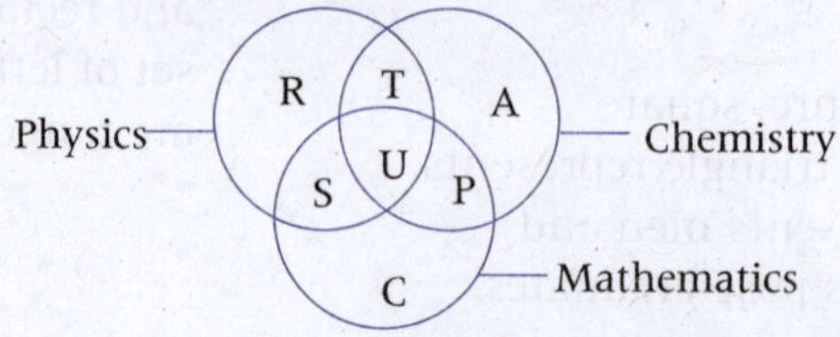

(a) T + S + U + P (b) C
(c) R + T + A + U + P + S (d) T

2 Marks Questions

Directions (Q. Nos. 16-18) Below is given a figure with four intersecting circles, each representing a group of persons having certain educational qualifications?

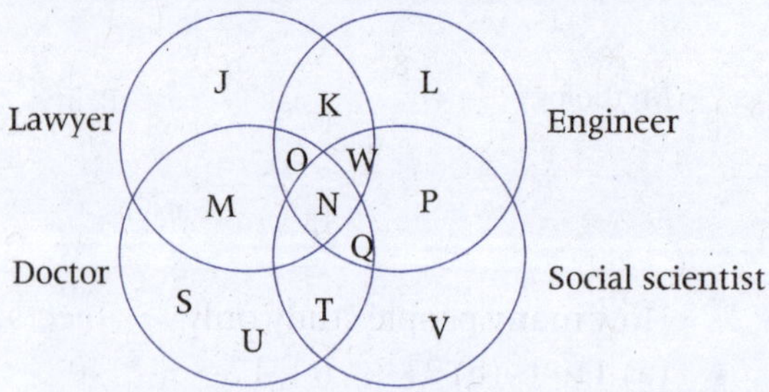

16. People who are not lawyers, engineers and doctors are represented by
(a) Q (b) T
(c) U (d) V

17. The region which represents people who are not social scientist but are lawyer, doctor and engineer is?
(a) M (b) N (c) O (d) W

18. People who are not social scientist and doctor but are lawyer and engineer both are represented by
(a) M (b) N
(c) P (d) K

Directions (Q. Nos. 19 and 20) Study the following diagram and answer the questions.

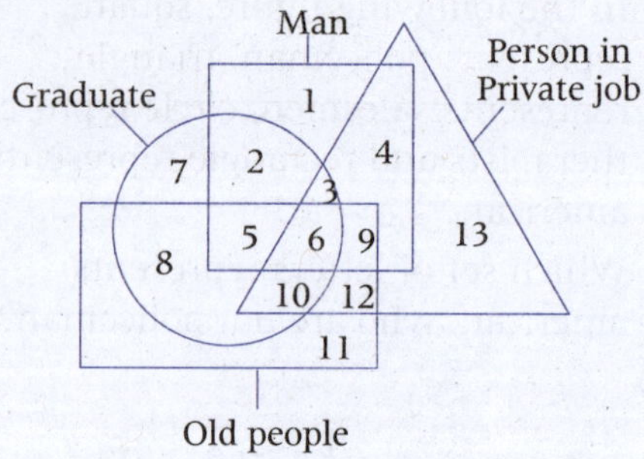

19. Which number represents graduate men, who are in private jobs?
(a) 2 (b) 3
(c) 6 (d) 4

20. Which number represents non-graduate men, who have private jobs as well as are old?
(a) 6 (b) 4
(c) 12 (d) 9

Chapter 11

Analytical Reasoning

Analytical Reasoning is a reasoning which tests the logical skills of students.

These types of questions are usually solved by applying logical thinking and skills on a particular problem.

Questions based on analytical reasoning arc basically of two following types.

1. Syllogism 2. Statement and Conclusion

1. Syllogism

Syllogism means inference or deduction.

In syllogism, conclusion are drawn from the given statements.

In this type of questions, a set of statements along with two or more conclusions is given. On the basis of these statements, candidates are required to find out which conclusion follows or which conclusion doesn't follow.

Venn Diagram Representation of Four Statements

Types of Statements	**Venn Diagram**		
A : All S are P	Always	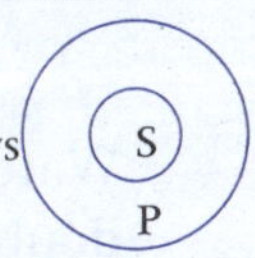	
E : No S is P	Always		
I : Some S are P	Either	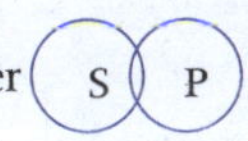	Some S are P [P are S]
	or	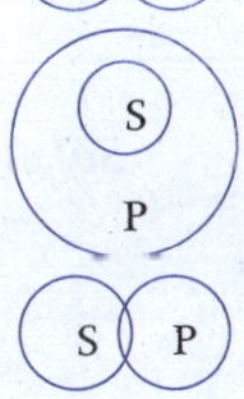	Some S are P [All S are P]
	or	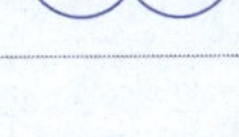	Some S not P [Some P are not S]

O Some S are not P

Either 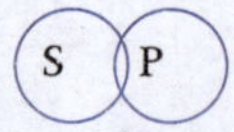

Some S not P [Some P are not S]

or 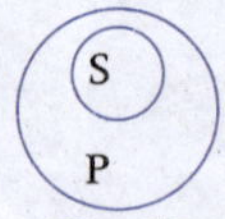

Some S are not P [Some P are not S]

or 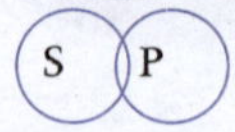

Some S are not P [No S are P]

Direction (Q. No. 1) In each of the following questions two or three statements along with a set of conclusion is given. You have to take the statements to be true even if they seem to be at variance from commonly known facts and decide which of the following conclusion logically follows from the given statements.

Give Answer

(a) If only Conclusion I follows

(b) In only Conclusion II follows

(c) If neither Conclusion I nor II follows

(d) If both Conclusions I and II follow

Example 1 **Statements**

Some stars are planets.

All planets are galaxies.

Conclusions

I. Some galaxies are planets.

II. Some stars are galaxies.

(a) None (b) One (c) Two (d) Three

Sol. (a) (d) According to the question,

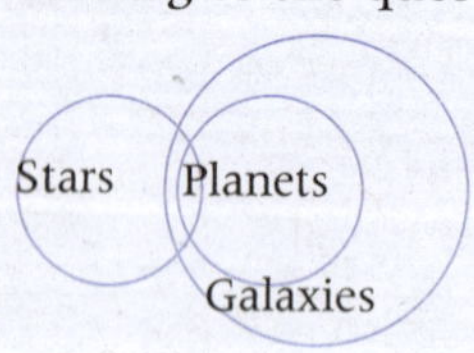

Conclusions I. ✓ II. ✓

Hence, both Conclusions I and II follow.

2. Statement and Conclusion

- Statement A statement is a group of words arranged to form a meaningful sentence.
- Conclusion A conclusion is a judgement or decisions reached after consideration about the given statement. It is an opinion or decision that is formed after a period of thought or research on some facts or sentence stated by some one. Students are required to analyse the given statements understand their direct/indirect implication and then decide which of the given conclusions follows logically.

Direction (Ex. No. 2) In the following question some statements with conclusions are given. Read the statements carefully and choose which of the conclusions logically follows from the statement.

Give answer

(a) Only Conclusion I follows

(b) Only Conclusion II follows

(c) Neither Conclusion I nor II follows

(d) Both Conclusions I and II follow

Example 2 **Statement**

Water consumption in society has been doubled during last 5 yr.

Conclusions

I. There is lot of developmental work going in the society like industrial set up, and plantation.

II. Water has become cheaper and easily accessible.

Sol. (a) Only Conclusion I follows because, industries and plantation activities requires a lot of water. Hence the consumption of water might have increased and infact doubled in the past 5 yr.

Let's Practice

1 Mark Questions

Directions (Q. Nos. 1-10) Which of the following conclusions can be concluded on the basis of given statements.

Give Answer

(a) If only Conclusion I follows
(b) If only Conclusion II follows
(c) If either Conclusion I or II follows
(d) If neither Conclusion I nor II follows

1. Statements

All birds are tall.
Some tall are dogs.

Conclusions

I. Some birds are dogs.
II. Some dogs are tall.

2. Statements

Some pastries are toffees.
All toffees are cookies.

Conclusions

I. Some cookies are toffees.
II. Some toffees are not pastries.

3. Statements

All umbrellas are aeroplanes.
Some aeroplanes are bus.

Conclusions

I. Some umbrellas are aeroplanes
II. All bus are umbrellas.

4. Statements

All books are pencils.
Some pencils are crayons.

Conclusions

I. Some crayons are pencils.
II. Some crayons are books.

5. Statements

All water is pure.
All temples are pure.

Conclusions

I. All water is temple.
II. All temples are water.

6. Statements

Some fathers are intelligent.
Some intelligent are fool.

Conclusions

I. Some father are fool.
II. No fool is father.

7. Statements

Some cities are villages.
Some temples are villages.

Conclusions

I. Some cities are temples.
II. No temple is city.

8. Statements

Some visitors are Italians.
Some visitors are American.

Conclusions

I. Some Italians are visitors.
II. All Italians are visitors.

9. Statements

Some Australian are boys.
Some boys are old.

Conclusions

I. Some Australian are not old.
II. All boys are old.

10. Statements

Some bands are tables.
Some tables are matchbox.

Conclusions

I. Some matchbox are bands.
II. No band is matchbox.

Directions (Q. Nos. 11-14) Consider the statement and following conclusion. Decide which of the conclusion follows from the statement.

Give answer

(a) If Conclusion I follows

(b) If Conclusion II follows

(c) If both Conclusions I and II follow

(d) If neither Conclusion I nor II follows

11. Statements

Animals breathe out carbon dioxide.

Conclusions

I. Plants do not breathe out carbon dioxide.

II. Anything that exhale carbon-dioxide is Animal.

12. Statements

The sun is the star at the leutre of the Solar system and it is a good source of light.

Conclusions

I. Sun is the only source of light.

II. Sun is a star.

13. Statement

He will definitely help you because all good men help.

Conclusions

I. He is a good man.

II. Woman are generally not good.

14. Statement

India is in the way to progress, due to proper maintenance of law and order in the country.

Conclusions

I. Maintenance of law and order is the only thing which is need to be done for the progress of a nation.

II. China is progressing due to maintenance of law and order.

15. Read the following statements and choose the conclusions which follows.

Statements

For protection of India's zoo, central government is responsible.
Delhi zoo is a national property.

Conclusion

I. Indian zoos are national property.

II. Property of a nation is a public property and always protected by the central government.

(a) Only Conclusion I follows

(b) Only Conclusion II follows

(c) Both Conclusions I and II follow

(d) None of the Conclusion follows

16. Read the following statement and choose the conclusion which follows.

Statement

He is lucky because he won the prize.

Conclusions

I. All those who win prize are lucky

II. Only those who win prize are lucky

III. All lucky persons win prize

IV. Some lucky persons have won prize

(a) Only Conclusion I follows

(b) Only Conclusion II follows

(c) Both Conclusions I and II follow

(d) None of the Conclusion follows

2 Marks Questions

Directions (Q. Nos. 17-18) Which of the following conclusions can be conclude on the basis of following statements.

Give answer

(a) If only Conclusion I follows
(b) If only Conclusion II follows
(c) If neither Conclusion I nor II follows
(d) If either Conclusion I or II follows

17. Statements All roses are red.
Some red are blue.
All blue are black.

Conclusions

I. Some red are black.
II. All red are blue.

18. Statements All bees are fishes.
All fishes are sloth.
No sloth is mammal.
All mammals are meat.

Conclusions

I. Some meat are sloth.
II. No meat is sloth.

19. Statements

Some fans are AC's.
Some AC's are machines.
Some machines are computer.
All computers are TV.

Conclusions

I. No machine is AC.
II. Some TV are machines.

20. Statements

All cities are towns.
Some cities are good

Conclusions

I. Some good is a town
II. No good is a town

Directions (Q. Nos. 21 and 23) Consider the statement and the following conclusion. Decide which of the conclusions follows from the statement.

Give Answer

(a) If Conclusion I follows
(b) If Conclusion II follows
(c) If either Conclusion I or II follows
(d) If neither Conclusion I nor II follows

21. Statement Meditation provide the means for attaining eternal peace. People should follow these mean.

Conclusions

I. Meditation ensures prosperous life.
II. Meditation help people to eradicate poverty.

22. Statements

A. Singing is an art.
B. Dancing is also an art.

Conclusions

I. All artists are singers.
II. All artists are well known dancers.

Give Answer

(a) Only Conclusion I follows
(b) Only Conclusion II follows
(c) Neither Conclusion I nor II follows
(d) Both Conclusions I and II follow

23. Statements

Happiness derived from external material is momentary.
Ever lasting happiness has to come from within

Conclusions

I. Nobody can experience happiness from outside.
II. Happiness experienced from cinema is not long lasting.

Give Answer

(a) Only I follows
(b) Only II folows
(c) Neither I nor II follow
(d) Both I and II follow

Chapter 12

Mirror and Water Images

Mirror Images

'Mirror Image' of an object is the virtual image formed by reflection of the object in a plane mirror.

It is of the same size as the object and seems to be an exact replica of the object but actually it is not. The left half of the object becomes the right half of the mirror image and the right half becomes the left half.

Water Image

'Water Image' of an object is the upside down (vertically inverted) image formed due to reflection of the object in water.

Water image is similar to the image of the object formed in a plane mirror when kept horizontally below the object.

Questions based on mirror and water images are of following types

1. Picture Based Image

In this type of questions a picture is given

Example 1 Find the correct mirror image of the figure given below.

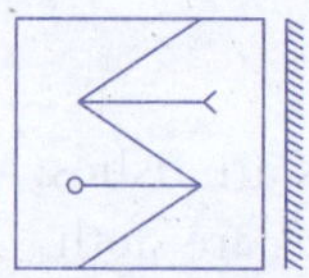

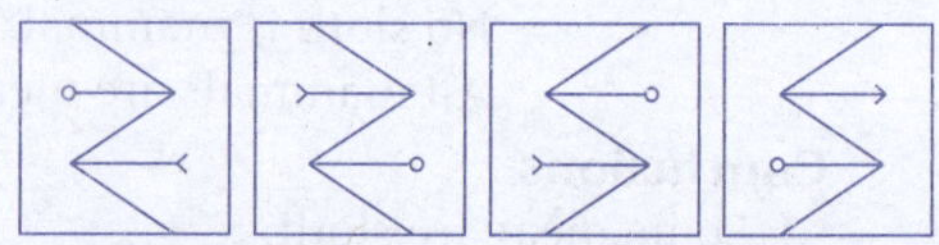

(a) (b) (c) (d)

Sol. *(b)* The mirror image of the figure is

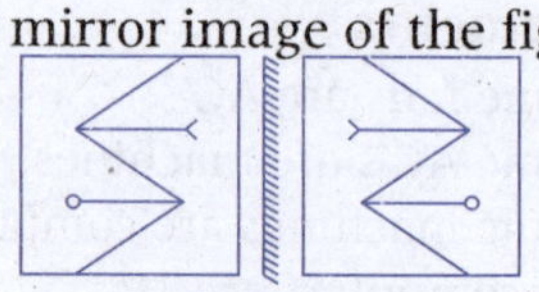

Mirror

Hence, option (b) is correct.

Example 2 Choose the correct water image of the given figure.

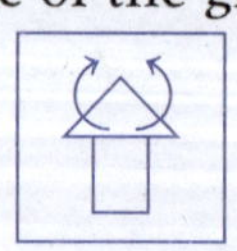

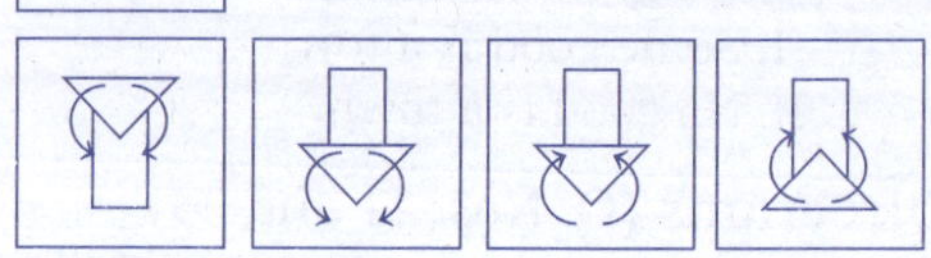

(a) (b) (c) (d)

Sol. *(b)* Here, the triangle will get vertically inverted and appears below the rectangle in the water image.

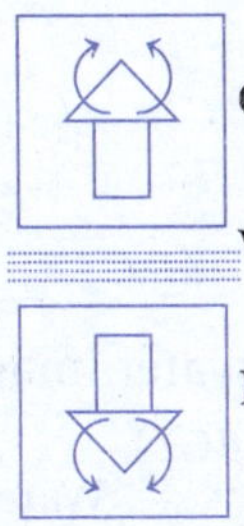

Hence, option (b) is correct.

2. Letter/Word Based Image

In this type of questions a combination of letters or number is given.

Example 3 Find the mirror image of the letters given below.

TDZP

(a) PDZT (b) ꟼZDT
(c) ꟼƧDT (d) ꟼƧTD

Sol. *(b)* The correct mirror image of the letters is

TDZP ꟼZDT

Hence, option (b) is correct.

Example 4 Choose the correct water image of the given letter set.

ZABXQ

(a) ƩABXQ (b) ZⱯBXϘ
(c) ƩⱯBXϘ (d) None of these

Sol. *(c)* Here, to get the correct water image of the given letter set, we should find out the water image of each letter

ZABXQ
Water
ƩⱯBXϘ

So, the required water image is ƩⱯBXϘ.

Hence, option (c) is correct.

3. Number Based Image

In this type of questions a combination of numbers are given and students are asked to find its correct mirror or water image.

Example 5 Find the mirror image of the number given below.

7385

(a) ƨ8Ꞁ3 (b) ƨ87Ɛ (c) ƨ8ƐꞀ (d) ƨ83Ꞁ

Sol. *(c)* The correct mirror image of the number is

7385 ƨ8ƐꞀ

Hence, option (c) is correct.

Example 6 Find the correct water image of the following number.

5 4 3 2

(a) 2ᔭ3Ƽ (b) 2ᔭƐ2 (c) 2ᔭ3Ƨ (d) 5ᔭ32

Sol. *(a)* Number given in option (a) is the correct water image.

5432
Water
2ᔭ3Ƽ

4. Mixed Based Image

In this type of questions, a combination of letters and numbers are given and students are asked to find its correct mirror and water image.

Example 7 Identify the correct mirror image of the given figure.

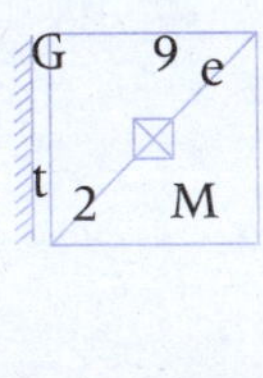

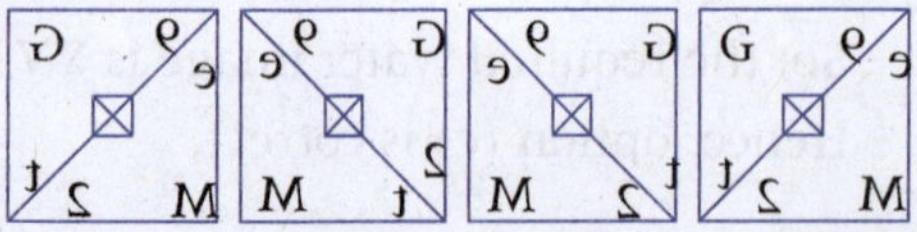

(a) (b) (c) (d)

Sol. (c) The letters and the digits given in the figure will be seen in the mirror as shown below

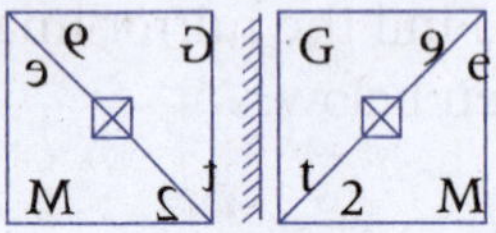

Mirror

Hence, option (c) is correct.

Example 8 Choose the correct water image of the following figure.

T20B4CZ1

(a) IZƆ4B0ZT

(b) IZCꟻB02T

(c) ꓕZ0BꟻCZI

(d) IZƆ4B0Zꓕ

Sol. (c) The correct water image is

T20B4CZ1

Water

ꓕZ0BꟻCZI

Hence, option (c) is correct.

Let's Practice

1 Mark Questions

Directions (Q. Nos. 1-11) Choose the correct mirror image of the following figure/ Letters/Numbers.

1.

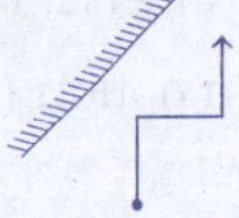

(a)

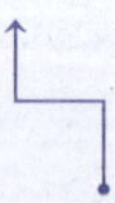

(b)

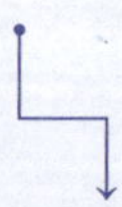

(c)

(d)

2.

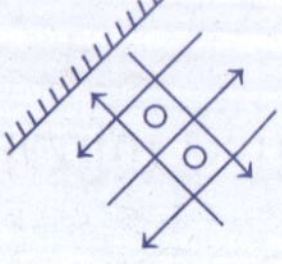

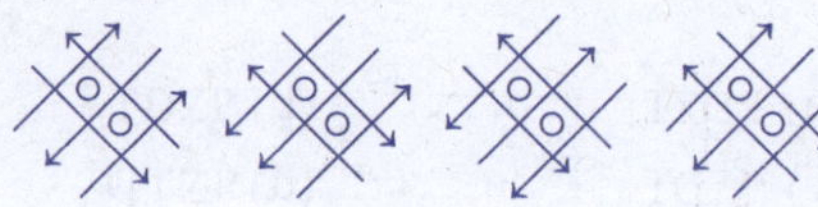

(a) (b) (c) (d)

3.

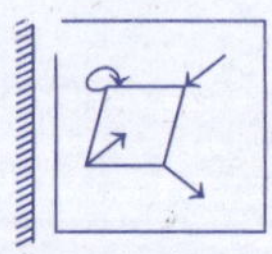

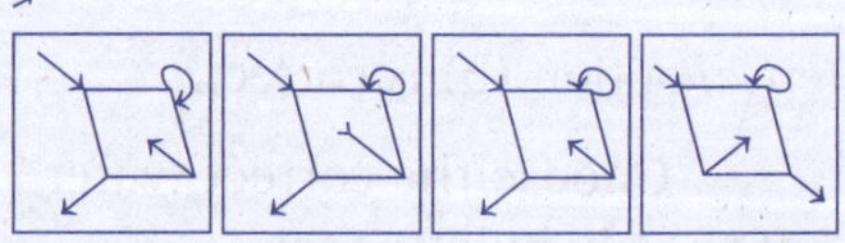

(a) (b) (c) (d)

4.

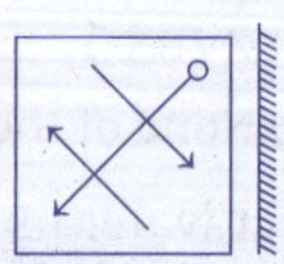

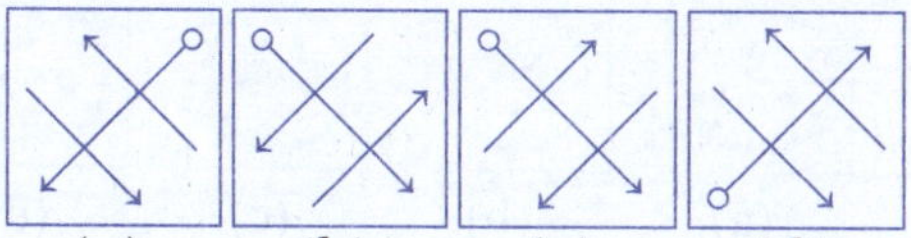

(a) (b) (c) (d)

5.

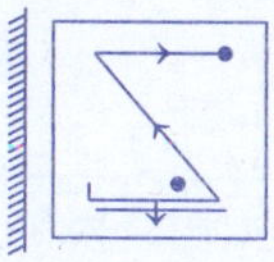

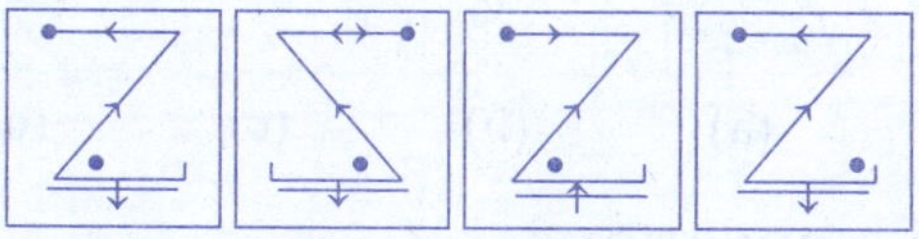

(a) (b) (c) (d)

6. MIRROR

(a) ꟽIꓤꓤOꓤ (b) ЯOЯЯIM

(c) ЯOЯЯOM (d) ЯOЯЯIM

7. ASSOCIATION

(a) ∀SSOƆIATIOИ (b) ИOITAIƆOSSA

(c) ИOITAIƆOƧƧA (d) ИOITAICOSSA

8. 9876

(a) ƍ8⅂9 (b) ɘ786 (c) ƍ8⅂6 (d) ɘ786

9. 1936

(a) ⇂ƍƐƍ (b) ɘƐ9⇂ (c) ɘƐ9⇂ (d) ƍƐ9⇂

10. C4Z2S68

(a) B9SZZ4Ɔ (b) C4ZZS9B

(c) B9SZZ4Ɔ (d) B6SZZ4Ɔ

11.

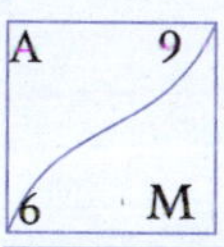

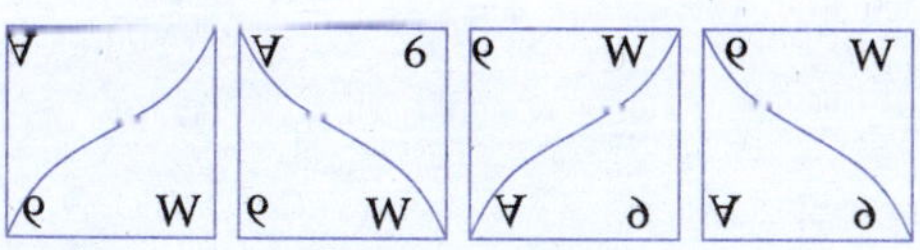

(a) (b) (c) (d)

Directions (Q. Nos. 12-25) Find the correct water image of the following figure.

12.

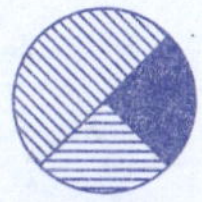

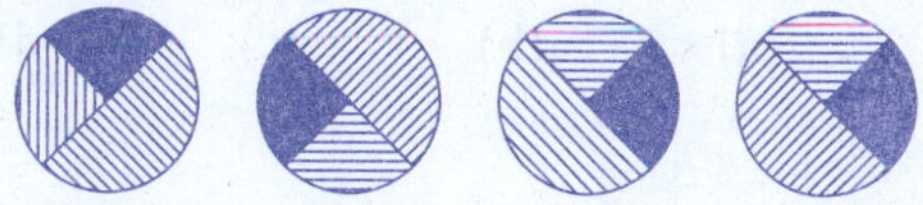

(a) (b) (c) (d)

13.

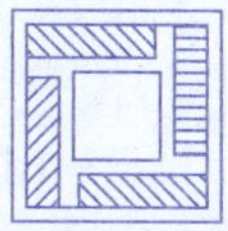

(a) (b) (c) (d)

14.

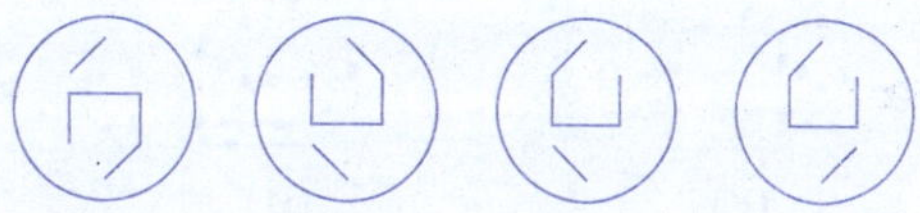

(a) (b) (c) (d)

15.

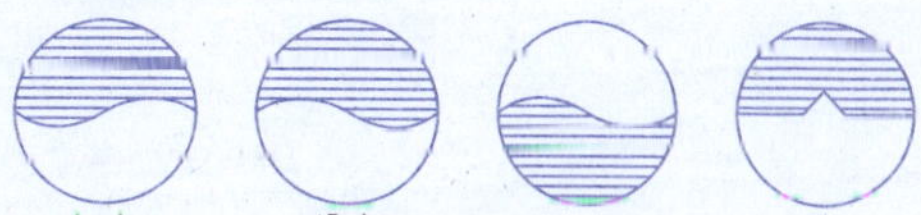

(a) (b) (c) (d)

16.

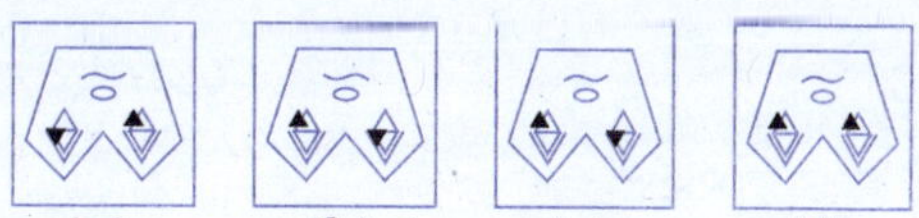

(a) (b) (c) (d)

17. 

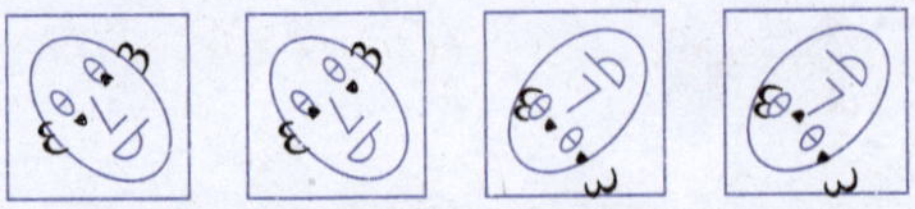

(a) (b) (c) (d)

18. 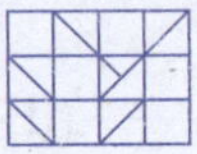

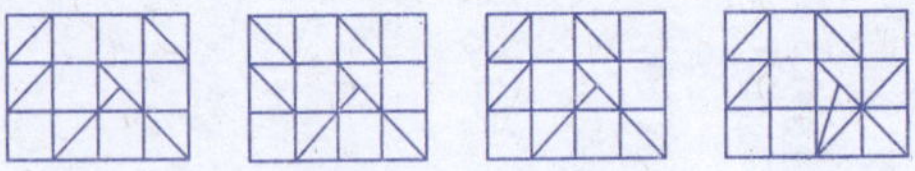

(a) (b) (c) (d)

19. 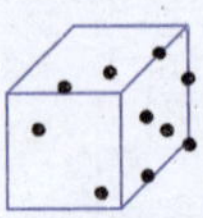

(a) (b)

(c) (d)

20. 

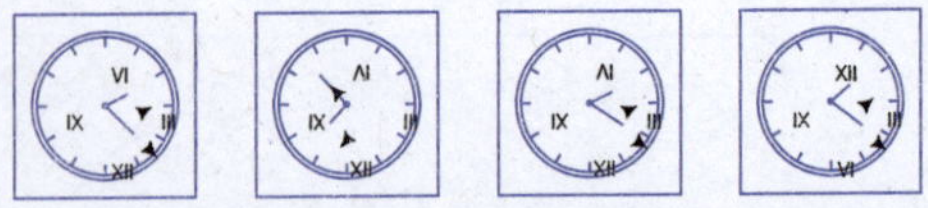

(a) (b) (c) (d)

21. 

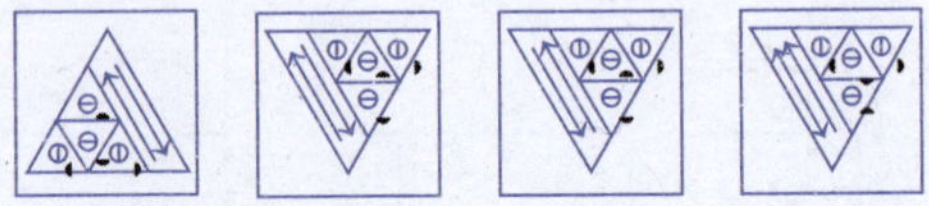

(a) (b) (c) (d)

22. QUESTIONS

(a) ϘUƎSTIOИ

(b) ϘUESTIONS

(c) ϘUESTIONS

(d) QUESTIONS

23. image

(a) ᴉɯage (b) ᴉɯagɐ

(c) ᴉɯage (d) ᴉɯagɐ

24. 8324

(a) 832ᔭ (b) 832ᔭ

(c) 8324 (d) 882ᔭ

25. K9J6F0

(a) K9ſ6F0 (b) K9ſ6F0

(c) K9ſ6F0 (d) K9ſ6F0

2 Marks Questions

26. Find the correct mirror image of the following figure.

(a) (b) (c) (d)

27. Find the correct mirror image of the following figure.

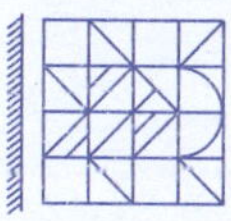

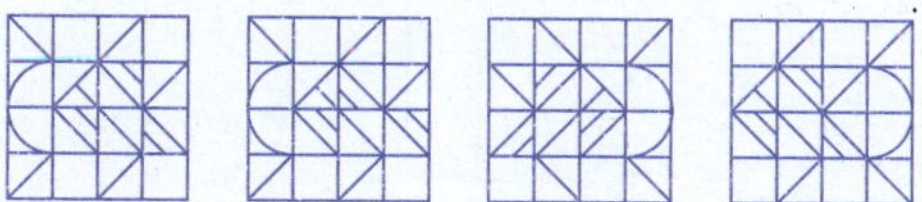

(a) (b) (c) (d)

28. Find the correct mirror image of the following figure.

12#3C%BA

(a) 12#3Ɔ%BA (b) AB%Ɔ3#21

(c) AB%Ɔ3#21 (d) 21#3Ɔ%BA

29. Find the correct water image of the following figure.

△⊕⊠ δ

(a) ▽⊕⊠ ƍ (b) ▽⊕⊠ ƍ

(c) ▽⊕ ⊠ ƍ (d) ▽⊕⊠ δ

30. Find the correct mirror image of the following figure.

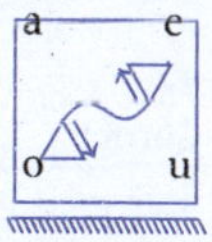

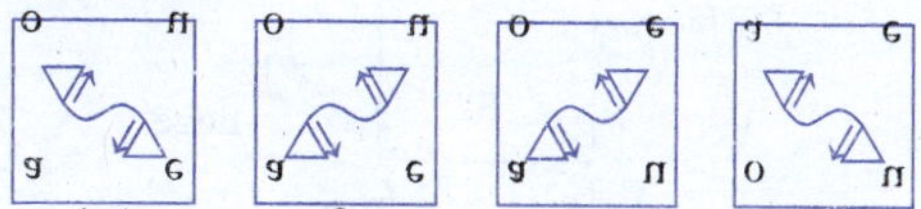

(a) (b) (c) (d)

Chapter 13

Cubes and Dice

Cubes

A 'Cube' is a three-dimensional solid having 8 corners, 12 edges and 6 surfaces as shown below

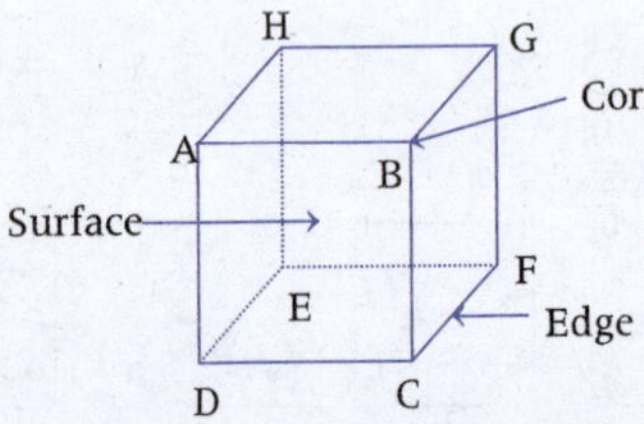

Corners = A, B, C, D, E, F, G and H

Edges = AB, BC, CD, DA, HG, GF, FE, EH, AH, BG, DE and CF

Surfaces = ABCD, EFGH, DCFE, ABGH, AHED and BGFC

In this topic, a cube (or a stack of cubes) is given and different types of questions asked based on the given arrangement.

Questions from this section can be divided into the following types

- Counting the number of small cubes in a regular/irregular arrangement of cubes.
- Counting the number of cubes having none (or more) of their faces coloured after a big coloured cube is cut into smaller cubes.
- Determining the number of small cubes required to complete a given shape as a perfect cube.

Example 1 Count the number of cubes in the given figure.

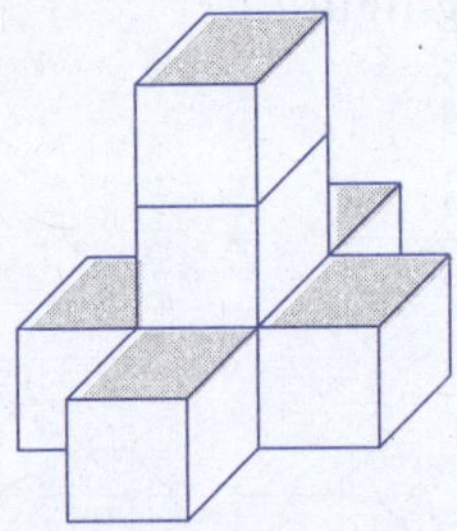

(a) 6

(b) 8

(c) 7

(d) None of the above

Sol. *(c)*

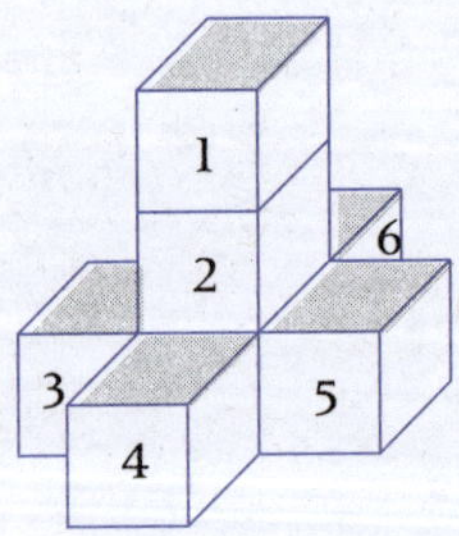

In the above figure, we see that there are 6 visible cubes and one is hidden cube below the cube number 2.

∴ Number of cubes in the given figure

$= 6 + 1 = 7$ cubes

Hence, option (c) is correct.

Example 2 A solid cube of each side 9 cm has been painted on all its faces. It is then cut into cubical blocks of each side 3 cm. The number of cubes having three faces painted and one face painted respectively, are

(a) 6 and 6 (b) 8 and 6
(c) 8 and 8 (d) None of these

Sol. *(b)*

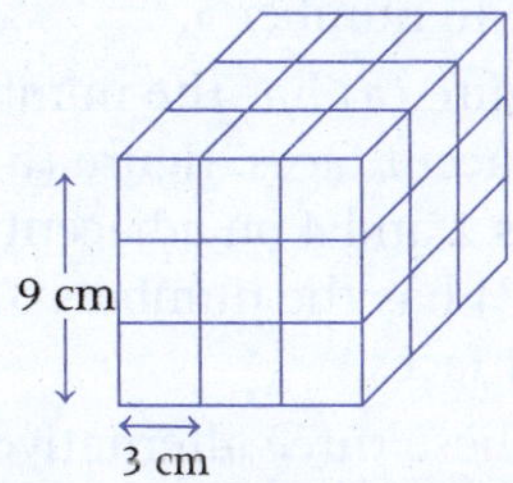

Now, smaller cubes having 3 faces painted will be at the corners of the original solid cube and there are 8 corners in a cube.

∴ Number of cubes having 3 faces painted = 8

Now, a cube having only 1 face painted will be at the centre of each face of the original solid cube. As there are 6 faces in a cube.

∴ Number of small cubes having single face painted = 6

Hence, option (b) is correct.

Dice

A 'Die', (plural dice) is a cube having 6 faces, each of which bears a distinct number of dots or numbers from 1 to 6.

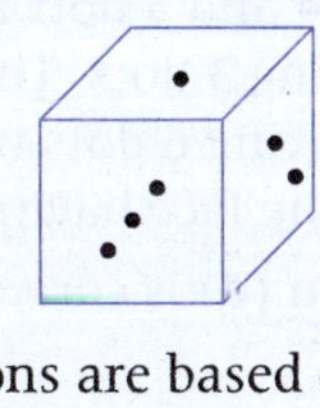

In dice, questions are based on the following types

Construction of Cubes (or Dice) from a Given Net (Unfolded Die)

If a die (or a cube) is unfolded, it can be represented as a net. Various nets can be obtained by unfolding a die in different ways.

Four such nets are as shown below

I

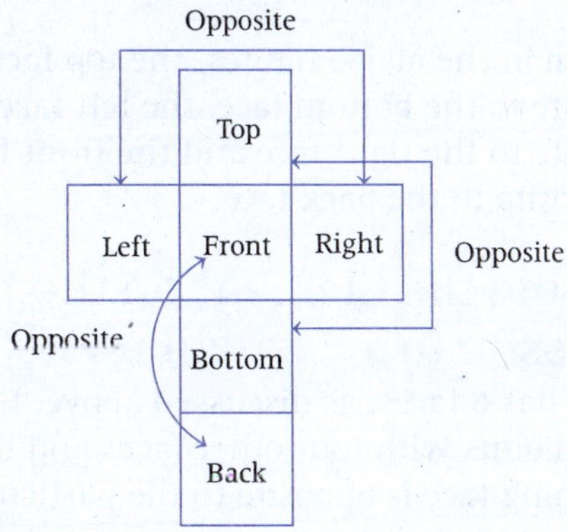

II

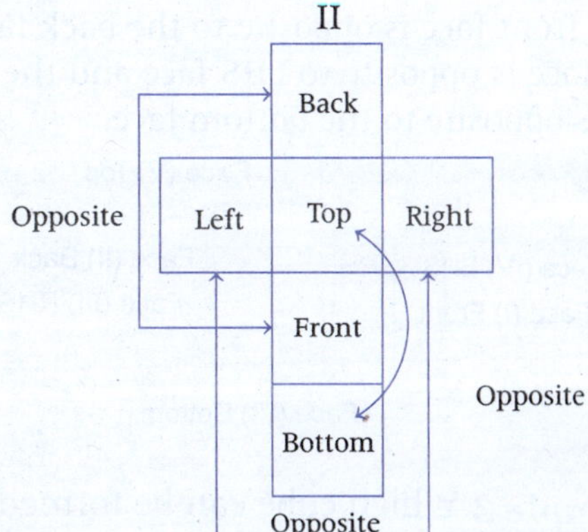

III

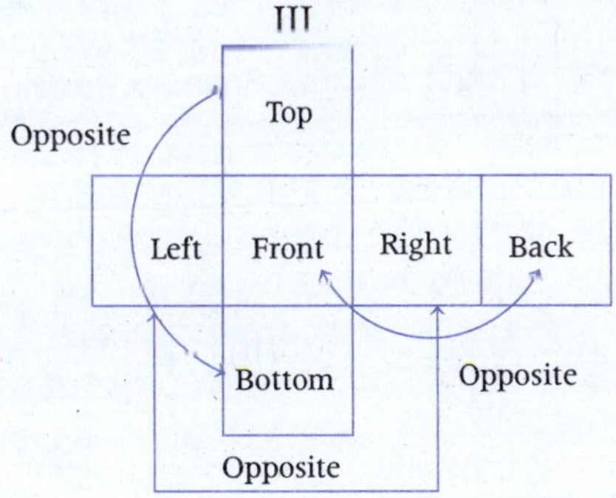

IV

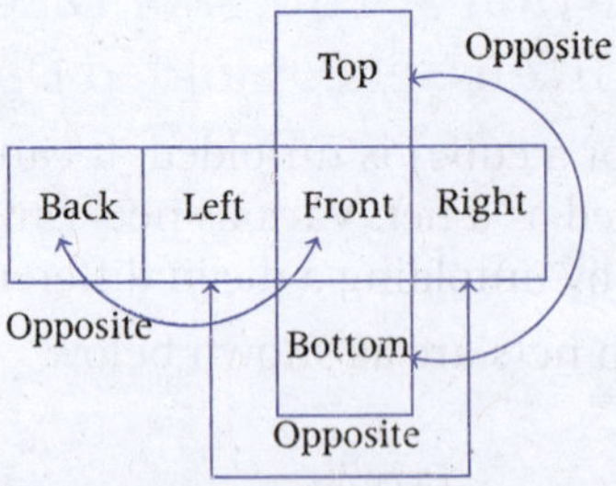

As seen in the above figures, the top face is opposite to the bottom face, the left face is opposite to the right face and the front face is opposite to the back face.

Finding the Element on the Face Opposite to a Particular Face

A dice has 6 faces, as discussed above. Each face adjoints with four other faces and the remaining face is opposite to the particular face.

Here, front face is opposite to the back face, RHS face is opposite to LHS face and the top face is opposite to the bottom face.

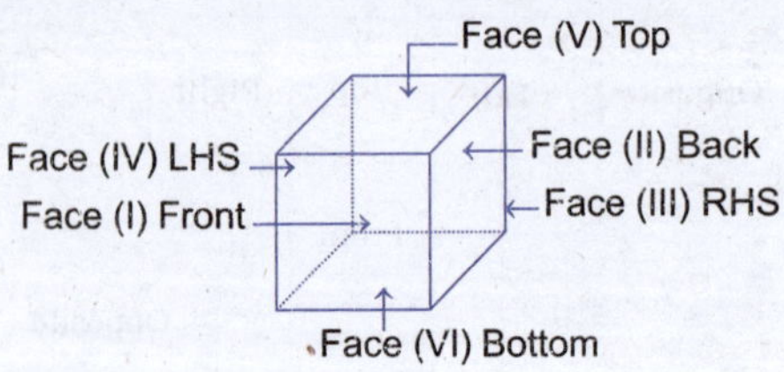

Example 3 Which cube can be formed by folding the given sheet of paper (X)?

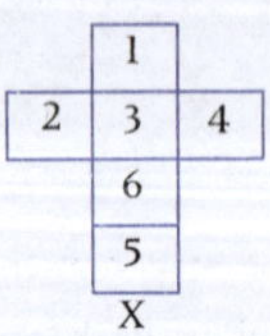

X

(a) 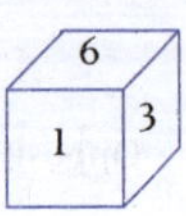

(b) 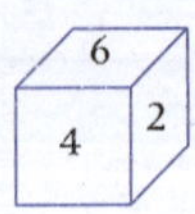

(c) 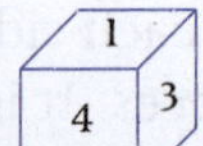

(d) 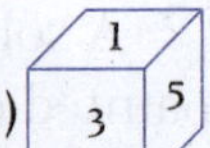

Sol. (c) When the sheet of paper represented by figure (X) is folded to form a cube, then number 2 will be opposite to number 4, number 1 will be opposite to number 6 and number 3 will be opposite to number 5.

Now, figure (a) has the numbers 1 and 6 on adjacent faces, figure (b) has the numbers 2 and 4 on adjacent faces and figure (d) has the numbers 3 and 5 on adjacent faces.

Hence, these three alternatives are not possible.

The only option left is figure (c), which can be formed by folding figure (X).

Hence, option (c) is correct.

Example 4 A die is rolled thrice and its three different positions are as shown below.

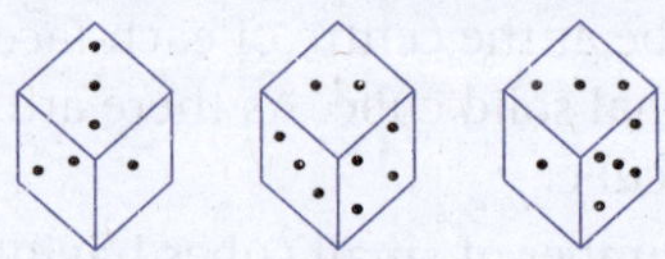

I II III

The number of dots on the face opposite to the face having 3 dots is

(a) 5 (b) 4
(c) 1 (d) 6

Sol. *(d)* The face with 3 dots appears in each of the three positions. Clearly, the faces having 1, 2, 4 and 5 dots are adjacent to the face having 3 dots. The only face left is the one having 6 dots which lies opposite to the face having 3 dots.

Hence, option (d) is correct.

Let's Practice

1 Mark Questions

Directions (Q. Nos. 1-4) Count the number of cubes in the following figures.

1.

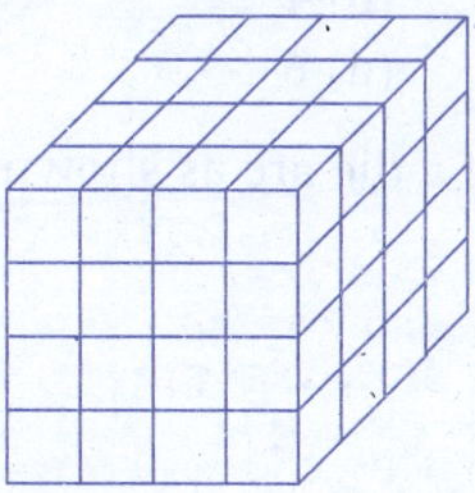

(a) 48 (b) 64
(c) 16 (d) None of these

2.

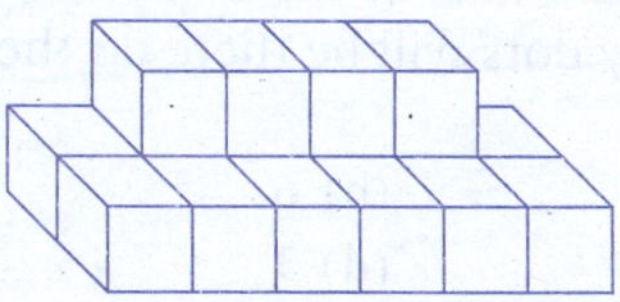

(a) 16 (b) 12
(c) 15 (d) None of these

3.

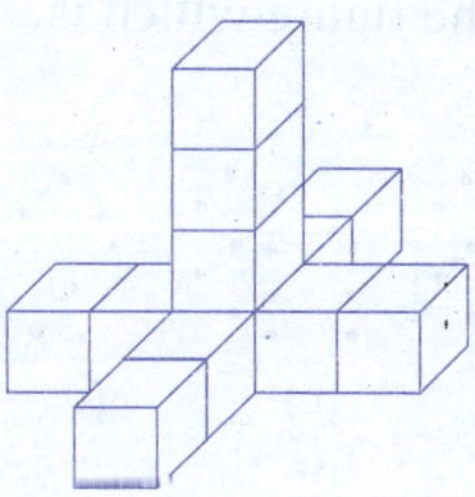

(a) 11 (b) 12
(c) 15 (d) None of these

4.

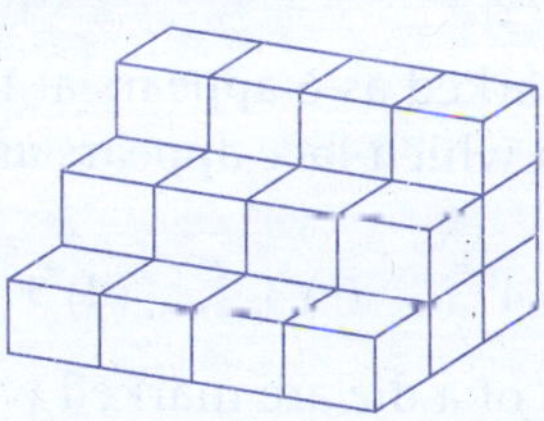

(a) 24 (b) 25
(c) 20 (d) None of these

Directions (Q. Nos. 5-8) Study the following information carefully and answer the given questions that follow.

A solid cube of each side 6 cm has been painted on all the faces. It is then cut into cubical blocks of each side 2 cm.

5. How many small cubes are there in the solid cube?
(a) 27 (b) 64
(c) 12 (d) None of these

6. How many small cubes have no faces painted?
(a) 0 (b) 1
(c) 2 (d) 3

7. How many cubes have only one face painted?
(a) 8 (b) 4
(c) 6 (d) None of these

8. How many cubes have only three faces painted?
(a) 12 (b) 6
(c) 8 (d) None of these

Directions (Q. Nos. 9-11) Which cube can be formed by folding the given sheet of paper (X)?

9.

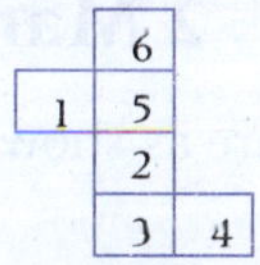

(X)

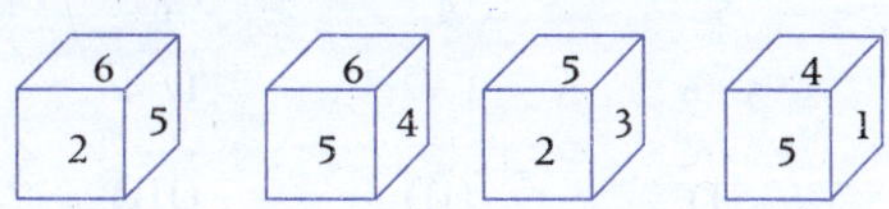

(a) (b) (c) (d)

10. 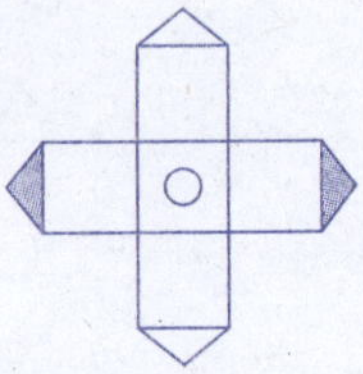

(X)

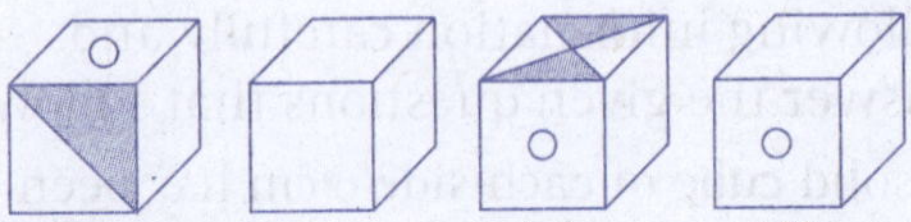

(a) (b) (c) (d)

11. 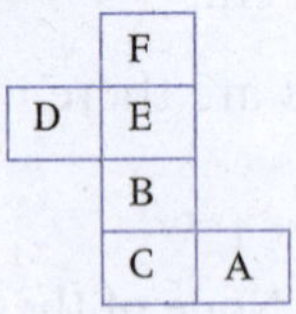

(X)

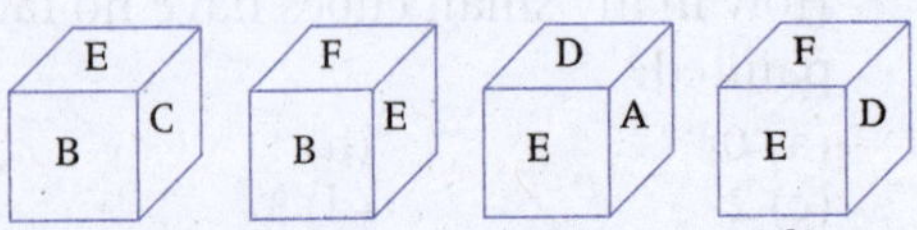

(a) (b) (c) (d)

12. The given figure shows the net of a cube. Which one of the faces is the base of the cube?

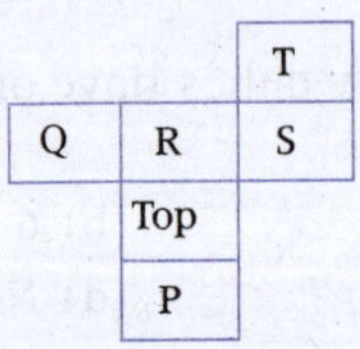

(a) P (b) T (c) R (d) S

13. How many dots lie opposite to the face having three dots, when the given figure is folded to form a cube?

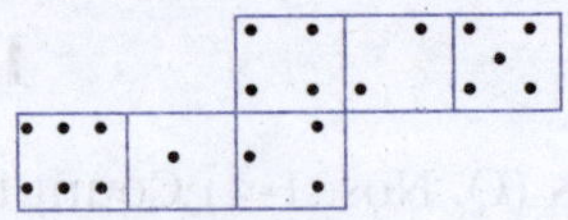

(a) 2 (b) 4
(c) 5 (d) 6

14. Two positions of a die are as shown below

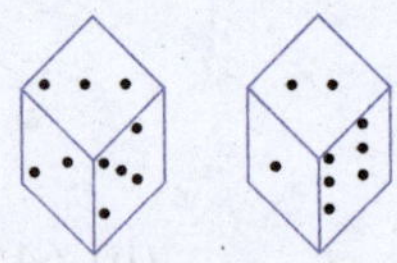

If there are 4 dots at the bottom, then how many dots will be there on the top face?

(a) 2 (b) 6
(c) 5 (d) 3

15. Given that the total number of dots present on opposite faces of a die is always 7, find the figure which is correct.

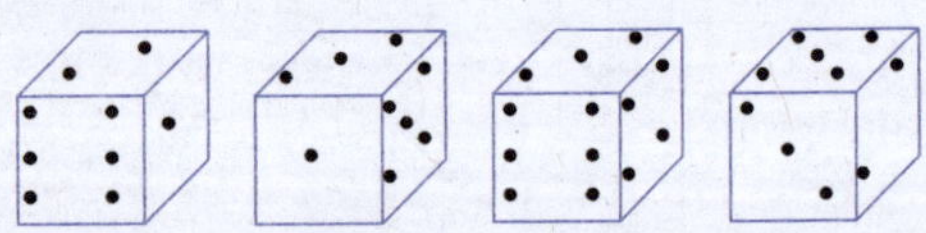

(a) (b) (c) (d)

2 Marks Questions

16. Three positions of a die are as shown below

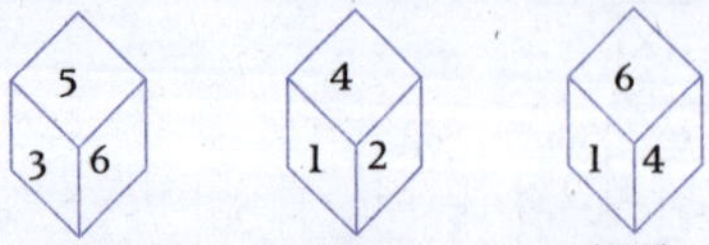

(I) (II) (III)

If the face marked as 6 appears at the bottom, then which face appears as the top face?

(a) 2 (b) 4 (c) 3 (d) 5

17. The six faces of a die are marked with letters A, B, C, D, E and F. The die is rolled three times and the positions obtained are shown as below

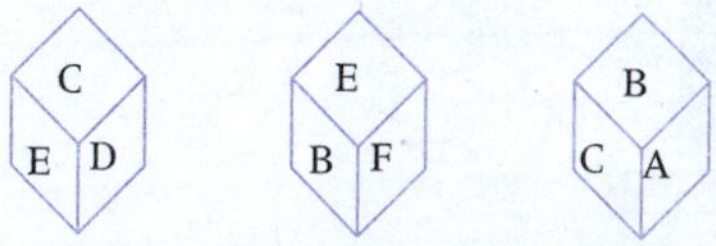

(I) (II) (III)

Which letter appears opposite A?

(a) E (b) D (c) C (d) F

18. Below are depicted the three different positions of a die. Find the number of dots on the face opposite to the face with 1 dot.

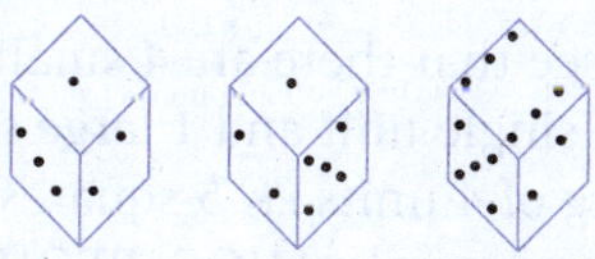

(I) (II) (III)

(a) 2 (b) 3
(c) 4 (d) 6

19. Calculate the number of cubes required to make the figure a perfect cube.

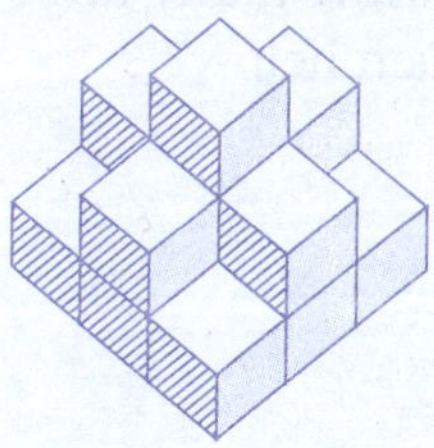

(a) 12 (b) 19
(c) 15 (d) None of these

20. Calculate the number of cubes required to make the figure a perfect cube.

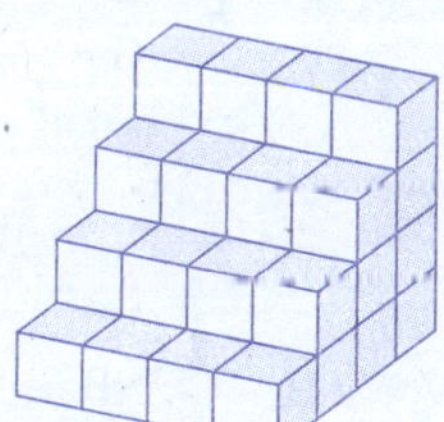

(a) 20 (b) 24 (c) 28 (d) 30

Direction (Q. No. 21) In each of the following questions, a sheet of paper represented as Figure (X) is folded to form a cube. From amongst the four alternatives (a), (b), (c) and (d), choose the cube which is similar to the cube that will be formed.

21.

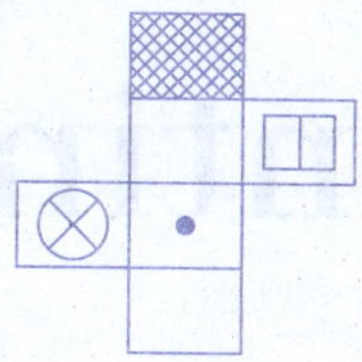

(X)

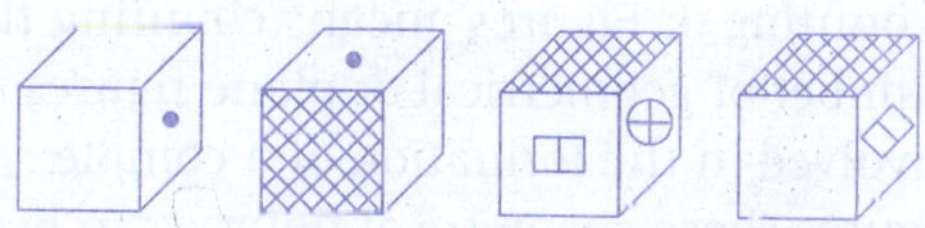

(a) (b) (c) (d)

Directions (Q.Nos. 22 and 23)Study the information given below carefully and answer the questions that follow.

The six faces of a cube have been marked with six different symbols

 and 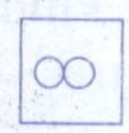

Three different positions of the cube are as shown below

(I) (II) (III)

22. Which symbol lies opposite the cross (×)?

(a) • (b) ✹
(c) □ (d) ×

23. Which symbol appears at the bottom of figure II?

(a) • (b) ✹ (c) □ (d) ∞

Chapter

14

Counting of Figures

'Counting of Figures' means counting the number of geometrical or plane figures involved in the formation of a complex figure. These geometrical figures can be lines, circles, rectangles, triangles, etc.

In such type of questions, a complex figure is given which consists of several small geometrical figures and the students are required to count these small geometrical figures to answer the question.

e.g. Find the number of squares in the given figure.

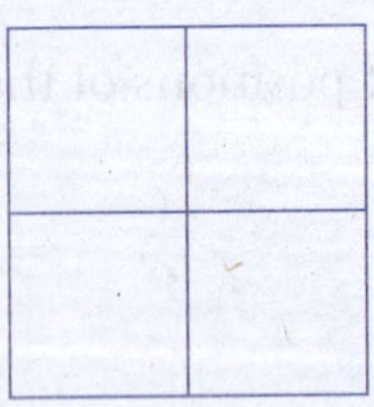

On labelling the above figure, we get

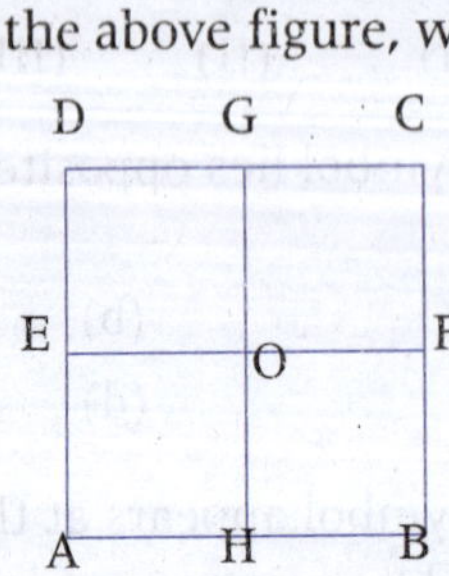

Here, we see that there are 4 small squares formed of single unit and 1 large square comprising of 4 units *i.e.* 5 squares in the above figure namely AHOE, BFOH, FOGC, DGOE and ABCD, respectively.

Hence, there are 5 squares in the above figure.

In counting of figures, following types of questions are generally asked

Example 1 How many lines are there in the figure given below?

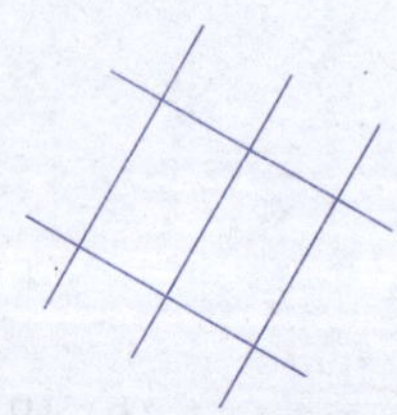

(a) 3 (b) 5

(c) 4 (d) None of these

Sol. (b) On labelling the given figure, we get

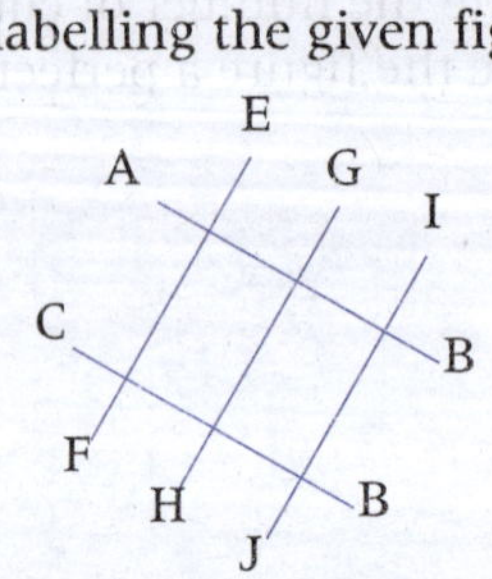

The lines in the figure are

AB , CD , EF , GH and IJ.

So, there are 5 lines.

Hence, option (b) is correct.

Example 2 How many circles are there in the figure given below?

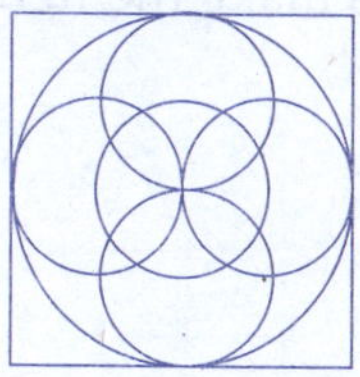

(a) 6 (b) 5 (c) 2 (d) 3

Sol. *(a)* There are two main circles and four smaller circles intersecting each other.

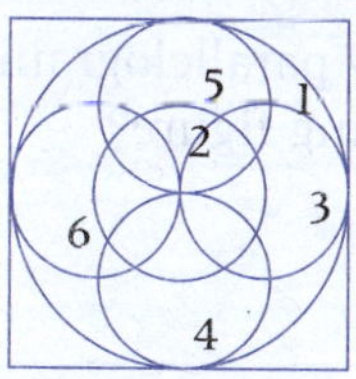

So, the total number of circles $= 2 + 4 = 6$

Hence, option (a) is correct.

Example 3 How many triangles are there in the figure given below?

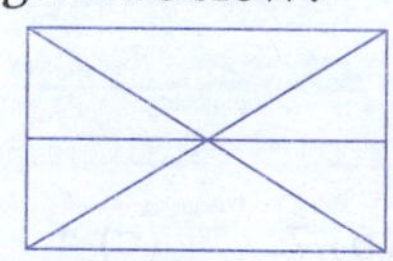

(a) 8 (b) 10 (c) 12 (d) 6

Sol. *(c)* To count the total number of triangles, count the number of triangles made up of 1 unit, 2 units, 3 units and so on.

On labelling the given figure, we get

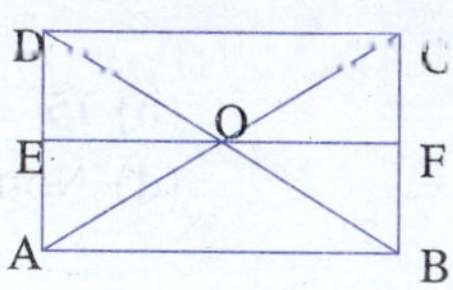

Triangles made up of 1 unit

$= \Delta AOB, \Delta BOF, \Delta FOC, \Delta COD, \Delta DOE$ and $\Delta EOA = 6$

Triangles formed by two small triangles

$= \Delta DOA$ and $\Delta BOC = 2$

Triangles formed by 3 small triangles

$= \Delta ABC, \Delta BCD, \Delta ACD$ and $\Delta ADB = 4$

$\therefore$ Total number of triangles

$= 6 + 2 + 4 = 12$ triangles

Hence, option (c) is correct.

Example 4 How many squares are there in the figure given below?

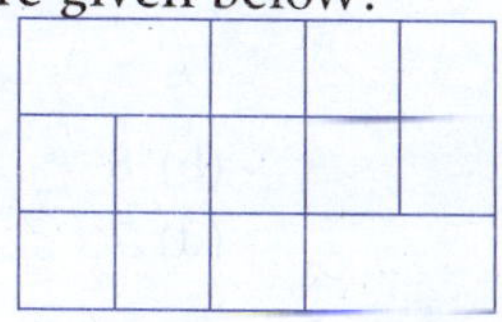

(a) 12 (b) 14 (c) 10 (d) 19

Sol. *(d)* On labelling the given figure, we get

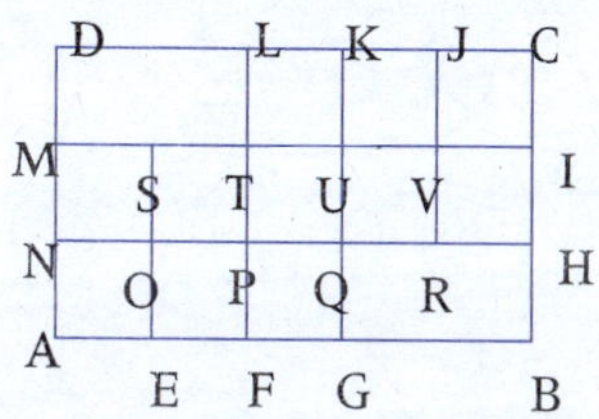

Squares made up of one unit

$=$ □ ANOE, □ NOSM, □ OPTS, □ OPFE, □ FGQP, □ PQUT, □ QRVU, □ RHIV, □ VICJ, □ VJKU and □ KUTL $= 11$

Squares formed by 3 figures (1 rectangle and 2 squares) $=$ □ DNPL and □ GUIB $= 2$

Squares formed by 4 small squares $=$ □ AMTF, □ ESUG, □ LPRJ and □ KQHC $= 4$

Squares formed by 8 figures (1 rectangle and 7 square) $=$ □ ADKG and □ LFBC $= 2$

$\therefore$ Total number of squares

$= 11 + 2 + 4 + 2 = 19$

Hence, option (d) is correct.

Let's Practice

1 Mark Questions

1. How many lines are there in the figure given below?

(a) 15 (b) 8
(c) 10 (d) 7

2. How many circles are there in the figure given below?

(a) 12 (b) 14
(c) 10 (d) None of these

3. Find the number of straight lines required to make the figure given below.

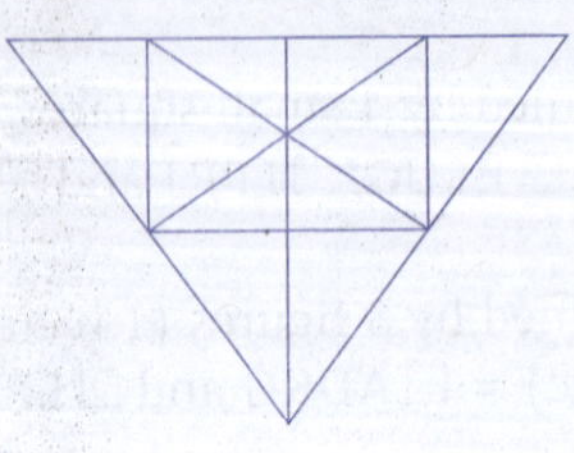

(a) 9 (b) 10
(c) 12 (d) None of these

4. Find the number of straight lines required to make the figure given below.

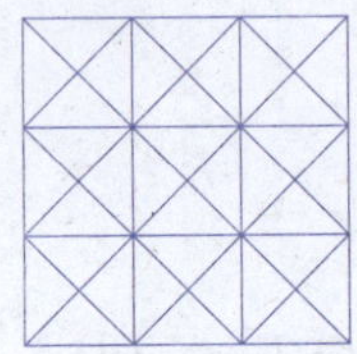

(a) 20 (b) 22
(c) 18 (d) None of these

5. How many parallelograms are there in the following figure?

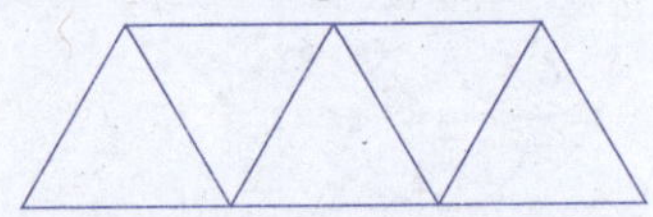

(a) 3 (b) 4 (c) 5 (d) 6

6. Find the number of squares in the figure given below.

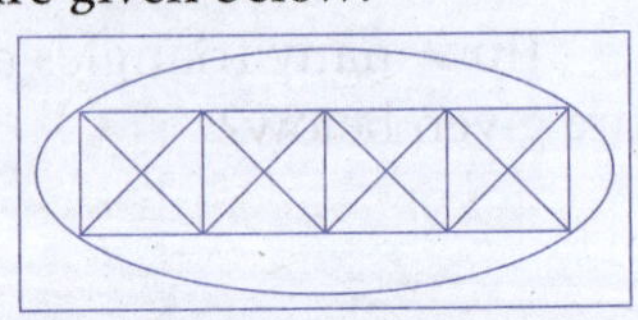

(a) 5 (b) 7 (c) 4 (d) 9

7. Find the number of triangles in the figure given below.

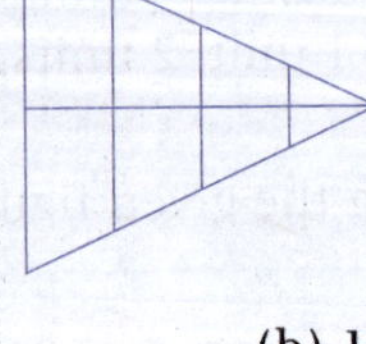

(a) 13 (b) 15
(c) 12 (d) None of these

8. Count the number of triangles in the given figure.

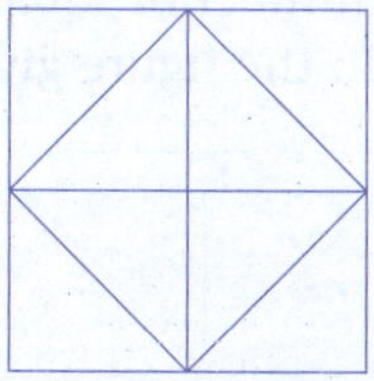

(a) 8 (b) 10
(c) 12 (d) None of these

9. Find the number of squares in the figure given below.

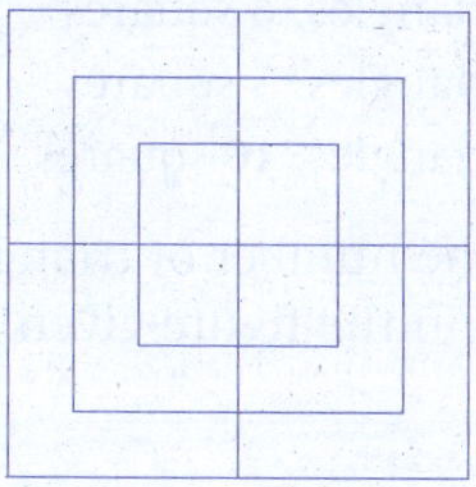

(a) 15 (b) 20
(c) 13 (d) None of these

10. How many triangles are there in the following figure?

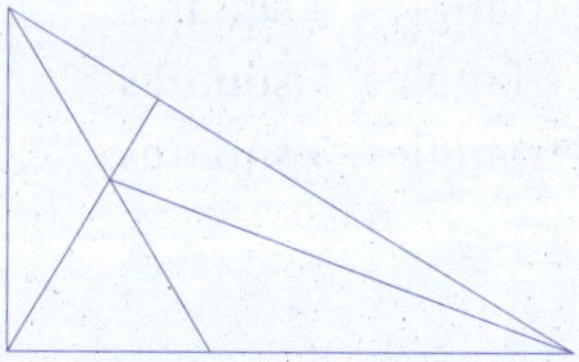

(a) 6 (b) 10
(c) 11 (d) 12

11. What is the number of rectangles in the following figure?

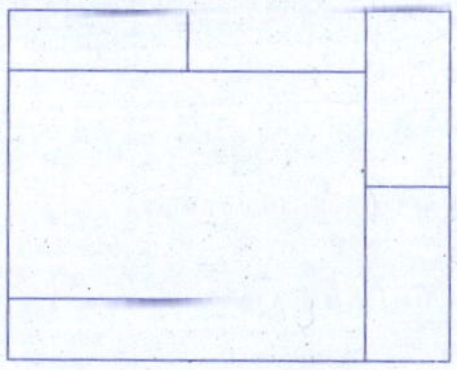

(a) 8 (b) 9
(c) 12 (d) 11

12. Find the number of triangles in the figure given below.

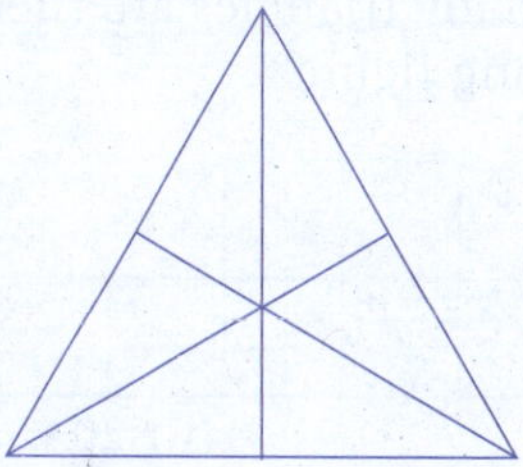

(a) 16 (b) 13 (c) 9 (d) 7

13. How many triangles are there in the following figure?

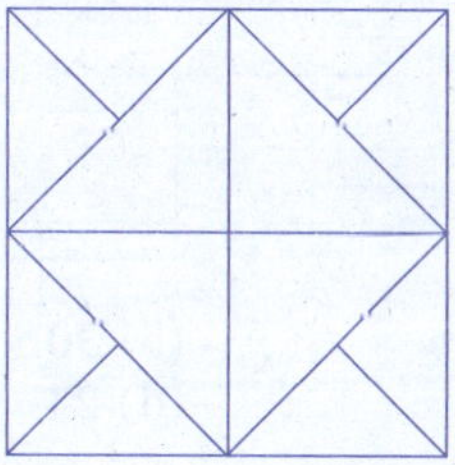

(a) 16 (b) 20
(c) 12 (d) 22

14. Identify the number of squares in the figure given below.

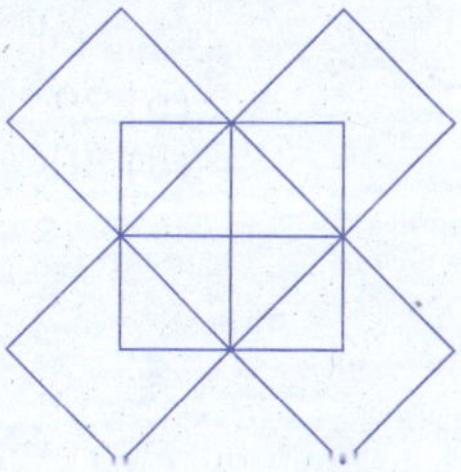

(a) 10 (b) 12
(c) 13 (d) 14

15. How many quadrilaterals are there in the following figure?

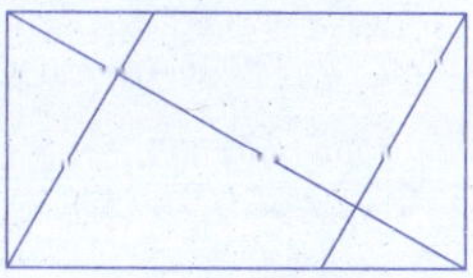

(a) 10 (b) 8
(c) 12 (d) 6

2 Marks Questions

16. How many triangles are there in the following figure?

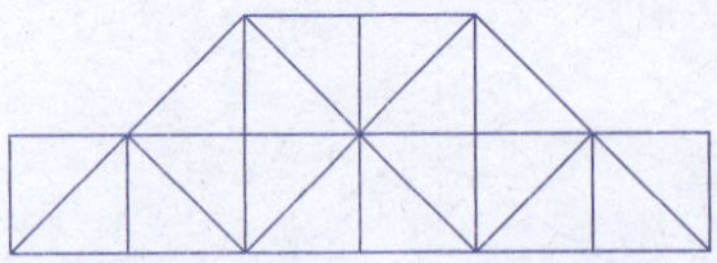

(a) 25 (b) 20
(c) 36 (d) None of these

17. Find the number of rectangles in the figure given below.

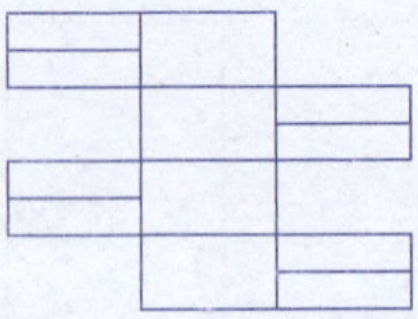

(a) 26 (b) 30
(c) 28 (d) 24

18. Find the number of parallelograms in the figure given below.

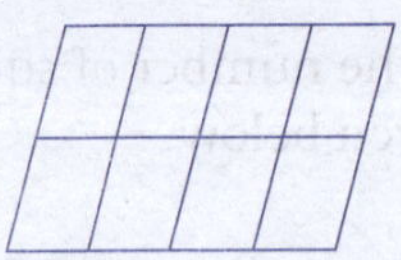

(a) 20 (b) 29
(c) 22 (d) 30

19. Find the number of squares and triangles in the figure given below.

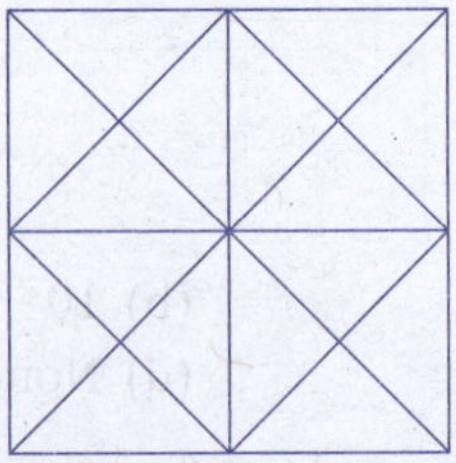

(a) 36 triangles, 10 squares
(b) 27 triangles, 6 squares
(c) 44 triangles, 5 squares
(d) 44 triangles, 10 squares

20. Count the number of triangles and squares in the figure given below.

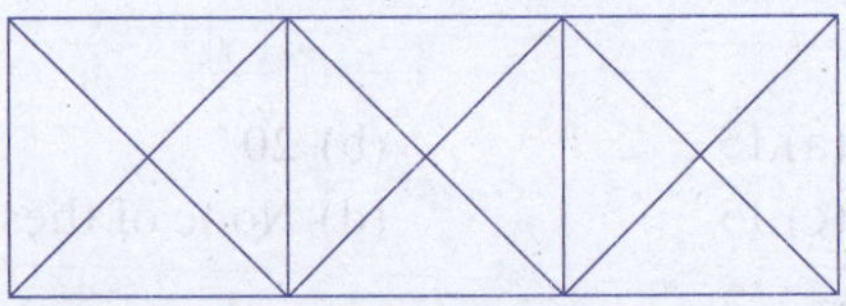

(a) 28 triangles, 2 squares
(b) 24 triangles, 5 squares
(c) 28 triangles, 5 squares
(d) 24 triangles, 3 squares

Chapter 15

Paper Folding and Paper Cutting

'Paper folding and Paper cutting' problems are based on a piece of paper which is folded along a dotted line or folded and cut (or punched) in a particular manner.

These questions are basically classified into following two types.

1. Paper folding (folded pattern)
2. Paper cutting (unfolded pattern)

1. Paper folding (folded pattern)

'Paper Folding' involves folding a transparent sheet along a dotted line, so that the design on one side of the dotted line gets superimposed on the design on the other side.

In such type of questions, students are required to select a figure from the given alternatives which closely resembles the pattern that would be formed when a transparent sheet of a paper, carrying a certain design is folded along the dotted line.

Direction (Ex. No. 1) In each of the following examples, a transparent sheet with a certain design and a dotted line is given. From amongst the four answer sheets, choose the one which resembles the transparent sheet after folding it along the dotted line.

Example 1

Transparent Sheet

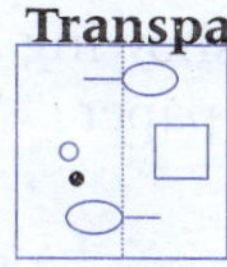

Answer Sheets

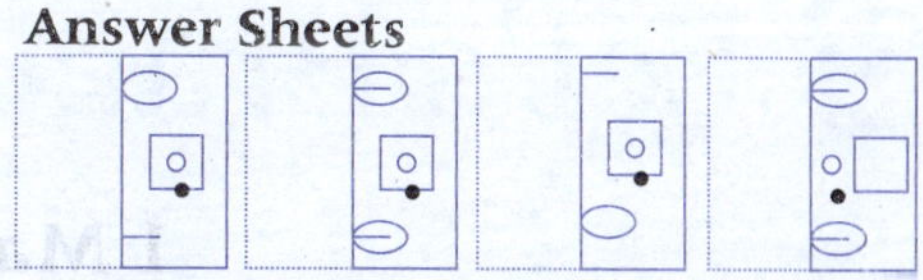

(a) (b) (c) (d)

Sol. (b) Clearly, the left half of the transparent sheet has been folded and placed over the right half.

The mirror image of the design on the left half of the sheet will get superimposed on the design on the right half. The folded transparent sheet will appear the same as figure (b).

Hence, option (b) is correct.

2. Paper Cutting

- 'Paper Cutting' involves folding a paper twice or thrice after which one or more cuts are made into it.
- In such type of questions, a set of three or more figures is given showing the manner in which a paper is folded and then cut. In each of the first two figures, a dotted line together with an arrow on it, is given. The paper is folded along with dotted line in the direction which is indicated by the arrow.
- Now, in third figure marks showing the position and nature of the cuts made in the folded sheet are given. The students are required to select one of the figures from the set of four answer figures that would most closely resemble the pattern of the paper when unfolded.

Direction (Ex. No. 2) Each of the following examples consists of a set of three sheets (X), (Y) and (Z) showing a sequence of folding a piece of paper. Sheet (Z) depicts the manner in which the folded paper has been cut. From amongst the four answer sheets (a), (b), (c) and (d), choose the one showing the unfolded form of sheet (Z).

Example 2

Transparent Sheet

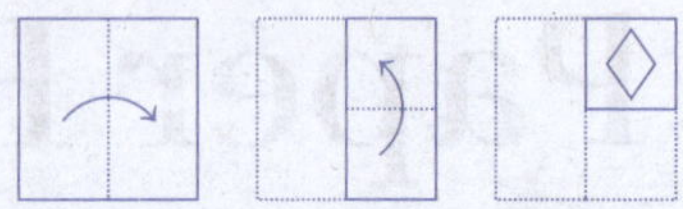

X Y Z

Answer Sheets

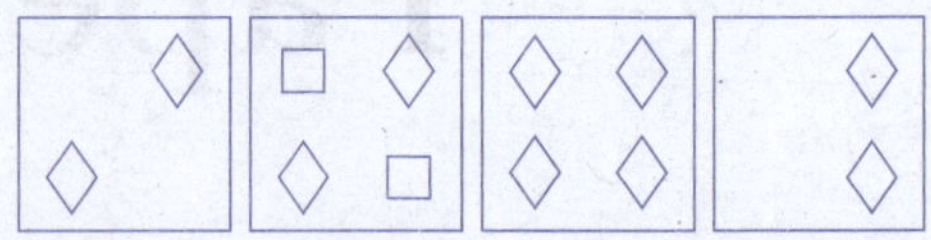

(a) (b) (c) (d)

Sol. *(c)* Upon unfolding the folded paper, represented by figure (Z), we get

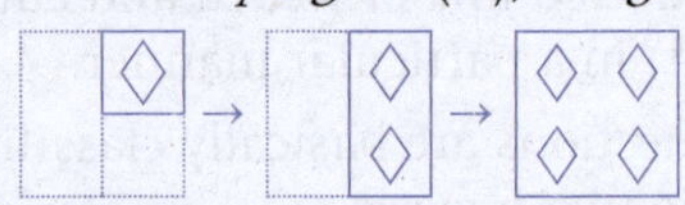

Z

Hence, option (c) is correct.

Let's Practice

1 Mark Questions

Directions (Q. Nos. 1-10) In each of the following questions, a transparent sheet with a certain design and a dotted line is given. From amongst the four answer figures, choose the one which resembles the transparent sheet after folding it along the dotted line.

1. Transparent Sheet

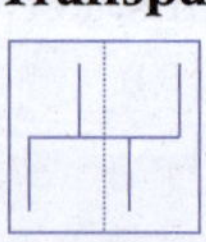

Answer Sheets

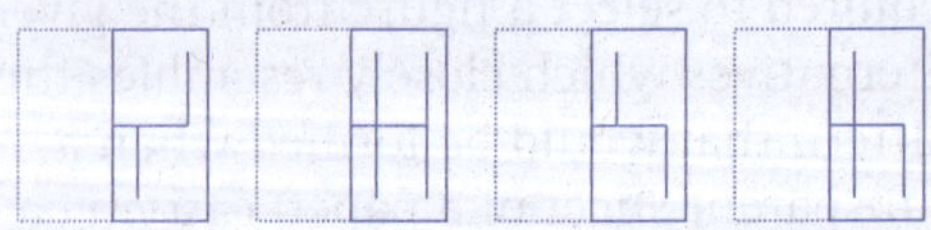

(a) (b) (c) (d)

2. Transparent Sheet

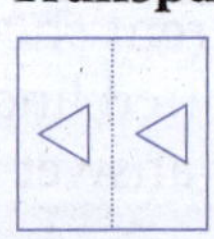

Answer Sheets

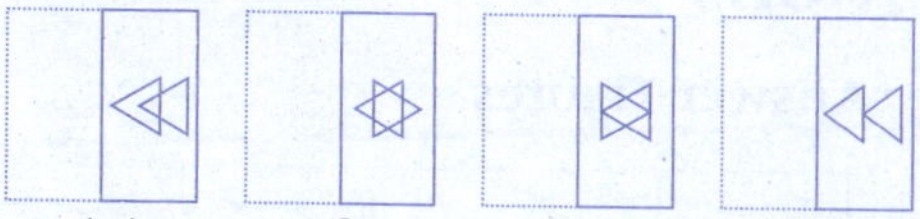

(a) (b) (c) (d)

3. Transparent Sheet

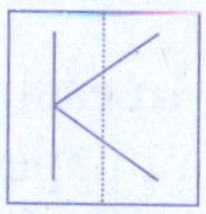

Answer Sheets

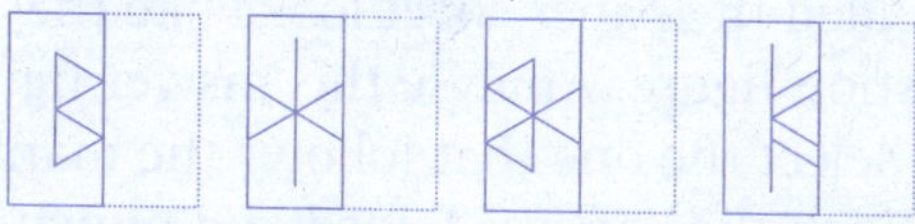

(a) (b) (c) (d)

4. Transparent Sheet

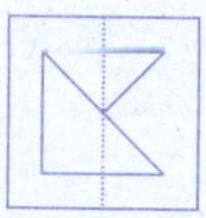

Answer Sheets

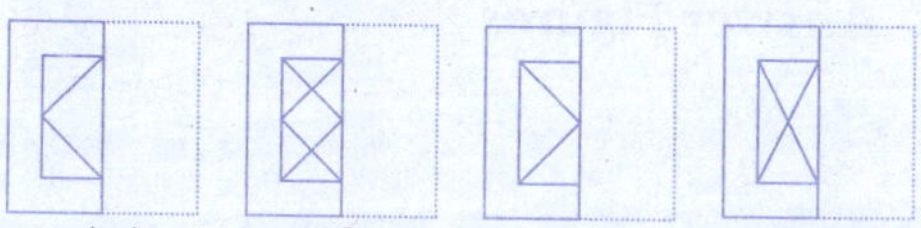

(a) (b) (c) (d)

5. Transparent Sheet

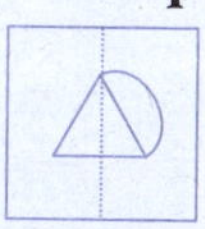

Answer Sheets

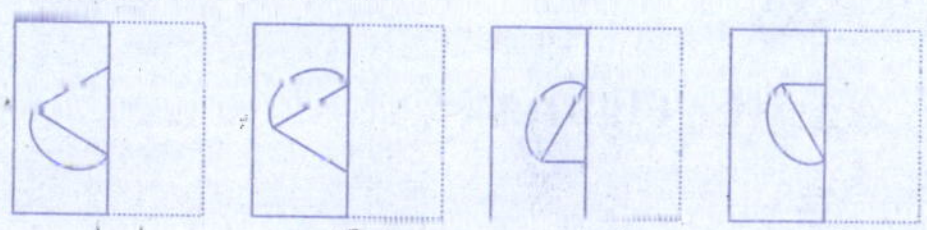

(a) (b) (c) (d)

Directions (Q. Nos. 6-8) Each of the following questions consists of a set of three transparent sheets (X), (Y) and (Z) showing a sequence of folding a piece of paper. Sheet (Z) depicts the manner in which the folded paper has been cut. From amongst the four answer sheets (a), (b), (c) and (d), choose the one showing the unfolded form of sheet (Z).

6. Transparent Sheets

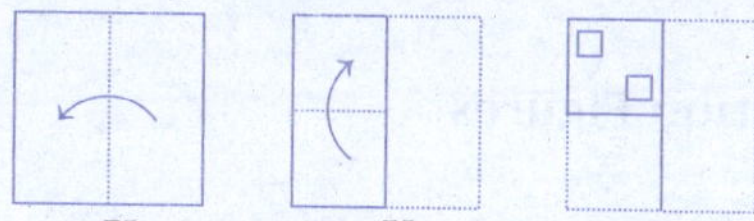

X Y Z

Answer Sheets

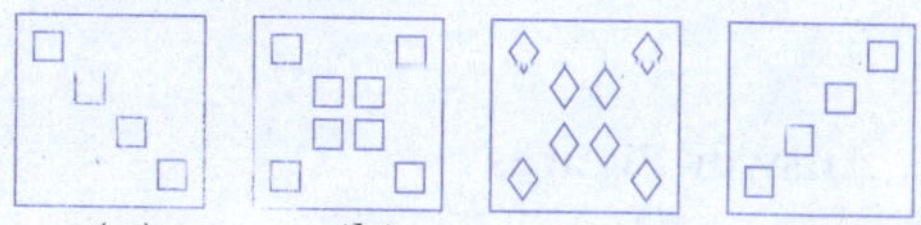

(a) (b) (c) (d)

7. Transparent Sheets

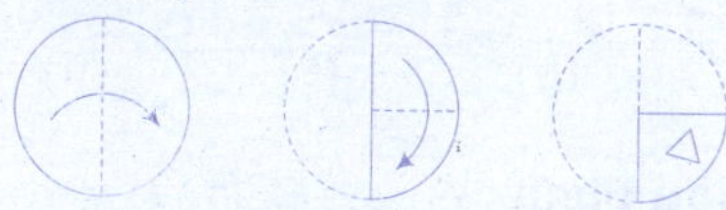

X Y Z

Answer Sheets

(a) (b) (c) (d)

8. Transparent Sheets

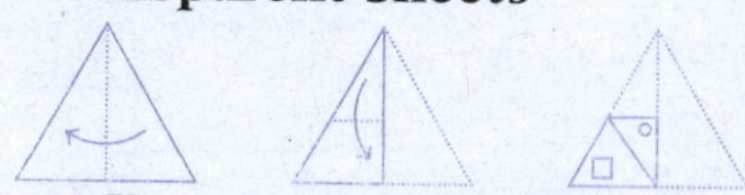

X Y Z

Answer Sheets

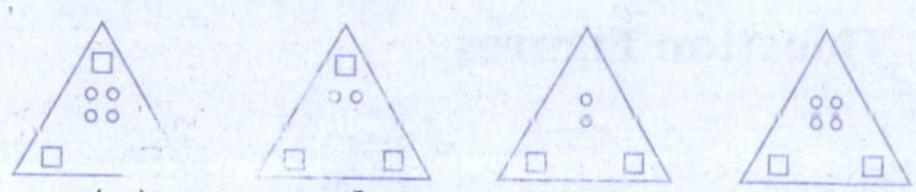

(a) (b) (c) (d)

2 Marks Questions

Directions (Q. Nos. 9-11) Each of the following questions consists of set of three sheets (X), (Y) and (Z), showing a sequence of folding a piece of paper, sheet (Z) depicts the manner in which the folded paper has been cut. From the given options select the one showing the unfolded form of sheet (Z).

9. Question Figures

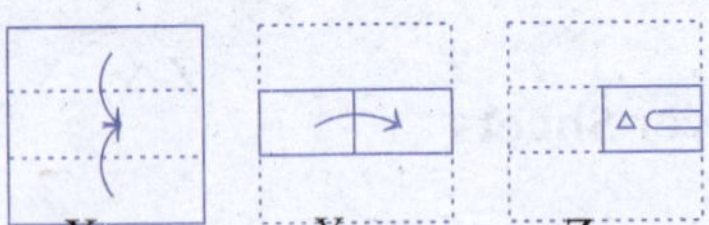

X Y Z

Answer Figures

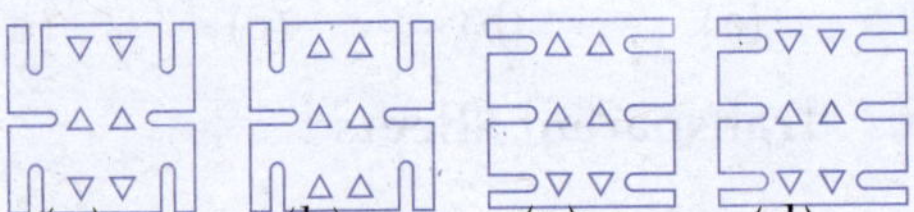

(a) (b) (c) (d)

10. Question Figures

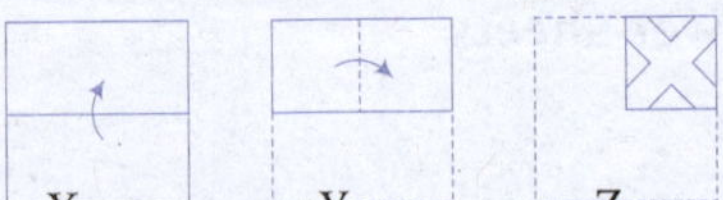

X Y Z

Answer Figures

(a) (b) (c) (d)

11. Question Figures

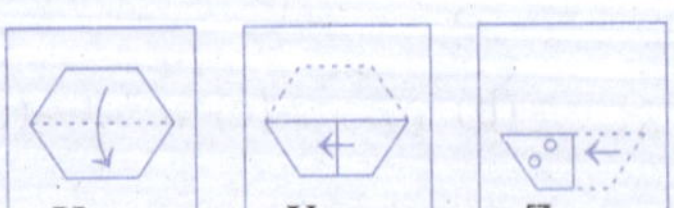

X Y Z

Answer Figures

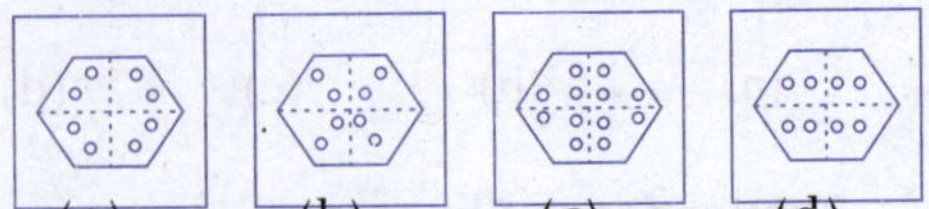

(a) (b) (c) (d)

Directions (Q. Nos. 12 and 13) In each of the following questions, a sheet of paper is folded and punch (cut) is made. When unfolded the paper sheet looks like the question figure. Analyse the answer figures and select the one that follows the manner in which the paper is folded and punch is made.

12. Question Figure

(X)

Answer Figures

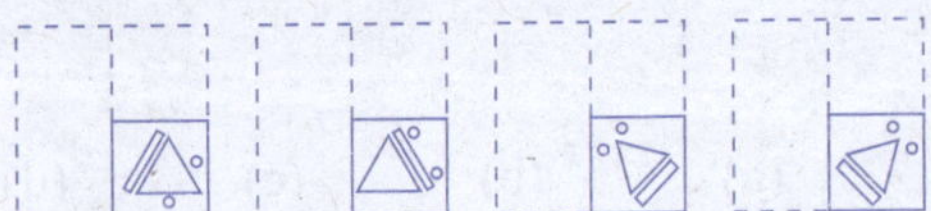

(a) (b) (c) (d)

13. Question Figure

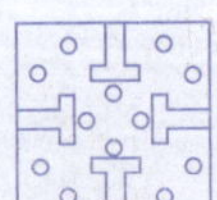

(X)

Answer Figures

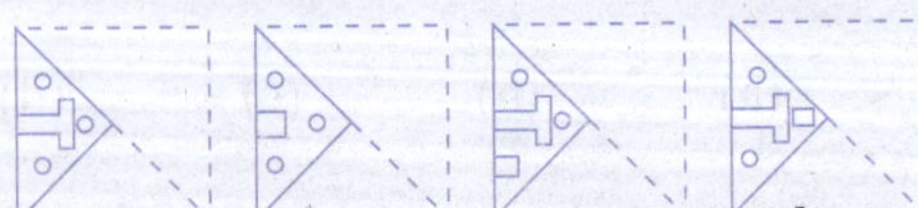

(a) (b) (c) (d)

Chapter 16

Dot Situation

The problems on 'Dot Position in Figures' involve the search of similar conditions in the alternative figures as indicated in the problem figure. In such type of questions, the problem figure contains dots(s) placed in the spaces(s) enclosed between the combination of three or more geometrical figures usually triangle, square, rectangle or/and circle.

There are basically two types of questions asked from this topic which are as follows

1. Double Dot Situation

These type of questions involve regions which is common to two dots. Students have to identify the regions in which two dots are placed.

Example 1 Choose the one figure from the four option figures, which best explains the characteristics given in question figure (X).

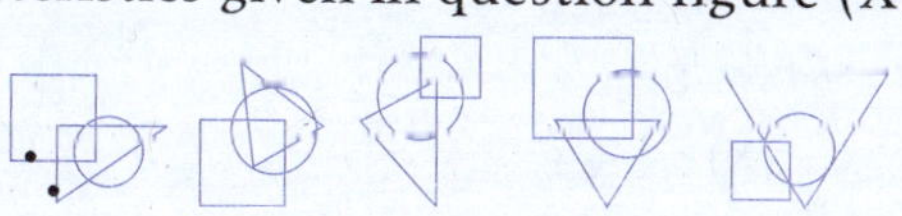

(X) (a) (b) (c) (d)

Sol. *(c)* Here, one dot is placed in the common region between square and triangle and another dot is placed in the common region between triangle and circle as shown

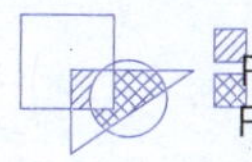

Now, from answer figures, option (c) represents such regions as shown

Hence, option (c) is correct.

2. Triple Dot Situation

These type of questions involves region which is common to three dots. Students have to identify the region in which three dots are placed.

Example 2 Choose the one figure from the four option figures, which best explains the characeristics given in the question figure (X).

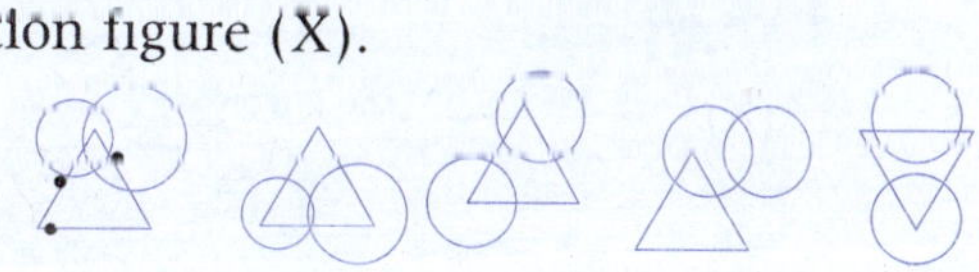

(X) (a) (b) (c) (d)

Sol. (a)

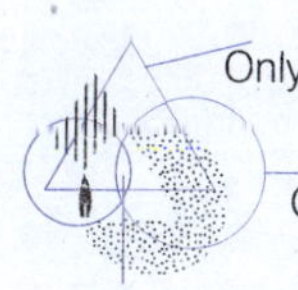

Let's Practice

1 Mark Questions

Directions (Q. Nos. 1-15) Choose the one figure from the four option figures, which best explains the characterstics given in the question figure (X).

1.

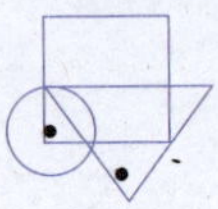

(X)

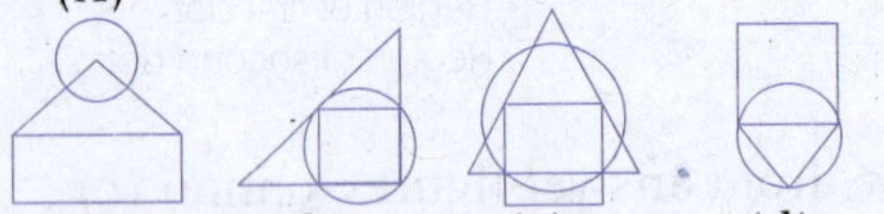

(a) (b) (c) (d)

2.

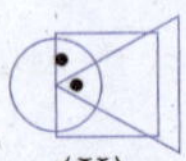

(X)

(a) (b) (c) (d)

3.

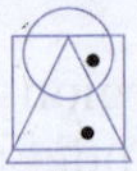

(X)

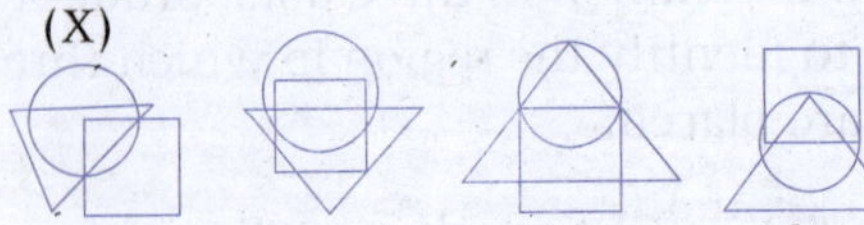

(a) (b) (c) (d)

4.

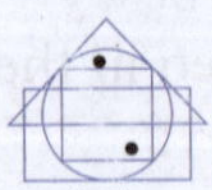

(X)

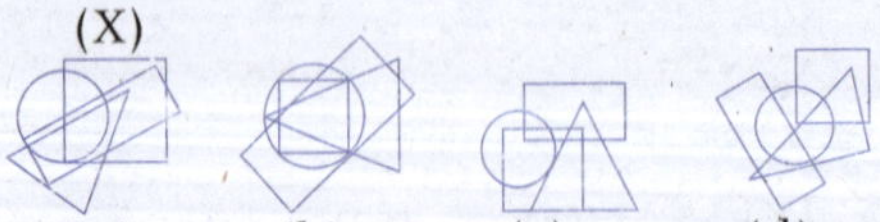

(a) (b) (c) (d)

5.

(X)

(a) (b) (c) (d)

6.

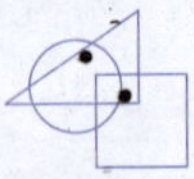

(X)

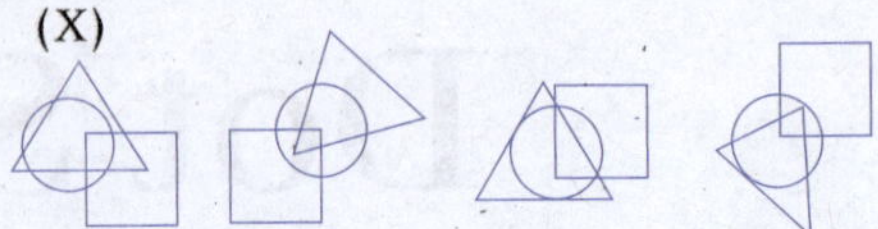

(a) (b) (c) (d)

7.

(X)

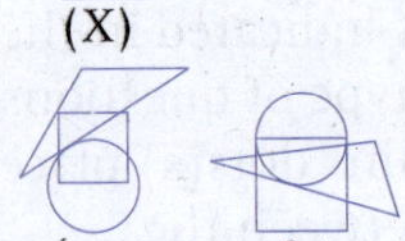

(a) (b) (c) (d)

8.

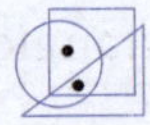

(X)

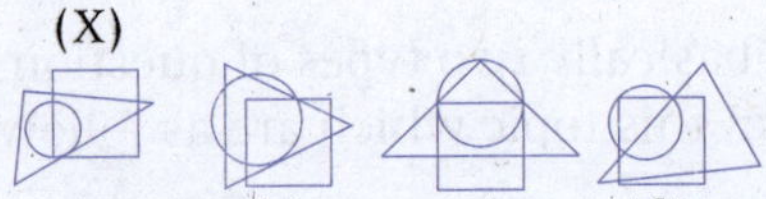

(a) (b) (c) (d)

9.

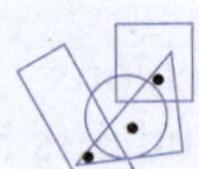

(X)

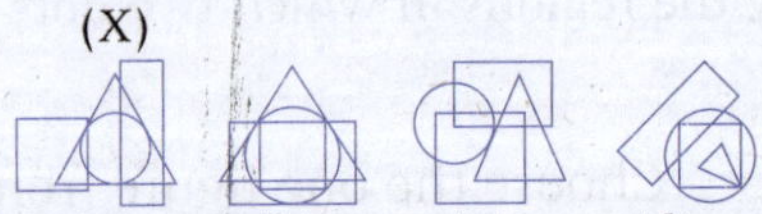

(a) (b) (c) (d)

10.

(X)

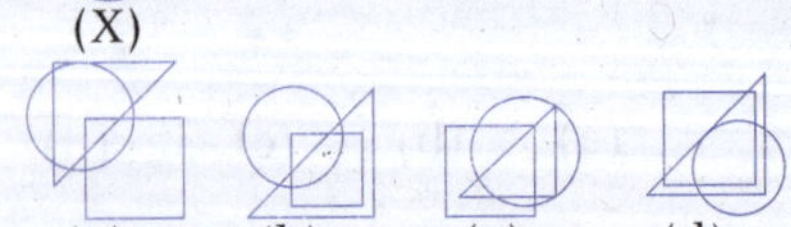

(a) (b) (c) (d)

11.

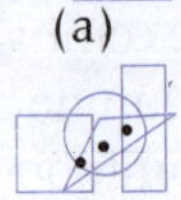

(X)

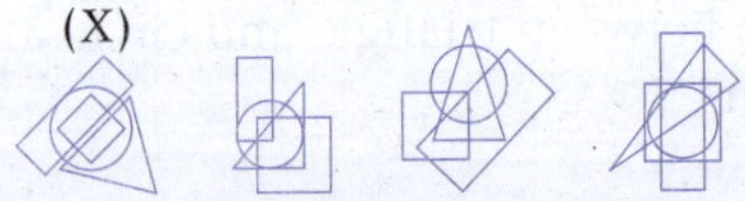

(a) (b) (c) (d)

12.

(X)

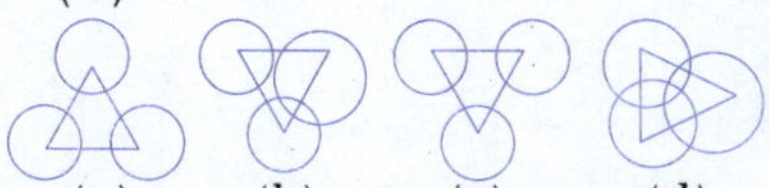

(a) (b) (c) (d)

13.

(X)

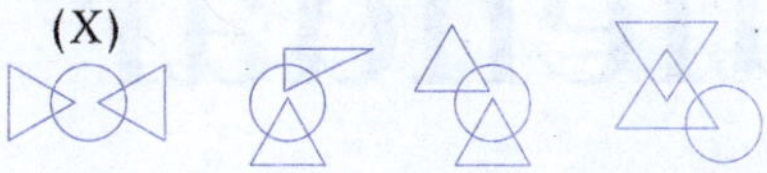

(a) (b) (c) (d)

14.

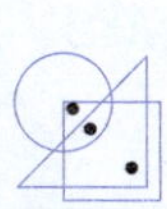

(X)

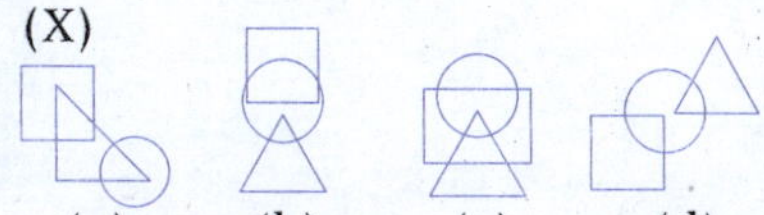

(a) (b) (c) (d)

15.

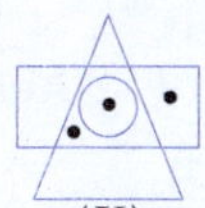

(X)

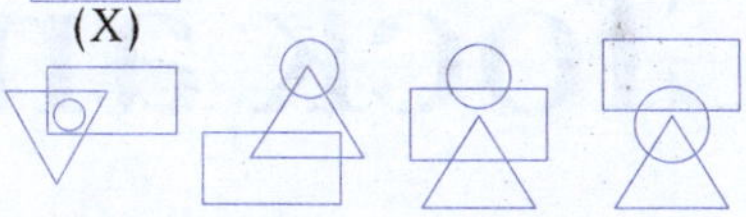

(a) (b) (c) (d)

2 Marks Questions

Directions (Q. Nos. 16-20) Choose the one figure from the four options that best explains the characteristics given in the question figure (X).

16.

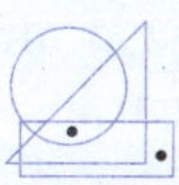

(X)

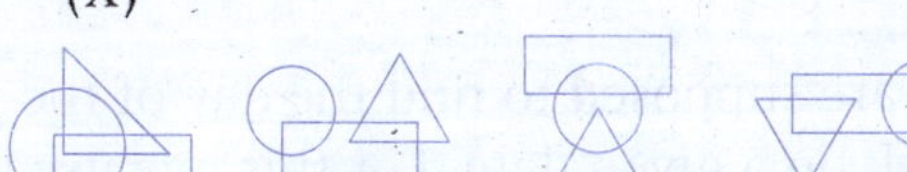

(a) (b) (c) (d)

17.

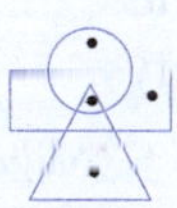

(X)

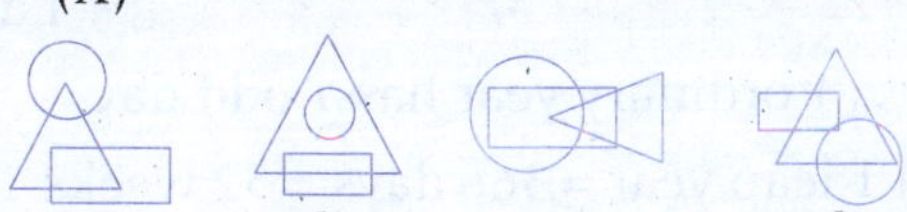

(a) (b) (c) (d)

18.

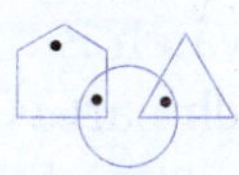

(X)

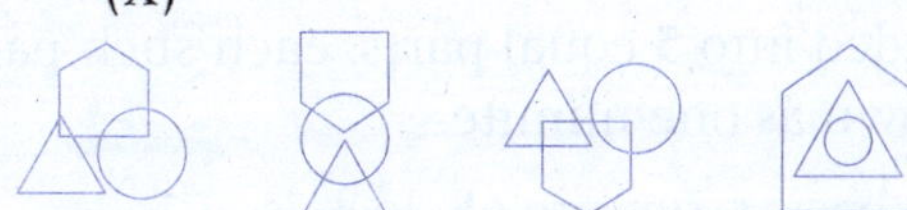

(a) (b) (c) (d)

19.

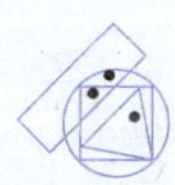

(X)

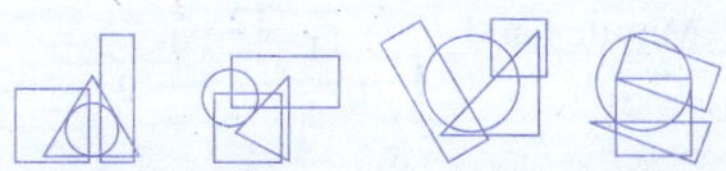

(a) (b) (c) (d)

20.

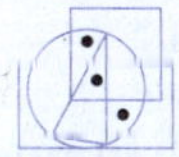

(X)

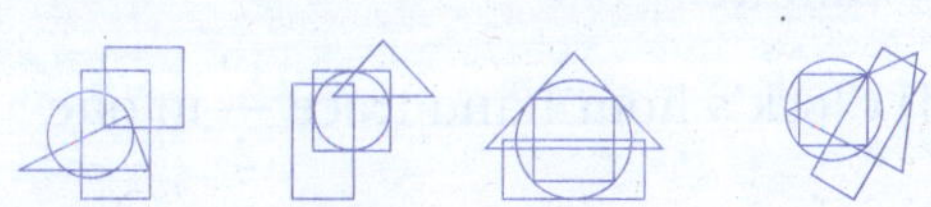

(a) (b) (c) (d)

Chapter 17

Clock and Calendar

Clock

A clock is an instrument used for indicating and maintaining the time. Dial, hour hand, minute hand and second hand are its components. Dial of a watch is divided into 12 equal parts, each part is known as one hour and one hour is also divided into 5 equal parts, each such part is known as one minute.

The basic structure of clock is as follow

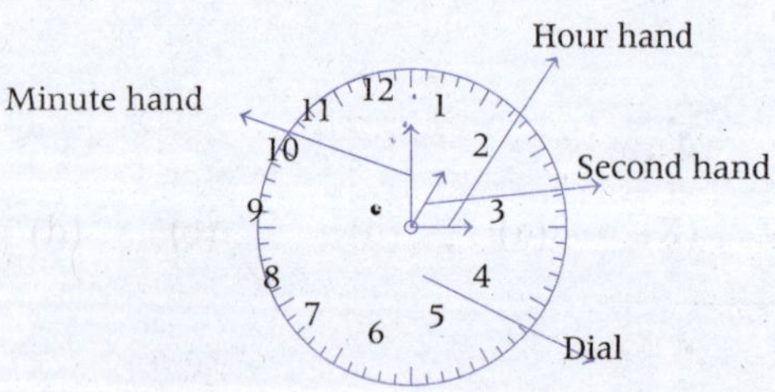

(i) Clock's minute hand trace 6° in one minute.

(ii) Clock's hour hand trace $\frac{1^{\circ}}{2}$ in one minute.

Calendar

Calendar measures a day, a month and a year. If clock decides our 24 hr daily routine, then calendar decides our 365 days of a year.

(i) Ordinary year : An ordinary year has 365 days (February has 28 days).

(ii) A leap year : A leap year has 366 days (February has 29 days).

(iii) Every year divisible by 4 is a leap year, if it is not a century.

(iv) Every 4th century is a leap year and no other century is a leap year.

Odd Days

We are supposed to find the day of the week on a given date. For this, we use the concept of 'odd days'. In a given period, the number of days more than the complete weeks are called odd days.

(i) 1 ordinary year = 365 days = 52 weeks + 1 day

$\therefore$ 1 ordinary year has 1 odd day.

(ii) 1 leap year = 366 days = 52 weeks + 2 days

$\therefore$ 1 leap year has 2 odd days.

Questions based on clock and calendar are basically divided into following three types.

1. Based on clock
2. Based on Finding angle between hour hand and minute hand
3. Based on calendars

1. Based on Clock

These type of questions are generally based on finding time with respect to certain events or given conditions.

Example 1 The priest told the devotee, "The temple bell is rung at regular intervals of 45 min. The last bell was rung 5 min ago. The next bell is due to be rung at 7:45 am."

At what time did the priest given this information to devotees?

(a) 7:40 am
(b) 7:05 am
(c) 7:00 am
(d) 6:55 am

Sol. *(b)* The last bell rang 45 min before 7:45 am i.e. at 7:00 am.

But it happened five minutes before the priest gave the information to the devotee.

So, the information was given at 7:05 am.

2. Based on Angle between the hand of Clock

In these type of questions, students are asked to find out the angle between the hands of a clock at a particular time.

To calculate the angle 'θ' between the hands of a clock, we use the following formulas

(i) $\theta = \frac{11}{2}m - 30\,h \left(\text{when } \frac{11}{2}m > 30\,h \right)$

(ii) $\theta = 30\,h - \frac{11}{2}m \left(\text{when } 30\,h > \frac{11}{2}m \right)$

where, m = minutes, h = hours.

Example 2 At what angle the hands of a clock are inclined at 3h 40 min?

(a) 150° (b) 120°
(c) 45° (d) 130°

Sol. (d) From the formula $\frac{11}{2}$ min − 30 hours

Here, min = 40, hour = 3

So, the required angle $= \frac{11}{2} \times 40 - 30 \times 3$

$= 220 - 90° = 130°$

So, the hands of a clock are inclined at 130° at 3 h 40 min.

3. Based on Calendar

These type of questions are generally based on finding day, month or year on which a particular event is held on the basis of certain given dates.

Example 3 If 18th February, 2005 falls on Friday, then what will be the day on 18th February 2007?

(a) Sunday (b) Wednesday
(c) Tuesday (d) Monday

Sol. (a) According to the question,

18th February, 2005 = Friday.

So, 18th February, 2006 = Friday + 1 day = Saturday.

So, 18th February 2007 = Saturday + 1 day = Sunday.

(∵ 2005, 2006 and 2007 are ordinary years).

Let's Practice

1 Mark Questions

1. How many times in a day are the hands of the clock at right angle in a day?

(a) 22 (b) 24 (c) 44 (d) 48

2. In how many times in a day, are the hands of a clock in straight line but opposite in direction?

(a) 20 (b) 22 (c) 24 (d) 48

3. The rotation undergone by the minute hand of a clock as it traverses a distance of 255 min.

(a) 810° (b) 1530°
(c) 450° (d) 90°

4. A clock shows 7 o'clock in the morning. By how much angle will the hour's hand rotate when the clock shows 9 o'clock in the morning.

(a) 40° (b) 60° (c) 45° (d) 90°

5. A clock shows 6:00 in the morning. By how much angle will the hour's hand rotate when the clock shows 12:00 in the noon?

(a) 160° (b) 120°
(c) 180° (d) 135°

6. Find the angle between the hands of the clock when the time is 10:30.

(a) 160° (b) 120° (c) 180° (d) 135°

7. What is the angle between the two hands of the clock is 6:24 pm?

(a) 0° (b) 50° (c) 30° (d) 158°

8. At what time between 3 o' clock and 4 o' clock is the angle between the hands of a watch one-third of a right angle?

(a) $3:\frac{120}{9}$ (b) $3:\frac{120}{11}$

(c) $3:\frac{100}{11}$ (d) $3:\frac{110}{11}$

9. At what time between 8 o' clock and 9 o' clock does the minute hand of a clock coincides with its hour hand?

(a) $8:43\frac{7}{11}$ (b) $8:43\frac{11}{7}$

(c) 8 : 44 (d) $8:45\frac{11}{7}$

10. At what time between 2 o' clock and 3 o' clock, will the minute hand and hour hand of the clock will be at right angles?

(a) 02 : 32 (b) $02:29\frac{6}{11}$

(c) $02:27\frac{3}{11}$ (d) 02 : 36

11. At what time between 2 o' clock and 3 o' clock will the minute hand and the hour hand of the clock will be exactly opposite to each other.

(a) 02 : 46 (b) $02:47\frac{6}{11}$

(c) $02:43\frac{7}{11}$ (d) 02 : 47

12. The calendar for the year 1988 is same as which up coming year?

(a) 2012 (b) 2014
(c) 2016 (d) 2010

13. If today is Monday, then what day will be after 63 days.

(a) Tuesday (b) Monday
(c) Sunday (d) Saturday

14. How many weekends are there in a normal year?
(a) 52 (b) 53
(c) 103 (d) 104

15. How many leap year does 100 yr have?
(a) 25 (b) 24 (c) 4 (d) 26

16. If today is Saturday. What will be the day 350 days from now?
(a) Saturday (b) Friday
(c) Sunday (d) Monday

17. It was Sunday on Jan 1, 2006. What was the day of the week Jan 1, 2010?
(a) Monday (b) Friday
(c) Sunday (d) Tuesday

18. On 8th Dec 2007 Saturday falls, what day of the week was it on 8th Dec, 2006?
(a) Saturday (b) Friday
(c) Monday (d) Tuesday

19. On 8th Feb 2005 it was Tuesday. What was the day of the week on 8th Feb 2004?
(a) Tuesday (b) Saturday
(c) Friday (d) Sunday

20. If January 1, 2007 was Monday. What day of the week lies on Jan 1, 2008?
(a) Monday (b) Tuesday
(c) Wednesday (d) Sunday

2 Marks Questions

21. Varun was born on 6th Dec, 1989. When was he 5 years 8 months and 22 days old?
(a) 28.05.1994
(b) 28.08.1995
(c) 28.08.1994
(d) 28.09.1995

22. If every second Saturday and all Sundays are holidays in a 30 days month beginning on Saturday, then how many working days are there in that month? (month starts from Saturday).
(a) 24 (b) 23
(c) 22 (d) 25

23. On which dates of April 2001 did Wednesday fall?
(a) 2nd, 9th, 16th, 23rd
(b) 4th, 11th, 18th, 25th
(c) 12th, 18th, 27th, 6 th
(d) 1st, 8th, 15th, 22nd

24. What will be the day of the week 15th August 2010?
(a) Sunday (b) Saturday
(c) Wednesday (d) Monday

25. How many degrees does a minute hand cover in same time, in which the hour hand covers 20°?
(a) 150° (b) 200°
(c) 180° (d) 240°

PRACTICE SET 01

1 Mark Questions

Directions (Q. Nos. 1-4) Select the related word from the given alternatives.

1. Maharashtra : India : : Texas : ?
(a) Canada (b) Mexico
(c) Brazil (d) USA

2. Heart : Cardiologist : : Kidney : ?
(a) Endocrinologist (b) Orthodontist
(c) Nephrologist (d) Neurologist

3. ACE : BDF : : MOQ : ?
(a) MZU (b) MVT (c) NPR (d) NZV

4. 8 : 48 : : 23 : ?
(a) 168 (b) 112 (c) 90 (d) 138

Directions (Q. Nos. 5-8) Find the odd one out from the given alternatives.

5. (a) Europe (b) Africa
(c) Asia (d) Canada

6. (a) Flute (b) Piano
(c) Violin (d) Sitar

7. (a) 53 (b) 98 (c) 83 (d) 64

8. (a) BCD (b) QRS
(c) KMN (d) WXY

Directions (Q. Nos. 9-11) Find out what will come at the place of '?' in the following series.

9. CE, GI, KM, OQ, ?
(a) TW (b) TV
(c) SU (d) RT

10. 23, 24, 27, 28, 31, 32, ?
(a) 30 (b) 33 (c) 29 (d) 35

11. A 1, C 4, E 7, G 10, ?
(a) I 13 (b) I 11 (c) J 11 (d) J 13

12. If 'water' is known as 'food', 'food' as 'tree' and 'tree' as 'sky', 'sky' as 'well' and 'well' as 'pond', then which of the following would yield fruits?
(a) Sky (b) Food (c) Well (d) Tree

13. In a code language FORGE is written as FPTJI. How should WATER be written in that code language?
(a) W B H H V (b) W B V H V
(c) W B H V V (d) B W H V V

14. Arrange the following words in a meaningful order.
1. Andhra Pradesh 2. Universe
3. Tirupati 4. World
5. India
(a) 3 1 4 5 2 (b) 1 3 5 4 2
(c) 3 1 5 4 2 (d) 3 1 2 4 5

15. In a class of 45 students, rank of Ayush is 15 from top. Then, rank of Ayush from bottom is
(a) 30 (b) 32
(c) 31 (d) 35

16. One morning Meena started walking towards the sun, after walking a while she turned towards her left and again towards her left. After walking a while, she turned left. In which direction is she facing now?
(a) North (b) East
(c) West (d) South

17. Town D is 12 km towards the North of town A. Town C is 15 km towards the West of town D. Town B is 15 km towards the West of town A. How far and in which direction is town B from town C?

(a) 15 km towards North
(b) 12 km towards North
(c) 13 km towards South
(d) 12 km towards South

18. Location of B is North of A and location of C is East of A. The distances AB and AC are 5 km and 12 km respectively. The shortest distance between the location, B and C are

(a) 60 (b) 13 (c) 17 (d) 7

19. Pointing to a girl in a bus, a man tells his friend, "She is the daughter of the only son of my father's wife". How is the girl related to the man?

(a) Cousin (b) Daughter
(c) Mother (d) Sister

20. Kannan is the brother of Kumar. Lakshmi is the daughter of Kumar. Kalai is the sister of Kannan and Govind is the brother of Lakshmi. Who is the uncle of Govind?

(a) Kumar (b) Kalai
(c) Lakshmi (d) Kannan

21. If '+' means ' ', '−' means '×', '÷' means '+' and '×' means '÷', then $10 \times 5 \div 3 - 2 + 3$ is equal to

(a) 5 (b) 53/3 (c) 21 (d) 36

22. If '+' and '−' are interchanged, similarly '×' and '÷' are interchanged, then find the answer of the following equation.

$10 - 2 \div 12 \times 1 \div 0$

(a) 8 (b) 12 (c) 1 (d) 0

23. Identify the diagram that best represents the relationship among the classes given below.
Oxygen, Carbon dioxide, Atmosphere.

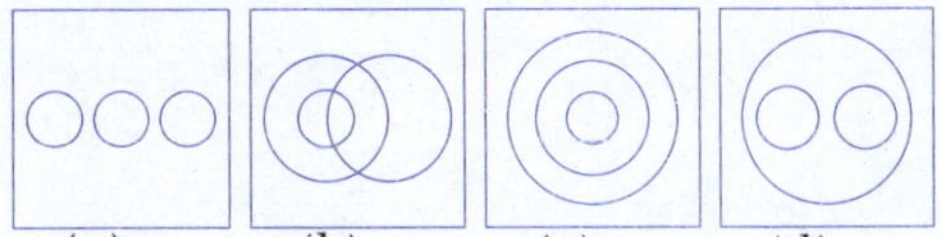

(a) (b) (c) (d)

24. Which of the following diagram best represents the relationship between Mammal, Dog and Bat.

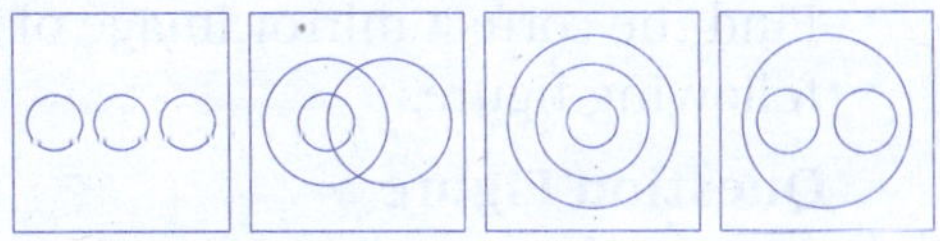

(a) (b) (c) (d)

25. In the following diagram, which alphabet represents athlete who are teachers but not woman?

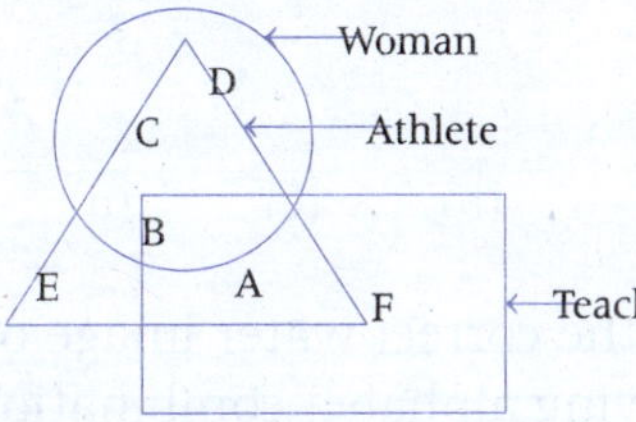

(a) A (b) B (c) C (d) D

26. Which conclusion is true with respect to following statements.

Statements

All crows are black.
Some black things are beautiful.

Conclusions

I. Some crows are beautiful.
II. Some beautiful are black.

(a) Only Conclusion I follows
(b) Only Conclusion II follows
(c) Both Conclusions I and II follows
(d) Neither Conclusion I nor II follows

27. Find the figure from the answer figures that will replace the '?' from the problem figure.

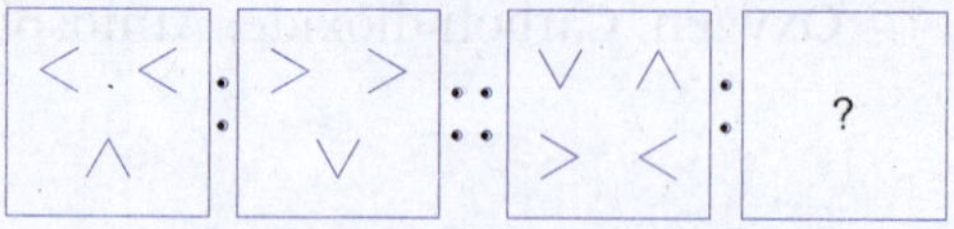

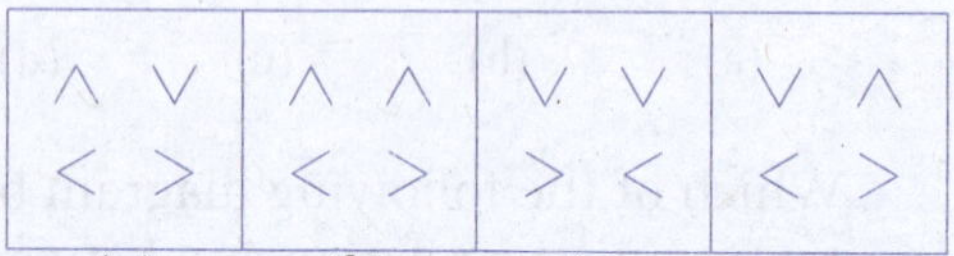

(a) (b) (c) (d)

28. Find the correct mirror image of the following figure.

Question Figure

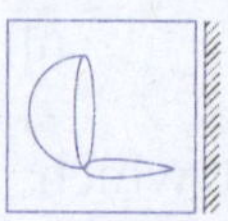

Answer Figures

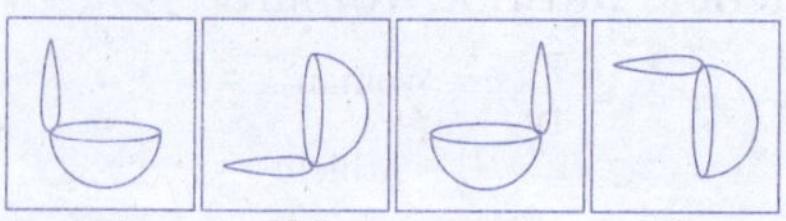

(a) (b) (c) (d)

29. Find the correct water image of the following alphabet combination.

CORDIAL

(a) COꓤDIⱯꓶ (b) COꓤDIⱯΓ

(c) COꓤDIⱯI (d) ꓶAIDꓤOƆ

30. How many rectangles are there in the given figure?

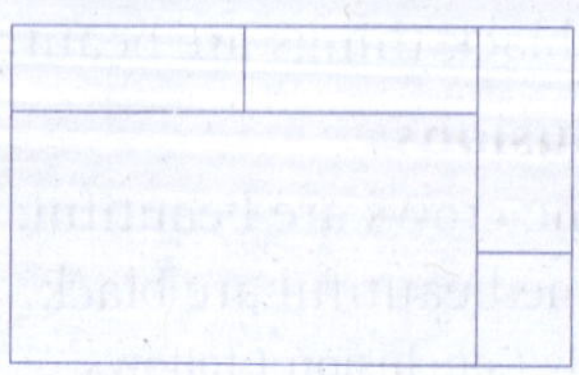

(a) 6 (b) 7

(c) 8 (d) 9

31. Which number is on the face opposite to 6 in the dice whose four views are given below?

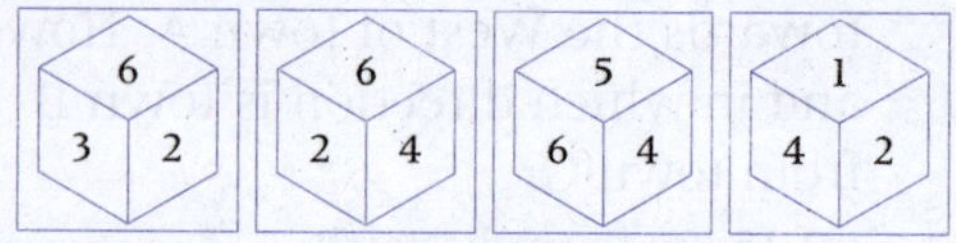

(a) 1 (b) 2

(c) 3 (d) 4

32. A solid cube of 4 inches have been painted red, green and black on pair of opposite faces. It has been cut into one inch cubes. How many cubes have only one face painted?

(a) 4 (b) 8

(c) 16 (d) 24

33. A piece of paper is folded and cut as shown below in the question figure. From the given answer figures indicate how it will appear when opened?

Question Figures

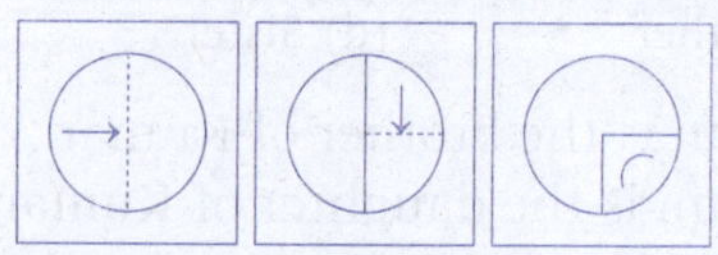

Answer Figures

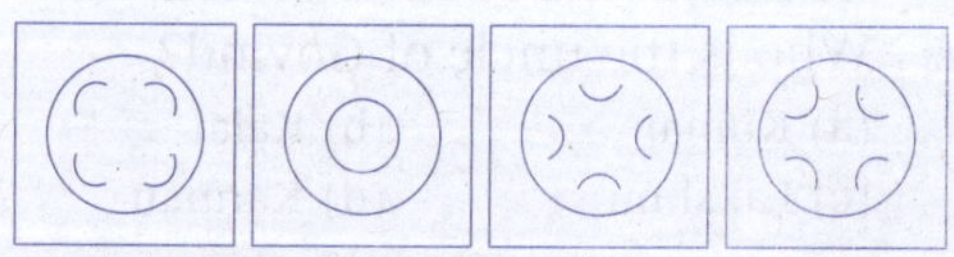

(a) (b) (c) (d)

34. A family consists of a man, his wife, his three sons, their wives and three children in each son's family. How many members are there in the family?

(a) 12 (b) 13

(c) 15 (d) 17

35. There are twelve dozen of apples in the basket. Two dozens are added later. Ten apples got spoilt and removed. The remaining are transferred equally into two baskets. How many apples are there in the each?

(a) 89 (b) 168 (c) 158 (d) 79

36. If 18th February, 2005 falls on Friday. Then, what will be the day on 18th February, 2007?

(a) Sunday (b) Wednesday
(c) Tuesday (d) Monday

37. If January 1 is a Friday. What is the first day of the month of March in a leap year?

(a) Tuesday (b) Wednesday
(c) Thursday (d) Friday

38. At what angle the hands of a clock are inclined at 3h 40 min?

(a) 150° (b) 120° (c) 45° (d) 130°

39. How many times are the hands of the clock at right angles in a day?

(a) 22 (b) 44 (c) 11 (d) 24

40. Choose the one figure from the four options figure, which best explains the characteriistics given in the question figure (X).

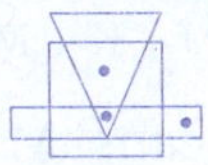

(X)

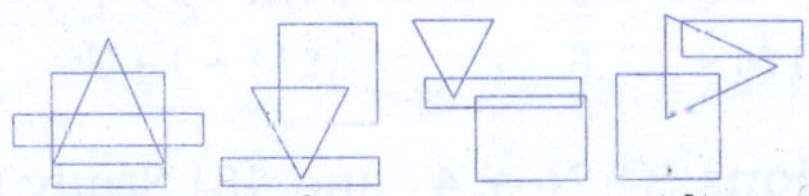

(a) (b) (c) (d)

2 Marks Questions

Directions (Q. Nos. 41and 42) Read the following information and answer the questions below it.

Four men Ram, Pramod, Vipul and Akash are friendly with four girls Sneha, Kavita, Veena and Priya. Sneha and Veena are friends. Vipul's friend who is a girl doesn't like Sneha and Veena. Kavita doesn't care for Vipul. Pramod's friend who is a girl is friendly with Sneha. Sneha doesn't like Ram.

41. With whom is Sneha friendly?

(a) Ram
(b) Pramod
(c) Vipul
(d) Akash

42. Which boy is Priya's friend?

(a) Akash
(b) Vipul
(c) Pramod
(d) Ram

43. Which statement is true with respect to the venn diagram?

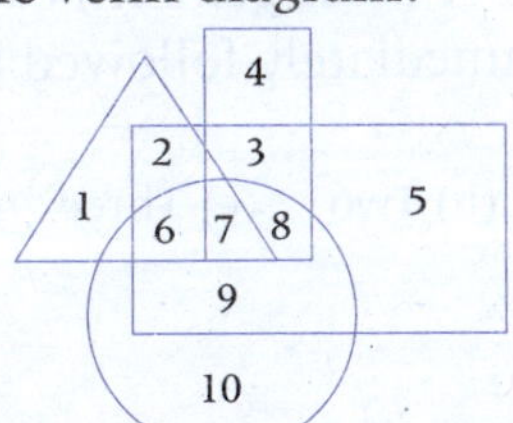

(a) 1, 9 and 10 are in all figures
(b) 1, 2 and 6 are in the triangle
(c) 6, 7and 8 are in all the figures
(d) 1, 5 and 9 are in all figures

44. If + stands for 'division', ÷ stands for 'multiplication', × stands for 'subtraction', – stands for 'addition'. Which of the following is correct?

(a) $18 \div 6 \times 7 + 5 - 2 = 22$
(b) $18 \times 6 + 7 \div 5 - 2 = 16$
(c) $18 \div 6 - 7 + 5 \times 2 = 20$
(d) $18 + 6 \div 7 \times 5 - 2 = 18$

Directions (Q. Nos. 45 and 46) Read the following information carefully and answer the questions that follow.

(i) P × Q means 'P is mother of Q'.
(ii) P ÷ Q means 'P is the sister of Q'.
(iii) P + Q means 'P is brother of Q'.
(iv) P − Q means 'P is father of Q'.

45. Which of the following means 'K is son of R'?
(a) R × K (b) R − K
(c) K + T × R (d) R − J ÷ K + M

46. Which of the following means 'M is paternal uncle of T'?
(a) M + J − T (b) M + J × T
(c) M ÷ J − T (d) M + J + T

Directions (Q. Nos. 47 and 48) Study the following information carefully and answer the given questions.

F 4 @ 3 J % Q M # 7 N P Z X ! V 6

47. How many such consonants are there in the above arrangement, each of which immediately followed by a symbol?
(a) One (b) Two (c) Three (d) Four

48. Which of the following is the 3rd to the right of 8th element from the left end of the above arrangement?
(a) # (b) 7
(c) N (d) Q

49. Which of the given conclusions can definitely be drawn from the given statements.

Statements

No super is man.
No man is guilty.
Some super are guilty.

Conclusions

(i) No guilty is super.
(ii) No guilty is man.
(iii) Some man are super
(iv) All guilty are super.

(a) None follows
(b) Only II follows
(c) II and III follow
(d) I and III follow

50. Find the number which will complete the following series.

4, 11, 30, 67, 128, ?

(a) 219 (b) 228 (c) 231 (d) 237

Answers

1. (d)	2. (c)	3. (c)	4. (d)	5. (d)	6. (a)	7. (d)	8. (c)	9. (c)	10. (d)
11. (a)	12. (a)	13. (b)	14. (c)	15. (c)	16. (d)	17. (d)	18. (b)	19. (b)	20. (d)
21. (a)	22. (b)	23. (d)	24. (d)	25. (a)	26. (b)	27. (a)	28. (b)	29. (b)	30. (c)
31. (a)	32. (d)	33. (d)	34. (d)	35. (d)	36. (a)	37. (a)	38. (d)	39. (b)	40. (a)
41. (d)	42. (b)	43. (b)	44. (d)	45. (d)	46. (a)	47. (c)	48. (c)	49. (b)	50. (a)

PRACTICE SET 02

1 Mark Questions

Directions (Q. Nos. 1-4) Select the related word from the given alternatives.

1. Doctor : Hospital : : Teacher : ?
   (a) School (b) Industry
   (c) Field (d) Laboratory

2. Smoke : Pollution : : War :?
   (a) Peace (b) Victory
   (c) Treaty (d) Destruction

3. ZX : AC : : VT : ?
   (a) AB (b) AE (c) EG (d) DF

4. 957 : 735 : : 833 : ?
   (a) 338 (b) 383 (c) 611 (d) 683

Directions (Q. Nos. 5-8) Find the odd one out from the given alternatives.

5. (a) Pond (b) River
   (c) Ocean (d) Waterfall

6. (a) Litre (b) Yard
   (c) Metre (d) Inch

7. (a) 2, 3 (b) 20, 21
   (c) 9, 10 (d) 24, 25

8. (a) QRS (b) XYZ (c) STU (d) MLN

Directions (Q. Nos. 9-11) Find out what will come at the place of '?' in the following series.

9. 1, 6, 13, 22, 33, ?
   (a) 46 (b) 44
   (c) 47 (d) 43

10. AZ, CX, FU, ?
    (a) IR (b) IV
    (c) JQ (d) KP

11. D 4, F 9, H 16, ?
    (a) J 24 (b) J 25 (c) K 25 (d) K 36

12. If SEVEN is coded as 23136 and EIGHT is coded as 34579. What will be the code for NINE?
    (a) 6463 (b) 6364
    (c) 6346 (d) 6436

13. If EARN is written as GCTP. How NEAR can be written in that code?
    (a) CTGP (b) GPTC
    (c) PGCT (d) PCGT

14. Arrange the following in ascending order.
    (1) Centimeter (2) Kilometer
    (3) Decimeter (4) Meter
    (a) 3 1 2 4 (b) 4 2 1 3
    (c) 1 3 4 2 (d) 2 4 3 1

15. In a queue, Soham is 10th from the left and 28th from right. How many people are there in the queue?
    (a) 38 (b) 35
    (c) 37 (d) 42

16. In the morning, Sheela walked 2 km facing the sun and stopped. From there, she walked 4 km on the right hand side, from there she walked 1 km again facing the sun, from there she walked on her right hand side. In which direction, she shall be walking now?
    (a) East (b) South-East
    (c) South-West (d) Right hand side

17. Ram goes 15 m North, then turns right and walks 20 m, then again turns right and walks 10 m, then again turns right and walks 20 m. How far is he from his original position?

(a) 5 m (b) 10 m
(c) 15 m (d) 20 m

18. At sunrise, Amit and Deepak are having a conversation standing in front of each other. The shadow of Deepak is formed towards the right hand of Amit. What direction is Deepak facing?

(a) North-East (b) South
(c) East (d) North

19. D's father's mother's son's wife is related to D as

(a) Grandmother
(b) Mother
(c) Aunt
(d) Cannot be determined

20. Pointing to Neeraj, Kavita said, "His mother's brother is the father of my son Pramod".
How is Neeraj related to Kavita?

(a) Niece (b) Nephew
(c) Sister-in-law (d) None of these

21. Which interchange of signs will make the following equation correct?
$(16-4)\times 6 \div 2 + 8 = 30$

(a) $\div$ and $-$ (b) 4 and 2
(c) $-$ and $+$ (d) 16 and 6

22. If $\times$ means $-$, $+$ means $\div$, $-$ means $\times$ and $\div$ means $+$, then
$15 - 2 \div 900 + 90 \times 100$ is equal to

(a) -2 (b) 2
(c) 4 (d) -60

23. Find the best relationship among the three classes in the following diagram.
Students, Children, Birds

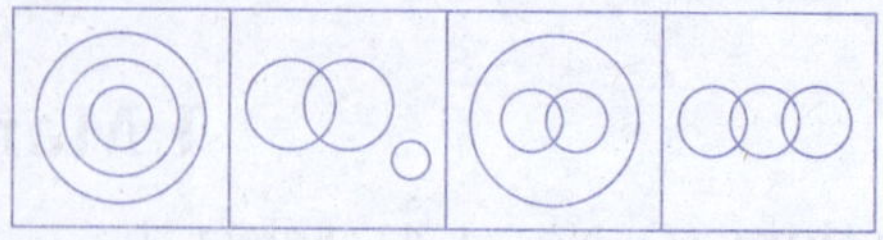

(a) (b) (c) (d)

24. Which of the following answer figures indicates best relation between Aeroplanes, Train, Travel.

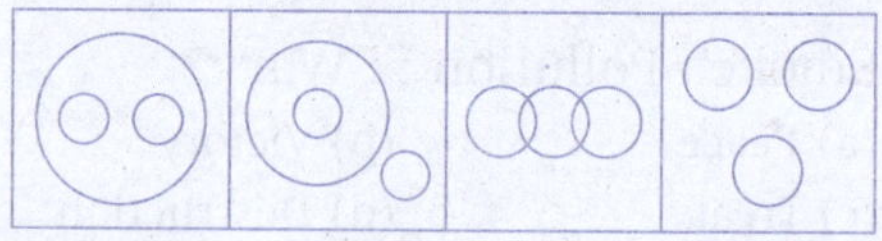

(a) (b) (c) (d)

25. How many backward uneducated people are employed according to the figure given below?

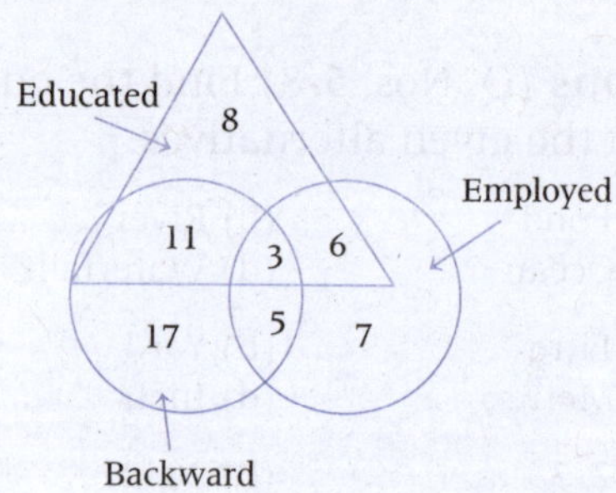

(a) 14 (b) 5 (c) 7 (d) 11

26. Which conclusion is true with respect to the given statements?

Statements Anandi is an artist.
Artists are beautiful.

Conclusions

(a) Anandi is not beautiful
(b) Beautiful persons are not artists
(c) All beautiful persons are artists
(d) Anandi is beautiful

27. Find the correct mirror image of the given question figure.

Question Figure

Answer Figures

(a) (b) (c) (d)

28. Find the odd figure out.

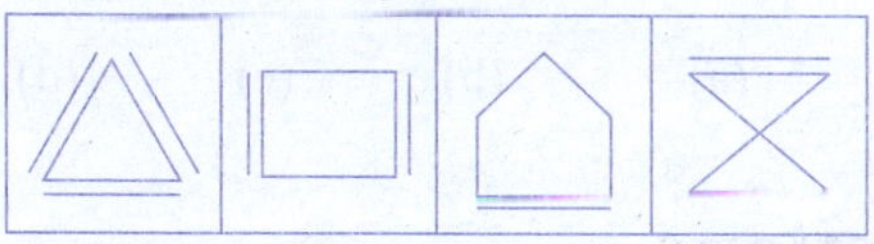

(a) (b) (c) (d)

29. Choose the correct water image of the figure (A) from the options.

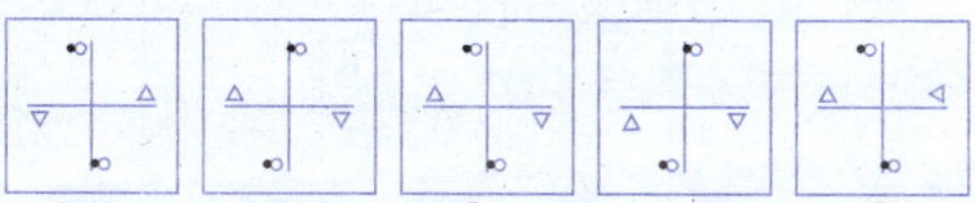

(A) (a) (b) (c) (d)

30. How many squares are there in the following figure?

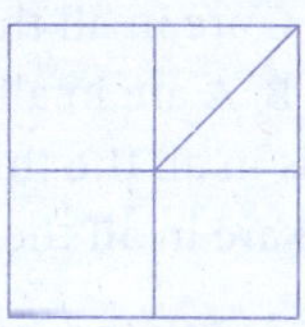

(a) 6 (b) 8
(c) 5 (d) 10

31. A solid cube of 4 inches has been painted red, green and black on pair of opposite faces. It has been, then cut into one inch cubes. How many cubes have only four faces painted?

(a) 0 (b) 4
(c) 8 (d) 16

32. Two positions of a dice are shown below when number 1 is on the top. What number will be there at the bottom?

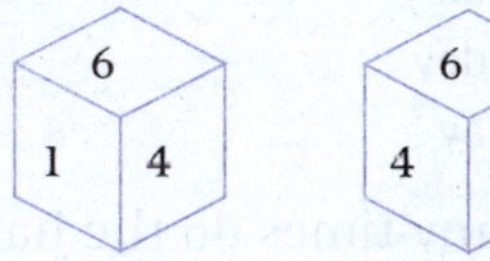

(a) 2 (b) 3
(c) 5 (d) Data Inadequate

33. A piece of paper is folded and cut as shown below in the question figure. From the given answer figures, indicate how it will appear when opened.

Question Figures

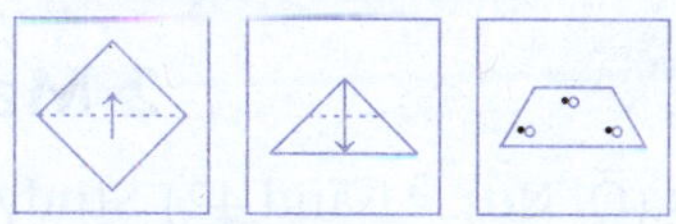

Answer Figures

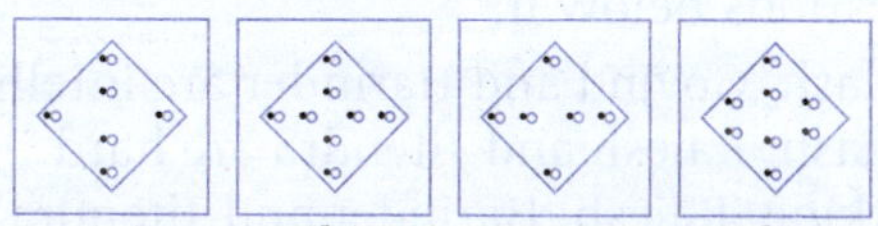

(a) (b) (c) (d)

34. In a group of buffaloes and ducks, the number of legs are 24 more than twice the number of heads. What is the number of buffaloes in the group?

(a) 6 (b) 12
(c) 8 (d) None of these

35. A frog has 18 eggs. All but nine are spoilt. How many are left?

(a) 17 (b) 9 (c) 0 (d) 8

36. If the day before yesterday was Wednesday, when will Sunday be?

(a) Today
(b) Tomorrow
(c) Day after tomorrow
(d) Two days after tomorrow

37. If 30th January, 2003 was Thursday. What was the day on 2nd March, 2003?

(a) Tuesday
(b) Thursday
(c) Saturday
(d) Sunday

38. How many times do the hands of the clock points towards each other in a day?

(a) 11 (b) 48
(c) 24 (d) 22

39. At what angle the hands of the clock are inclined at 30 min past 6?

(a) 45° (b) 15°
(c) 30° (d) 20°

40. Choose the one figure from the four answer figures, which best explains the characteristics given in the question figure (X).

Question Figure

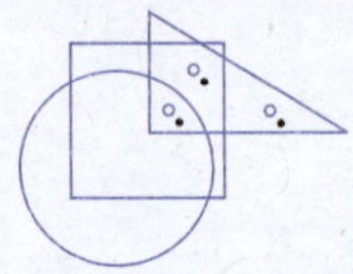

(X)

Answer Figures

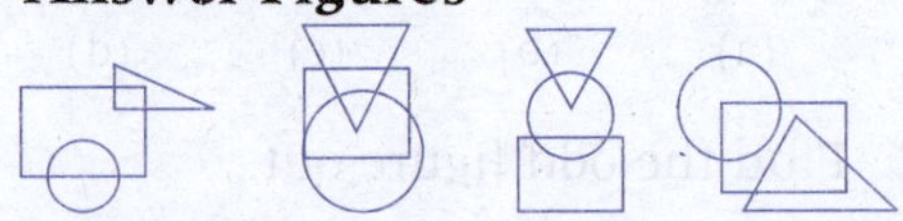

(a) (b) (c) (d)

2 Mark Questions

Directions (Q. Nos. 41 and 42) Study the following information and answer the questions below it.

Kailash, Govind and Harinder are intelligent. Kailash, Rajesh and Jitendra are hard working. Rajesh, Harinder and Jitendra are honest. Kailash, Govind and Jitendra are ambitious.

41. Which of the following persons is neither hard-working nor ambitious?

(a) Kailash
(b) Govind
(c) Harinder
(d) Rajesh

42. Which of the following persons in neither honest nor hard-working but is ambitious?

(a) Kailash (b) Govind
(c) Rajesh (d) Harinder

43. Which of the following statements is correct with regard to the given figure?

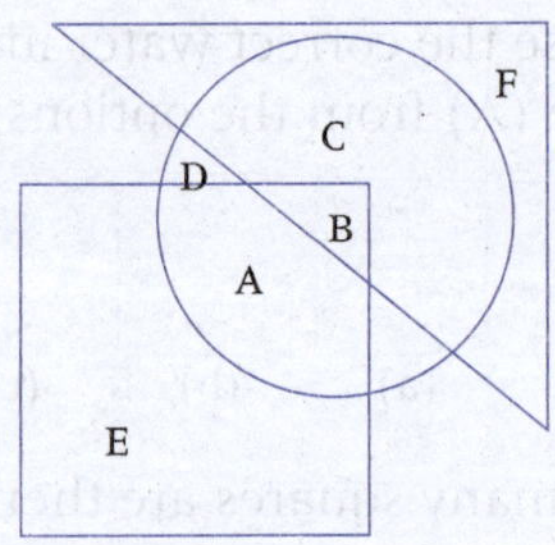

(a) E, A, B, C are in all the three shapes
(b) F, C, D, B, A are in all the three shapes
(c) Only B is in all the three shapes
(d) A and B are in all the three shapes

44. If '×' stands for 'addition', '<' for 'subtraction', '+' for 'division', '>' for multiplication, '–' for 'equal to', '÷' for 'greater than' and '=' for 'less than', then state which of the following is true?

(a) $3 \times 4 > 2 - 9 + 3 < 3$
(b) $5 \times 3 < 7 \div 8 + 4 \times 1$
(c) $5 > 2 + 2 = 10 < 4 \times 8$
(d) $3 \times 2 < 4 \div 16 > 2 + 4$

Directions (Q. Nos. 45 and 46) Read the following information carefully and answer the questions that follow.

(i) A + B means 'A is father of B'.
(ii) A × B means 'A is daughter of B'.
(iii) A ÷ B means 'A is brother of B'.
(iv) A – B means 'A is wife of B'.

45. In ' L – M + K ÷ F', how is 'F' related to 'L'?
(a) Son (b) Daughter
(c) Nephew (d) Cannot be determined

46. Which of the following expressions means 'J' is the son of 'D'?
(a) D + L × H ÷ J (b) J ÷ P × D
(c) J ÷ P – D (d) T – D + J

Directions (Q. Nos. 47 and 48) Study the following alphabet codes carefully and answer the given questions.

A	G	P	N	W	L	C	I	X	V	M	D	H	K
1	%	g	3	2	@	<	m	7	>	#	p	*	!

47. Which word can be decoded from the following?
< @ m # 1 7 3 m @
(a) CLIMATE VIP (b) CLIMAX NIL
(c) VIJAY SALE (d) CLIMAX MALP

48. The code 'p * g % 7 !' is stands for?
(a) DHPGXK (b) DHGXKM
(c) DHPHKN (d) DKLCIM

49. Sayani starts from her school towards North and reaches home. From there she turns towards North-West and reaches is temple. Then she turns towards South-West and walks to the mall. From there she turns towards North-West and finally reaches supermarket. Which of the following figures shows the movement of Sayani?

(a)
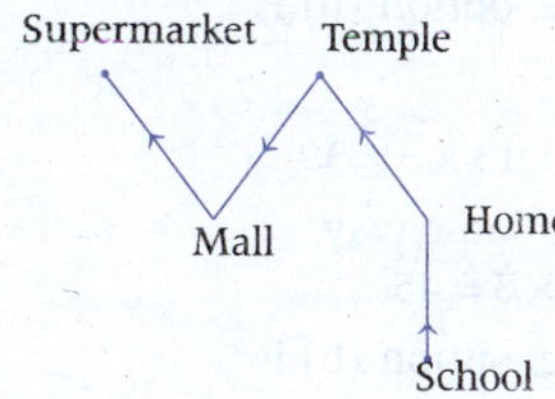

(b)
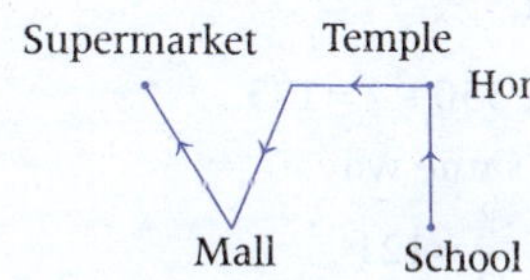

(c)
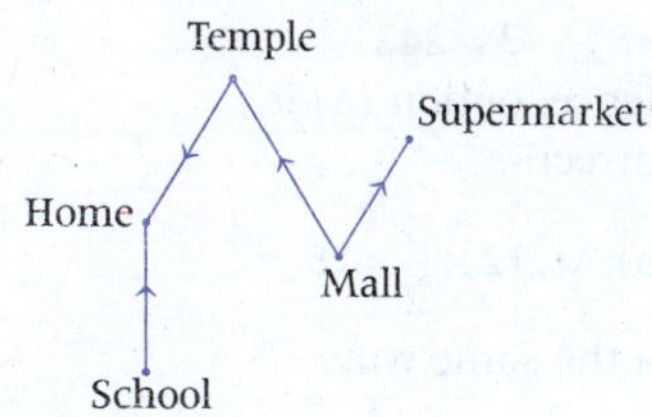

(d)
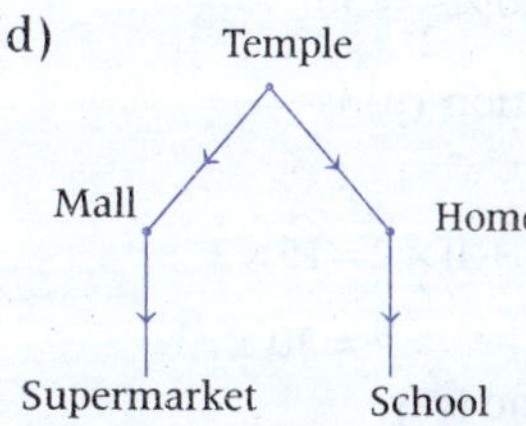

50. Find what will come at the place of '?' in the following question?
A B C D : N P R T : : F G H I : ?
(a) K L M N (b) O Q R T
(c) R T U W (d) S U W Y

Answers

1. (a)	**2.** (d)	**3.** (c)	**4.** (c)	**5.** (d)	**6.** (a)	**7.** (a)	**8.** (d)	**9.** (a)	**10.** (c)
11. (b)	**12** (a)	**13.** (c)	**14.** (c)	**15.** (c)	**16.** (d)	**17.** (a)	**18.** (d)	**19.** (d)	**20.** (b)
21. (a)	**22.** (d)	**23.** (b)	**24.** (a)	**25.** (b)	**26.** (d)	**27.** (b)	**28.** (b)	**29.** (a)	**30.** (c)
31. (a)	**32.** (c)	**33.** (d)	**34.** (b)	**35.** (b)	**36.** (c)	**37.** (d)	**38.** (d)	**39.** (b)	**40.** (b)
41. (c)	**42.** (b)	**43.** (c)	**44.** (c)	**45.** (d)	**46.** (b)	**47.** (b)	**48.** (b)	**49.** (a)	**50.** (d)

Hints & Solutions

1. Analogy

1. (b) As, $11+1=12$

In the same way, $15+1=16$

Hence, option (b) is correct.

2. (b) As, $13\times3=39$

In the same way,

$15\times3=45$

Hence, option (b) is correct.

3. (a) As, $350\div2=175$

In the same way,

$\frac{?}{2}=121$

$\Rightarrow ?=242$

Hence, option (a) is correct.

4. (b) As, $12\times\frac{3}{2}=18$

In the same way,

$20\times\frac{3}{2}=30$

Hence, option (b) is correct.

5. (a) As, $(14+1)\times2=15\times2$

$=30$

In the same way,

$(13+1)\times2=14\times2$

$=28$

Hence, option (a) is correct.

6. (d) Relation can be represented as

$600-25=575$

In the same way,

$450-25=425$

Hence, option (d) is correct.

7. (b) The relation can be represented as

$5^2-1=25-1$

$=24$

In the same way,

$8^2-1=64-1$

$=63$

Hence, option (b) is correct.

8. (b) The relation can be represented as

$65\div5=13$

In the same way,

$180\div5=36$

Hence, option (b) is correct.

9. (d) The relation can be as

1 1   1 0 1

In the same way,

7 3   7 0 3

Hence, option (d) is correct.

10. (c) The relation can be shown as

A P : B Q

+1 +1

In the same way,

W M : X N

+1 +1

Hence, option (c) is correct.

11. (a) The relation can be represented as

A D E : C F G

+2 +2 +2

Similarly,

P L K : R N M

+2 +2 +2

Hence, option (a) is correct.

12. (c) The relation can be represented as

A D E : F I J

+5 +5 +5

Similarly,

P Q S : U V X

+5 +5 +5

Hence, option (c) is correct.

13. (c) As,

a b c : b d f

+1 +2 +3

In the same way,

p q r : q s u

+1 +2 +3

Hence, option (c) is correct.

14. (a) Here, the relation can be represented as

H I J K : F G H I

−2 −2 −2 −2

In the same way,

Z Y X W : X W V U

−2 −2 −2 −2

Hence, option (a) is correct.

15. (b) As,

H → (+2) → J, I → (+2) → K, R → (+2) → T, O → (+2) → Q

Likewise,

L → (+2) → N, J → (+2) → L, F → (+2) → H, P → (+2) → R

Hence, option (b) is correct.

16. (a) Here, the relation can be represented as

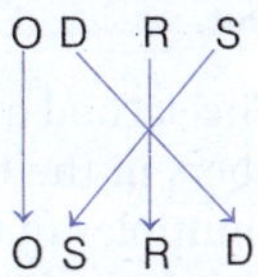

In the same way,

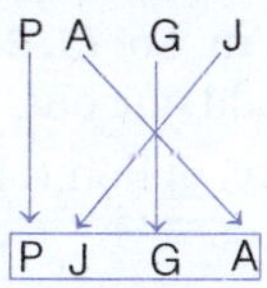

Hence, option (a) is correct.

17. (c) As NEEDLE is used for SEWING, in the same way SCISSOR is used for CUTTING.
Hence, option (c) is correct.

18. (c) As LINE is a part of SQUARE, in the same way ARC is a part of CIRCLE.
Hence, option (c) is correct.

19. (c) As DRAMA is directed by DIRECTOR, in the same way MAGAZINE is shaped up or edited by EDITOR.

Hence, option (c) is correct.

20. (b) TREE is a part of FOREST. Likewise, SOLDIER is a part of ARMY.

Hence, option (b) is correct.

21. (d) Raining slowly is called Drizzling. In the same way, Running slowly is called Jogging.
Hence, option (d) is correct.

22. (b) Jaundice is a disease which effects the Liver. In the same way, Rash is a disease which effects the Skin.
Hence, option (b) is correct.

23. (b) As Pen is used by a Writer for writing, in the same way Brush is used by an Artist for creating his art form.

Hence, option (b) is correct.

24. (a) As, in the first pair

M 5 : P 10 (M +3 → P; 5 × 2 → 10)

[∵ P is three places ahead of M in alphabet series]

Similarly, T 20 : W 40 (T +3 → W; 20 ×2 → 40)

[∵ W is three places ahead of T in alphabet series].

25. (d) As, in the first pair

J 24 : G 12 (J −3 → G; 24 ÷2 → 12)

[∵ G is three places before J in alphabet series]

Similarly,

L 18 : I 9 (L −3 → I; 18 ÷2 → 9)

[∵ I is three places before L in alphabet series]

26. (c) As, in the first pair
H = 8 [position of H in alphabet series is 8]

$8^2 = 64$

Similarly, in the second pair E = 5 [position of E in alphabet series is 5]

$5^2 = 25$

$\therefore \quad ? = 25$

27. (d) Second figure of each pair is mirror image of first figure.

28. (a) The outer figure comes inside and becomes shaded. The inner figure comes outside.

29. (c) First design of first pair of problem figures is inverted and then placed on the original design to get the second figure. Similar concept is used in second pair.

30. (b) The symbol '◯' is moving from one corner to another in clockwise direction and one line is removed to get the second figure of the pair.

31. (c) As, $16 \times 2 - 2 = 32 - 2$

$= 30$

In the same way,

$17 \times 2 - 2 = 34 - 2 = 32$

Hence, option (c) is correct.

32. (d) In the given set, each successive number is four times of the previous number, as shown

$6 \times 4 = 24$

and $\quad 24 \times 4 = 96$

In the same way,

$2 \times 4 = 8$
and $8 \times 4 = 32$
Hence, option (d) is correct.

33. (c) Here, the relation can be represented as

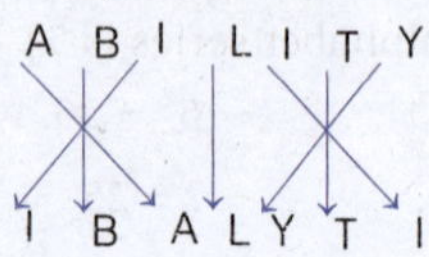

In the same way,

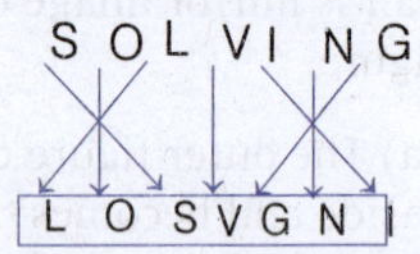

Hence, option (c) is correct.

34. (d) As SODIUM is a component of SALT, in the same way OXYGEN is a component of WATER.
Hence, option (d) is correct.

35. (a) In word GREAT, the number of alphabets = 5,
$\therefore$ GREAT $= (5)^2 = 25$
In the same way, in word NUMBER, the number of alphabets = 6
$\therefore$ NUMBER $= 6^2 = 36$

36. (d) The figure is rotated 45° clockwise in such a way that one curved line is deleted and one arrow is added. The arrows get inverted to form their new position.

37. (d) The larger figure becomes small, gets inverted and occupies the top position inside the small figure which gets enlarged.

38. (a) In first pair of problem figures, one more arm/side is added to the first figure and the half-circle at the corner of the sides, which were at the outside, comes inside. Similarly, in second pair of problem figures, one more side is added to the first figure and the half-circle at the corner of the sides, which were at the inside, comes outside.

39. (b) Here, the relation can be represented as

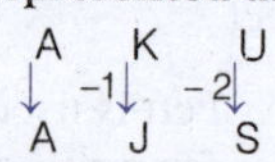

In the same way,

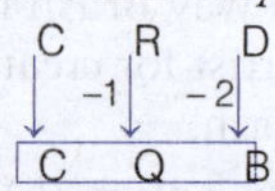

Hence, option (b) is correct.

2. Classification

1. (c) Numbers 4, 20 and 40 are even numbers but 25 is not an even number, it is an odd number.
So, 25 is odd one out.
Hence, option (c) is correct.

2. (c) Numbers 7, 21 and 35 are multiples of 7 but 27 is not a multiple of 7.
So, 27 is odd one out.
Hence, option (c) is correct.

3. (d) The number on right side is multiple of the number on the left side.
$15\text{-}45 = 15 \times 3 = 45$,
$12\text{-}72 = 12 \times 6 = 72$,
$13\text{-}169 = 13 \times 13 = 169$
But 11-90 does not follow this pattern.
So, 11-90 is odd one out.
Hence, option (d) is correct.

4. (c) Except (45, 53), numbers given in each of the pairs are even numbers but option (c) pair does not follow this pattern.
So, (45, 53) is the odd one out.
Hence, option (c) is correct.

5. (c) The second and third numbers in the triplets are the multiples of the first number but triplet (5, 25, 53) does not follow this pattern. So, (5, 25, 53) is the odd one out.
Hence, option (c) is correct.

6. (d) Except 36, all others are squares of odd numbers, 36 is the square of an even number i.e. 6.
So, 36 is odd one out.
Hence, option (d) is correct.

7. (c) The sequence can be represented as

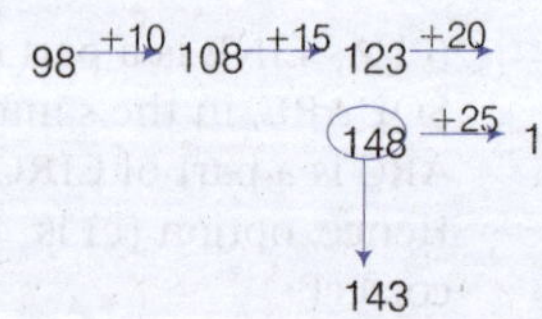

Here, 143 should come in place of 148. So, 148 is odd one out.
Hence, option (c) is correct.

8. (b) Numbers 5, 7, 11 and 13 are prime numbers but 9 is not a prime number.
So, 9 is odd one out.
Hence, option (b) is correct.

9. (b) Here, third digit of the number is obtained by dividing the first digit by the second digit.

This can be represented as

$4 \div 2 = 2$; $8 \div 2 = 4$;
$9 \div 3 = 3$, $2 \div 1 = 2$
but $6 \div 3 = 2 \neq 3$

So, 633 is odd one out.
Hence, option (b) is correct.

10. (c) Letters OD, IK and UP have vowels in their first place and consonants in their second place but letters EA do not follow this relationship. In EA, both letters are vowels. So, EA is odd one out.
Hence, option (c) is correct.

11. (d) Here, the relation between letters is shown as

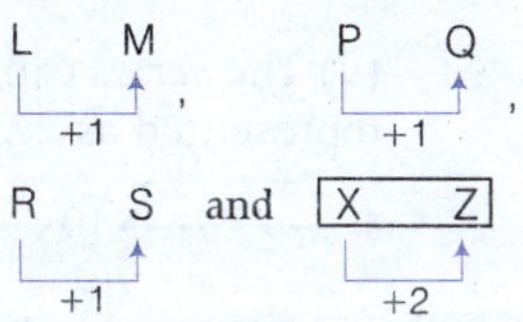

So, XZ is odd one out.
Hence, option (d) is correct.

12. (d) Here, the relation between the letters is shown as

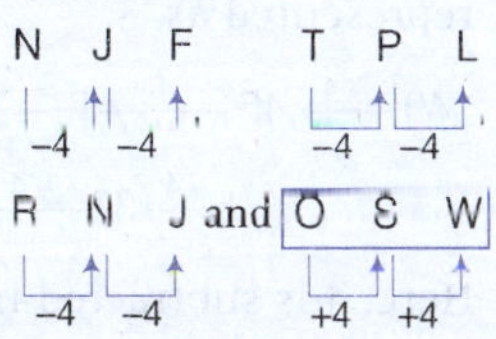

So, OSW is odd one out.
Hence, option (d) is correct.

13. (b) Except PQR, in all other groups the letters are written right to left in alphabetical order.
So, PQR is odd one out.

Hence, option (b) is correct.

14. (b) Except TOU, all other terms have 1 vowel but TOU contains two vowels.

Hence, option (b) is correct.

15. (b) Letters DA, KU and ME have consonants at their first place and vowels at their second place but letters FC do not follow this relationship. In FC, both letters are consonants.

So, FC is odd one out.

Hence, option (b) is correct.

16. (b) Here, the relation between the letters is shown as

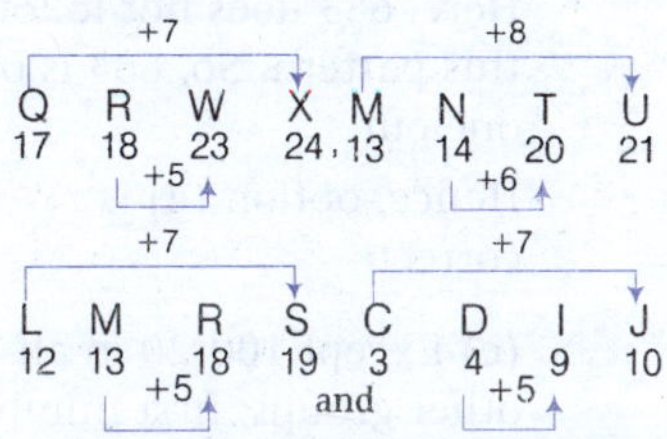

So, MNTU is odd one out.
Hence, option (b) is correct.

17. (c) The words swimming, boating and diving are related to water i.e. they are water activities but driving is not a water activity as it is done on roads.

So, driving is odd one out.

Hence, option (c) is correct.

18. (a) Here, only kilogram is measuring unit of weight.
So, kilogram is odd one out.
Hence, option (a) is correct.

19. (d) Rickshaw, cart and cycle do not require any engine to operate but taxi requires engine to operate.
So, taxi is odd one out.

Hence, option (d) is correct.

20. (d) The words goal, red card and penalty shoot are terms used in football but 'no ball' term is not used in football, it is used in cricket.

So, no ball is odd one out.
Hence, option (d) is correct.

21. (d) The words know, recognise and identify are similar in meaning but unaware is opposite in meaning.

So, unaware is odd one out.

Hence, option (d) is correct.

22. (d) Except 19T, in all the terms number written on the left side is the positional value of the letter written on the right side in English alphabetical order but 19T does not follow this pattern, since the positional value of T is 20 in English alphabetical order.
So, 19T is odd one out.

Hence, option (d) is correct.

23. (c) Here, the result of the multiplication of the numbers written on either sides of the letter is the positional value of the letter written in the middle.

This can be represented as

$4 \times 2 = 8 = H$
$5 \times 2 = 10 = J$
$4 \times 4 = 16 = P$

but $5\times3=15=O\neq N$
So, 5N3 is odd one out.

Hence, option (c) is correct.

24. (d) All the figures except figure (d) are made of straight lines. But figure (d) is not, thus, it is different.

25. (d) Except figure (d), all other figures are made up of four lines.

26. (b) Figure (b) is divided into two parts while others are being divided into four parts.

27. (c) Figure (c) has one closed loop while others do not have such loop.

28. (c) Direction of arrows in all figures except figure (c), is in clockwise direction.

29. (d) In all the figures except figure (d), there are two pins and three arrows: In figure (d), there are three pins and two arrows, thus it is different from the others.

30. (c) Except figure (c), in all other figures, the inner design consists of less number of sides than that of the outer design.
In option (c), the inner design has more sides than outer design.

31. (c) Here, we find that in each number, first and second digits are multiplied to get the third digit, as shown

$236:2\times3=6$

$155:1\times5=5$

$717:7\times1=7$

$428:4\times2=8$

But $328:3\times2=6\neq8$

Here, 328 does not follow this pattern.

So, 328 is odd one out.

Hence, option (c) is correct.

32. (a) Here, we see that in each number, first and third digits are added to get the second digit as shown

$396:3+6=9$

$682:6+2=8$

$792:7+2=9$

$374:3+4=7$

$683:6+3=9\neq8$

$781:7+1=8$

Here, 683 does not follow this pattern. So, 683 is odd one out.

Hence, option (a) is correct.

33. (c) Except 100-20 in all other groups, first number when divided by 4 gives the second number.
So, 100-20 is odd one out.
Hence, option (c) is correct.

34. (c) In all other groups, number at the end is half of the positions of sum of first and second letters in the alphabet, except (c).

$KQ14\Rightarrow\frac{K+Q}{2}$

$\Rightarrow\frac{11+17}{2}=14$

$AY13\Rightarrow\frac{A+Y}{2}$

$\Rightarrow\frac{1+25}{2}=13$

$GW15\Rightarrow\frac{G+W}{2}$

$\Rightarrow\frac{7+23}{2}=15$

But in option (c),

$MR11\Rightarrow\frac{M+R}{2}$

$\Rightarrow\frac{13+18}{2}=\frac{31}{2}=15.5\neq11$

Therefore, MR11 is the different term.

35. (d) Except figure (d), all other figures have four black and three white squares.

36. (d) All the figures except figure (d) are rotated forms of the same figure. i.e. all are same when rotated. But in figure (d), the shaded portion is at opposite side.

3. Series

1. (d) The series can be represented as

$4\xrightarrow{+3}7\xrightarrow{+3}10\xrightarrow{+3}13\xrightarrow{+3}16\xrightarrow{+3}\boxed{19}$

Here, 3 is added to each term to get the next term.
Hence, option (d) is correct.

2. (a) The series can be represented as

$49\xrightarrow{-4}45\xrightarrow{-4}41\xrightarrow{-4}37\xrightarrow{-4}33\xrightarrow{-4}\boxed{29}$

Here, 4 is subtracted from each term to get the next term.
Hence, option (a) is correct.

3. (a) The series can be represented as

$567\xrightarrow{\div3}189\xrightarrow{\div3}63\xrightarrow{\div3}21\xrightarrow{\div3}\boxed{7}$

Here, each term is obtained by dividing the previous term by 3 to get the next term.
Hence, option (a) is correct.

4. (c) The series can be represented as

$$1 \xrightarrow{\times 2} 2 \xrightarrow{\times 3} 6 \xrightarrow{\times 4} 24 \xrightarrow{\times 5} \boxed{120} \xrightarrow{\times 6} \boxed{720}$$

Hence, option (c) is correct.

5. (b) The series can be represented as

$$3 \xrightarrow{+1} 4 \xrightarrow{+1} \boxed{5} \xrightarrow{+1} 6 \xrightarrow{+1} 7$$
$$5 \xrightarrow{+1} 6 \xrightarrow{+1} \boxed{7} \xrightarrow{+1} 8 \xrightarrow{+1} 9$$
$$8 \xrightarrow{-1} 7 \xrightarrow{-1} \boxed{6} \xrightarrow{-1} 5 \xrightarrow{-1} 4$$

Hence, option (b) is correct.

6. (b) The series can be represented as

$$5 \xrightarrow{+2} 7 \xrightarrow{+2} 9 \xrightarrow{+2} 11 \xrightarrow{+2} \boxed{13}$$
$$25 \xrightarrow{-1} 24 \xrightarrow{-1} 23 \xrightarrow{-1} 22 \xrightarrow{-1} \boxed{21}$$
$$19 \xrightarrow{-2} 17 \xrightarrow{-2} 15 \xrightarrow{-2} 13 \xrightarrow{-2} \boxed{11}$$

Hence, option (b) is correct.

7. (b) The series can be represented as

$$P \xrightarrow{+2} R \xrightarrow{+2} T \xrightarrow{+2} V \xrightarrow{+2} \boxed{X}$$
$$F \xrightarrow{-1} E \xrightarrow{-1} D \xrightarrow{-1} C \xrightarrow{-1} \boxed{B}$$

Hence, option (b) is correct.

8. (b) The series can be represented as

$$P \xrightarrow{+3} S \xrightarrow{+3} V \xrightarrow{+3} Y \xrightarrow{+3} \boxed{B}$$
$$r \xrightarrow{+3} u \xrightarrow{+3} x \xrightarrow{+3} a \xrightarrow{+3} \boxed{d}$$

Hence, option (b) is correct.

9. (d) The series can be represented as

$$B \xrightarrow{+1} C \xrightarrow{+1} D \xrightarrow{+1} E \xrightarrow{+1} \boxed{F}$$
$$P \xrightarrow{+1} Q \xrightarrow{+1} R \xrightarrow{+1} S \xrightarrow{+1} \boxed{T}$$
$$L \xrightarrow{+1} M \xrightarrow{+1} N \xrightarrow{+1} O \xrightarrow{+1} \boxed{P}$$

Hence, option (d) is correct.

10. (a) The series can be represented as

$$J \xrightarrow{+1} K \xrightarrow{+2} M \xrightarrow{+3} P \xrightarrow{+4} T$$
$$Z \xrightarrow{-1} Y \xrightarrow{-1} X \xrightarrow{-1} W \xrightarrow{-1} V$$

Hence, option (a) is correct.

11. (a) The series can be represented as

$$O \xrightarrow{+2} Q \xrightarrow{+2} S \xrightarrow{+2} U \xrightarrow{+2} \boxed{W}$$
$$J \xrightarrow{-1} I \xrightarrow{-1} H \xrightarrow{-1} G \xrightarrow{-1} \boxed{F}$$

Hence, option (a) is correct.

12. (b)

$$D \xrightarrow{+2} F \xrightarrow{+2} H \xrightarrow{+2} J \xrightarrow{+2} \boxed{L}$$
$$K \xrightarrow{-1} J \xrightarrow{-1} I \xrightarrow{-1} H \xrightarrow{-1} \boxed{G}$$
$$Y \xrightarrow{-2} W \xrightarrow{-2} U \xrightarrow{-2} S \xrightarrow{-2} \boxed{Q}$$

Hence, option (b) is correct.

13. (c)

$$Y \xrightarrow{-2} W \xrightarrow{-2} U \xrightarrow{-2} \boxed{S}$$
$$V \xrightarrow{-2} T \xrightarrow{-2} R \xrightarrow{-2} \boxed{P}$$
$$P \xrightarrow{-2} N \xrightarrow{-2} L \xrightarrow{-2} \boxed{J}$$

Hence option (c) is correct.

14. (c) The series can be represented as

$$C \xrightarrow{+2} E \xrightarrow{+2} G \xrightarrow{+2} I \xrightarrow{+2} \boxed{K}$$
$$8 \xrightarrow{+3} 11 \xrightarrow{+3} 14 \xrightarrow{+3} 17 \xrightarrow{+3} \boxed{20}$$
$$W \xrightarrow{-1} V \xrightarrow{-1} U \xrightarrow{-1} T \xrightarrow{-1} \boxed{S}$$

Hence, option (c) is correct.

15. (a) The series can be represented as

$$J \xrightarrow{+1} K \xrightarrow{+1} \boxed{L} \xrightarrow{+1} M \xrightarrow{+1} N$$
$$6 \xrightarrow{-1} 5 \xrightarrow{-1} \boxed{4} \xrightarrow{-1} 3 \xrightarrow{-1} 2$$

Hence, option (a) is correct.

16. (b) In this series, every letter is given its alphabetical position and one letter is skipped in between each term.

$$C\text{-}3 \xrightarrow{+2} E\text{-}5 \xrightarrow{+2} G\text{-}7 \xrightarrow{+2} I\text{-}9 \xrightarrow{+2} \boxed{K\text{-}11} \xrightarrow{+2} \boxed{M\text{-}13}$$

(letters +2, numbers +2)

Hence, the missing terms are K-11 and M-13.

17. (d) Here, from figure (1) to (2), an identical shape is added but in 90° the opposite direction. This pattern follows from figure (3) to (4) and figure (5) to the answer figure. On following this pattern, we see that option figure (d) will come next.
Hence, option (d) is correct.

18. (a) Here, the dot, square and shaded portions are moving in 90° clockwise direction. On following this pattern, we see that option figure (a) will come next.

Hence, option (a) is correct.

19. (d) Here, we see that a circle is added in horizontal and vertical direction and they all are connected by lines. On following this pattern, we see that option figure (d) will come next. Hence, option (d) is correct.

20. (b) Here, the outer arc is moving 90° in anti-clockwise direction and middle arc is moving 90° in clockwise direction and the small arc is moving 90° in anticlockwise. On following this pattern, we see that option figure (b) will complete the given series. Hence, option (b) is correct.

21. (a) Here, the circles are moving in clockwise direction and the shaded portion in both circles is also moving in clockwise direction. On following this pattern, we see that option figure (a) will complete the series. Hence, option (a) is correct.

22. (b) The series can be represented as

$$1 \xrightarrow{+1.25} 2.25 \xrightarrow{+2.25} 4.5 \xrightarrow{+3.25} 7.75 \xrightarrow{+4.25} \boxed{12}$$

Here, each time a number to be added is increased by 1 and gives the next term.

Hence, option (b) is correct.

23. (d) The series can be represented as

$$6^3 \xrightarrow{-1} 5^3 \xrightarrow{-1} 4^3 \xrightarrow{-1} 3^3 \xrightarrow{-1} 2^3$$

$$216 \quad 125 \quad 64 \quad 27 \quad \boxed{8}$$

Here, the cubes of natural numbers in decreasing order are given.

Hence, option (d) is correct.

24. (c) The series can be represented as

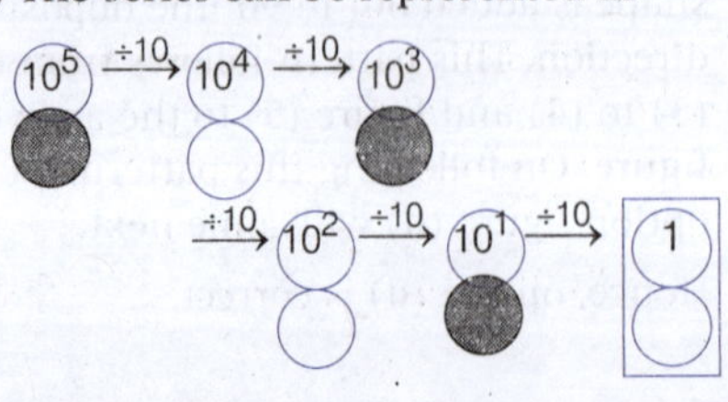

Here, each term is obtained by dividing the previous term by 10 to get the next term. The lower circle is shaded in every alternative step.
Hence, option (c) is correct.

25. (a) The series can be represented as

$$12 \xrightarrow{+5} 17 \xrightarrow{+5} 22 \xrightarrow{+5} 27 \xrightarrow{+5} \boxed{32}$$

$$77 \xrightarrow{-7} 70 \xrightarrow{-7} 63 \xrightarrow{-7} 56 \xrightarrow{-7} \boxed{49}$$

$$3 \xrightarrow{+8} 11 \xrightarrow{+8} 19 \xrightarrow{+8} 27 \xrightarrow{+8} \boxed{35}$$

Hence, option (a) is correct.

26. (b) The series can be represented as

$$\text{YXW} \xrightarrow{-2} \text{UTSR} \xrightarrow{-2} \text{PONML} \xrightarrow{-2} \text{JIHGFE} \xrightarrow{-2} \boxed{\text{CBAZYXW}}$$

Here, the first letter of each next term is obtained by subtracting 2 from the place value of last letter of the previous letter group. Also, in each step one letter is increased in each letter group of the series.

Hence, option (b) is correct.

27. (a) The series can be represented as

Upper: Q $\xrightarrow{-5}$ L $\xrightarrow{-4}$ H $\xrightarrow{-3}$ E $\xrightarrow{-2}$ C $\xrightarrow{-1}$ B

15 Q 10 L 6 H $\boxed{3}$ E 1 C 0 B

Lower: 15 $\xrightarrow{-5}$ 10 $\xrightarrow{-4}$ 6 $\xrightarrow{-3}$ 3 $\xrightarrow{-2}$ 1 $\xrightarrow{-1}$ 0

Hence, option (a) is correct.

28. (b) Here, the circle, square, cross and star are moving in clockwise direction. On following this pattern, we see that option figure (b) will complete the given series.

Hence, option (b) is correct.

29. (a) Here, everytime line segment is changed into a square which appears with pre-existing signs in each of the subsequent figures. On following this pattern, we see that option figure (a) will complete the series.
Hence, option (a) is correct.

4. Coding-Decoding

1. (a) The code for each of the letters 'S', 'E', 'V' and 'N' are as shown below

Word	T	E	L	E	V	I	S	I	O	N
Code	A	N	C	N	L	B	Z	B	T	D

Clearly, S→ Z, E→ N , V→ L, N→ D

Therefore, SEVEN would be written as ZNLND.

Hence, option (a) is correct.

2. (b) As, M I S I R A L → S I M I L A R

Similarly, N I W D S W O → W I N D O W S

Hence, option (b) is correct.

3. (c) As, RIDER → QHCDQ (each letter −1)

Similarly, HONDA → GNMCZ (each letter −1)

Hence, option (c) is correct.

4. (a)

Letters	A	B	C	D	---	W
Codes	C	D	E	F	---	Y

Clearly, P I L A T E S (+2 each) → R K N C V G U

Hence, option (a) is correct.

5. (b) As, W A T E R (+2 each) → Y C V G T

Similarly, H K T G (+2 each) → J M V I

Hence, option (b) is correct.

6. (b) As, R E A S O N → 6 2 1 7 5 4

and T R U T H → 8 6 9 8 3

Therefore, T R E A S O N → 8 6 2 1 7 5 4

7. (c) Here each alphabet is coded with corresponding positions of letters.

As, R A M A N → 18 1 13 1 14

Similarly,

K A P I L A → 11 1 16 9 12 1

∴ KAPILA ⇒ 111169121

8. (b) Here each letter is coded with corresponding positions in alphabetical series.

As, H I G H → 8 9 7 8

Similarly, D E A F → 4 5 1 6

∴ DEAF ⇒ 4516

9. (b) Here each letter is coded with their corresponding positions in alphabetical series.

As, H A C B → 8 1 3 2

Similarly,

D	E	F	A
4	5	6	1

∴ DEFA ⇒ 4561

10. (b) As,

S	T	A	R
5	$	*	2

and

T	O	R	E
$	3	2	@

Similarly,

O	A	T	S
3	*	$	5

∴ OATS ⇒ 3 * $ 5

11. (d) As,

R	O	P	E	D	O	U	B	T
%	5	7	$	3	5	#	8	*

and

L	I	V	E
@	2	4	$

Similarly,

T	R	O	U	B	L	E
*	%	5	#	8	@	$

∴ TROUBLE ⇒ * % 5 # 8 @ $

12. (a) As,

B	A	S	K	E	T
5	$	3	%	#	1

and

T	R	I	E	D
1	4	*	#	2

Similarly,

S	K	I	R	T
3	%	*	4	1

∴ SKIRT ⇒ 3%*41

13. (d) As,

R	A	T,	C	A	T
*	Δ	%	#	Δ	%

and

F	A	T
$	Δ	%

Similarly,

C	A	R
#	Δ	*

∴ CAR ⇒ #Δ*

14. (d) Colour of 'Lady Finger' is green but here green is called yellow. Hence, colour of 'Lady Finger' is yellow.

15. (b) 'Lion' is a wild animal but here 'lion' is called 'buffalo'. Hence, in this case 'buffalo' is a wild animal.

16. (c) 'Train' is associated with 'railways' but here train is called 'aeroplane'. Hence, in this case 'aeroplane' is associated with railways.

17. (c) Sachin is great ⟶ ga ma ra ...(i)

is he poor ⟶ ta sa ga ...(ii)

From Eqs. (i) and (ii),

is ⇒ ga

18. (c) pick and choose ⟶ ko ho po ...(i)

pick up and come ⟶ to no ko po ...(ii)

From Eqs. (i) and (ii),

pick and ⇒ ko po

∴ pick ⇒ ko or po

19. (a) open the door ⟶ ka te jo ...(i)

door is closed ⟶ jo pa ma ...(ii)

this is good ⟶ la ra pa ...(iii)

From Eqs. (i) and (ii),

door ⇒ jo

From Eqs. (ii) and (iii),

is ⇒ pa

∴ closed ⇒ ma

20. (b) where are you → pit ka ta ...(i)

are they there → sa da ka ...(ii)

they may come → da na ja ...(iii)

From Eqs. (i) and (ii),

are ⇒ ka

From Eqs. (ii) and (iii),

they ⇒ da

∴ there ⇒ sa

21. (a) Here, M O N K E Y → α γ θ 8 7 @

22. (a) According to the given alphabet code table.

1 6 3 5 1 4 → A N I M A L

9 7 8 4 2 → W O R L D

23. (d) As, M I N G L E → E I G N L M

Similarly, B R A Z I L → L R Z A I B

So, BRAZIL would be written as LRZAIB.

Hence, option (d) is correct.

24. (d) Each letter is coded with its opposite letter in alphabetical series.

As, C E R T A I N → X V I G Z R M

and S E Q U E N C E → H V J F V M X V

Similarly, R E Q U I R E D → I V J F R I V W

25. (c) As, H E A R T → @ 8 5 3 1

and F E A S T → # 8 5 4 1

Similarly, F A R T H E S T → # 5 3 1 @ 8 4 1

∴ FARTHEST ⇒ #531@841

26. (d)

Sue Re Nik → She is brave ...(i)

Pi Sor Re Nik → She is always smiling ...(ii)

Sor Re Zhi → is always cheerful ...(iii)

From Eqs. (i), (ii) and (iii),

∴ Smiling = Pi.

27. (a) nik ma de → he has come ...(i)

de lit pa → come here tast ...(ii)

ma la se → she has gone ...(iii)

From Eqs. (i) and (ii),

come ⇒ de

From Eqs. (i) and (iii),

has ⇒ ma

∴ he ⇒ nik

28. (c) Here, B E A S T → I ÷ + # II

29. (c) Clearly we have

Letter	A	B	C	D	E	F	G	G	I	J	K
Value	1	3	5	7	9	11	13	15	17	19	21

So, DICE = 7 + 17 + 5 + 9 = 38

30. '786' → Study very nice ...(i)

'958' → hard work nice ...(ii)

'645' → study and work ...(iii)

From Eqs. (ii) and (iii) we get the code of 'work' is '5'.

5. Alphabet and Number Sequence Test

1. (b) 7th letter from left = G

∴ 8th letter to the right of G

= (7 + 8) th letter from left

= 15th letter from left = O

2. (d) 7th letter to the right of K in backward order
= 7th letter to the left of K in forward order
= 7th letter before K in forward order
= (11 − 7)th letter in the forward order
= 4th letter in the forward order = D

3. (a) 7th letter from right = (27 − 7)th = 20th letter from left = T

$\therefore$ Required middle letter $= \frac{8+20}{2} = 14$th letter from left = N

4. (c)

Original word M [O] [N] K E Y

Word after arranging in descending order Y [O] [N] M K E

So, such two type of letters are O and N.

5. (c) XUVMRSTMWNVMWOPMWUVMWAC (WMV) HPNVWMWTUN

Clearly, there is one M which is preceded by W and followed by V.

6. (b)

M L K J I H G F (E) D C B [A] N O
→ 9th   Middle
P (Q) R S T U V W X Y Z
10th ←

The 9th letter from the left is E and 10th letter from the right is Q and therefore we see that A lies exactly in middle between E and Q.

7. (d)

D I S T U R B A N C E ⟶ E C N A B R U T S I D

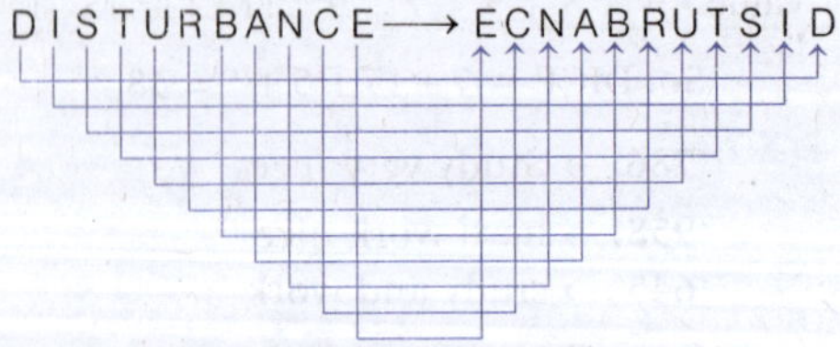

E C N A B R U T (S) I D

8. (c) Let us see

The given number 8 [2] 4 7 [5] 3 1

Ascending order arrangement 1 [2] 3 4 [5] 7 8

So, position of two digits remain unchanged.

9. (a) Let us see

Original number 8 3 1 4 6 7 5 9

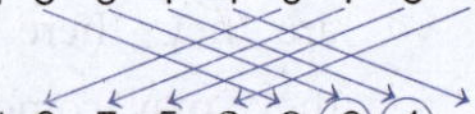

New arrangement 6 7 5 9 8 (3) (1) 4

3rd from right

So, the required digit is 3.

10. (b) Let us see

(7) 4 2 (7) 6 4 3 6 (7) 5 3 5 (7) 8 4 3

7 6 (7) 2 4 0 6 (7) 4 3

✓ = Condition fulfilled

× = Condition not fulfilled

Clearly, there are two such 7's.

11. (a)

(5) [4] △3 △3 (5) [4] 8 8 △3 2 (5) △3 6 (5) (5)

8 = 2 times, 6 = 1 time; 5 = 5 times, 4 = 2 times
3 = 4 times, 2 = 1 times

Clearly, 5 has come maximum times.

12. (c)

(8) [4] 6 7 △3 [4] △3 7 (8) △3 [4] [4] 5 6
△3 [4] 6 [4] △3 [4] (8)

8 = 3 times, 7 = 2 times, 6 = 3 times,
5 = 1 time, 4 = 7 times, 3 = 5 times.

Clearly, 5 is minimum.

13. (a) 2 X [4 Y 3] A B D 7 F [2 M 9] Z

Hence, there are two such letters Y and M, which are immediately preceded by an even number and immediately succeeded by an odd number.

14. (b) X Y A 2 E P I 8 O [P 7 U] 9 E X E 5 O

Hence, there is only one number '7', which is immediately preceded by a consonant and immediately followed by a vowel.

15. (d) On dropping all the vowels and even numbers from the given sequence. We get

t 3 9 [r] q p 7

$\therefore$ Fourth element from the left is r.

16. (d) The given sequence contains two such elements.

$ A a 5 # 6 b C 1 [d m 6] M $ 9 [d = 8]

Hence, option (d) is correct.

17. (b) The given sequence contains two such elements.

E G 4 B H 7 5 [@ K 8] D N £ Q Z [$ W 3] C 1 9 * L B 2 S 6

Hence, option (b) is correct.

18. (b) There is only one such consonant [8 V #].

19. (b) 10th to the right of 19th from the right end = (19 – 10)th from right end

= 9th from right end = T

20. (d) According to the question,

Given word C O M M U N I C A T I O N S

New word O C M M [N] U C I T A O I S N

K ← 10th from right

Hence, required letter is N

21. (b) Original word, T O L E R A N T

I. Change, S P K F Q B M S

II. Change, B F K M (P) Q S S

Fourth from the right

Clearly, P will be fourth from the right.

22. (c) Let us see

Original number 3 8 5 6 4 9 0 2 7 1

New arrangement 8 3 6 5 (9) 4 2 0 1 7

from left 5th

So, the required digit is 9.

23. (c) Highest number = 846

∴ Sum of the first two digit of 846 = 8 + 4 = (12)

24. (a) Given sequence

8 C L M @ N £ T 2 Y 6 S £ Q $ 7 * W # Z 3 U ε % A 4

Applying the given operation we get

C L M N T Y [S] Q W Z U E A

7th from left

Hence, 'S' is seventh from the left.

25. (a) The symbols are E % V

Hence, only one such symbol.

6. Direction and Distance Sense Test

1. (b) The direction diagram can be drawn as shown below

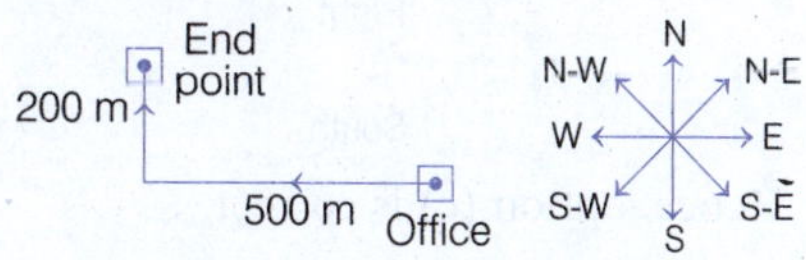

Now, comparing the above diagram with the standard direction graph, we see that Raju is now facing towards North.

Hence, option (b) is correct.

2. (a) The direction diagram can be drawn as shown below

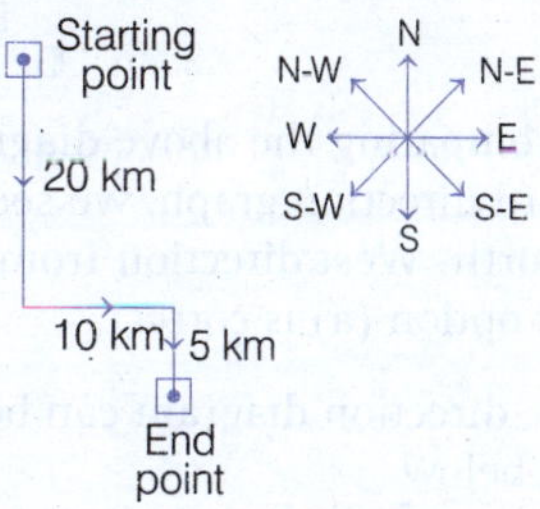

Now, comparing the above diagram with the standard direction graph, we see that the person is now facing towards South.

Hence, option (a) is correct.

3. (a) The direction diagram can be drawn as shown below

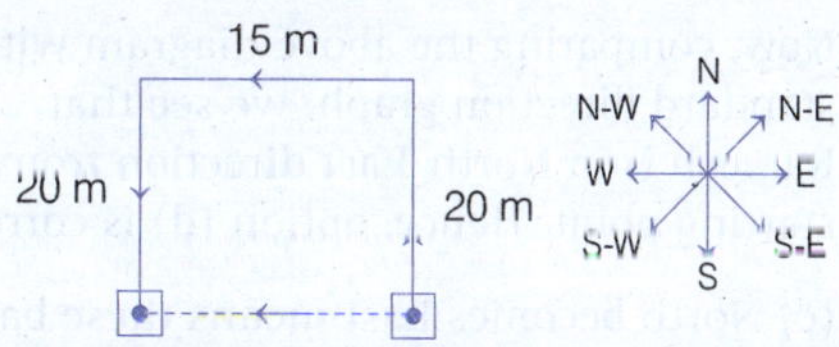

Now, comparing the above diagram with the standard direction graph, we see that, Rohit is in West direction from his starting point.

Hence, option (a) is correct.

4. (c) In the given question, when Mohit is facing in East direction, then his left hand is towards the North direction and his right hand is towards the South direction as shown below

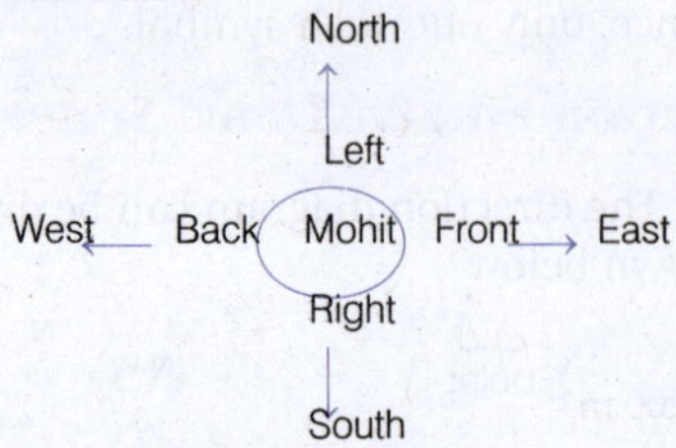

Hence, option (c) is correct.

5. (a) The direction diagram can be drawn as shown below

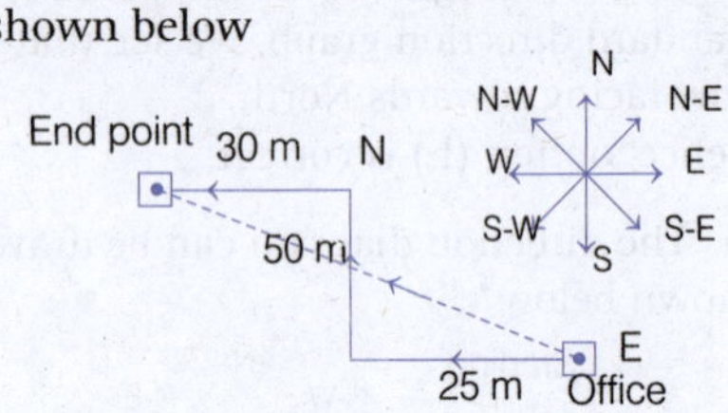

Now, comparing the above diagram with the standard direction graph, we see that Jitesh is in North- West direction from his office. Hence, option (a) is correct.

6. (d) The direction diagram can be drawn as shown below

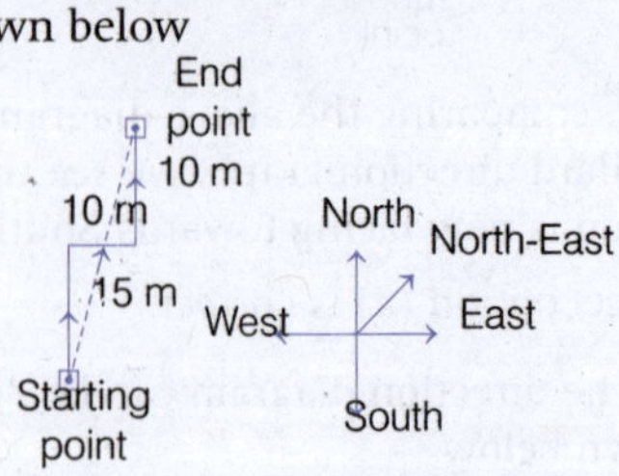

Now, comparing the above diagram with the standard direction graph, we see that Ramesh is in North-East direction from his starting point. Hence, option (d) is correct.

7. (c) North becomes East means these basic directions are moving anti-clockwise through an angle of 90° as shown below

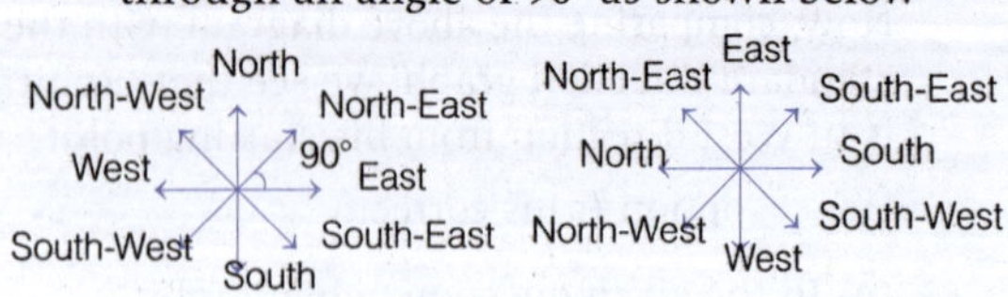

Now, from the above diagram, it is clear that North-East becomes South-East.
Hence, option (c) is correct.

8. (b) The direction diagram can be drawn as

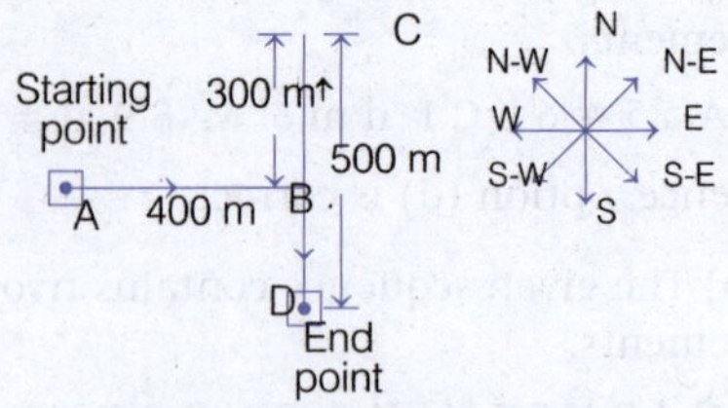

∴ Total distance travelled by Rajesh

$= AB + BC + CD = 400 + 300 + 500$

$= 1200\text{ m} = 1.2\text{ km}$

Hence, option (b) is correct.

9. (b) The direction diagram can be drawn as

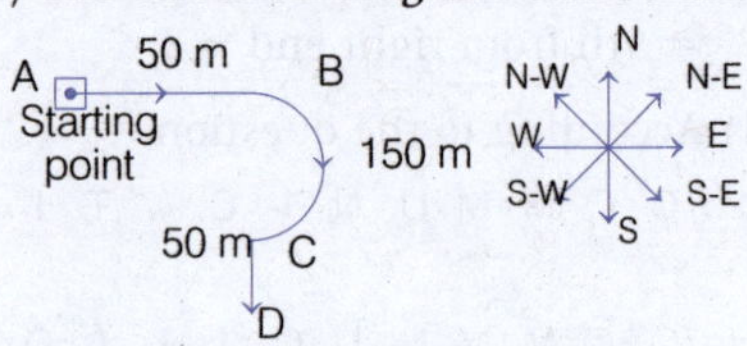

∴Total distance travelled by Shivam
$= AB + BC + CD = 50 + 150 + 50 = 250\text{ m}$
Hence, option (b) is correct.

10. (b) The direction diagram can be drawn as

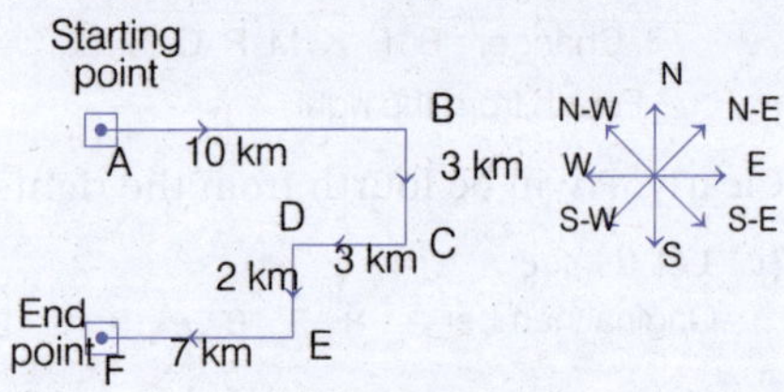

Now, the distance between starting and end point $AF = BC + DE = 3 + 2 = 5\text{ km}$
Hence, option (b) is correct.

11. (c) The figure below shows the path travelled by Ramesh from node A to B via D.

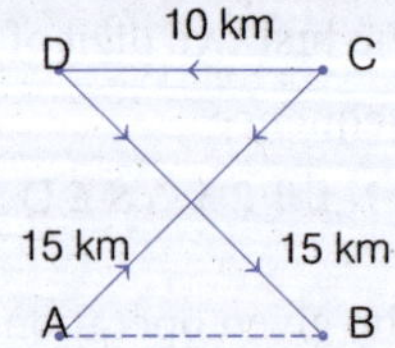

∴ Total distance travelled by Ramesh

$= AC + CD + DB$

$= 15 + 10 + 15 = 40\text{ km}$

Hence, option (c) is correct.

12. (d) The direction diagram can be drawn as

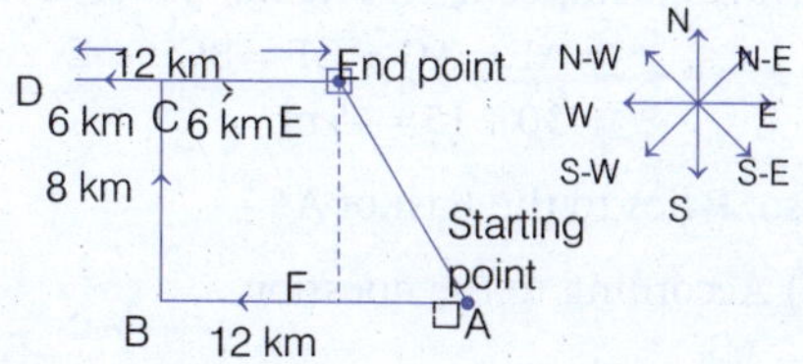

Now, from the above direction graph, short distance is AE.

Using Pythagoras theorem,

$(AE)^2 = (EF)^2 + (AF)^2 = 8^2 + 6^2$

$[\because EF = CB \text{ and } AF = AB - CE]$

$= 64 + 36 = 100 \Rightarrow AE = 10$

So, the shortest distance between her starting point and present position = 10 m

Hence, option (d) is correct.

13. (b) At 8:00 am the sun is in the East direction.

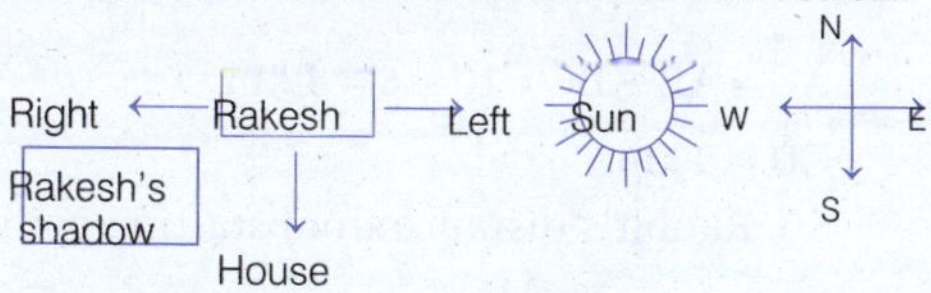

Clearly, Rakesh is walking towards the South direction.

14. (c) According to the question,

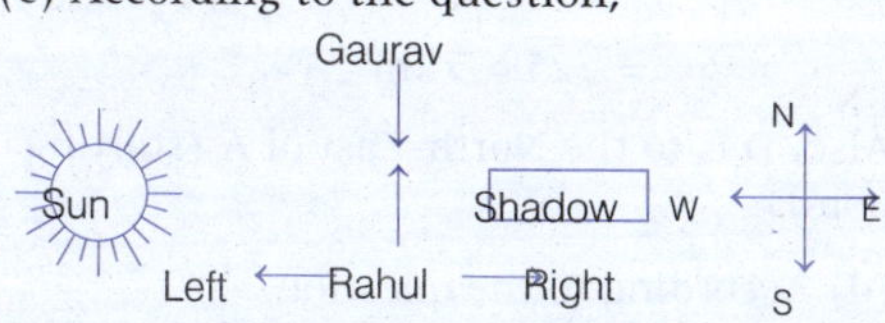

From the diagram it is clear that Gaurav is facing South.

15. (c) According to the question,

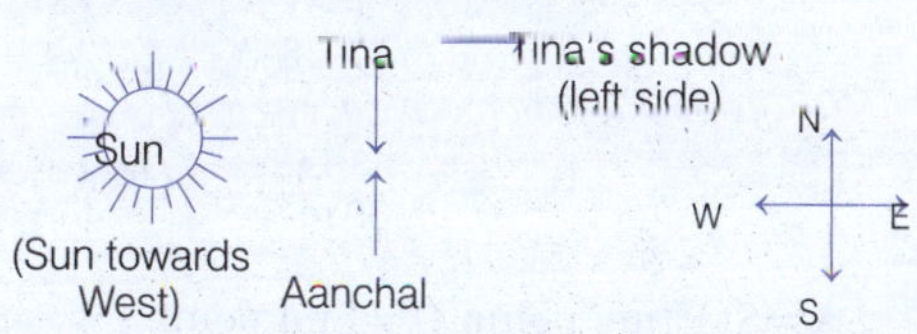

So, Aanchal was facing North.

16. (d) Movement in clockwise direction = 90°

Movement in anti-clockwise direction

$= 180° + 90° = 270°$

We can say, she turns $(270° - 90°) = 180°$ in anti-clockwise direction.

Initially she was facing North-West direction. So, now she is facing South-East direction.

17. (c) According to the question, the direction diagram is as given below,

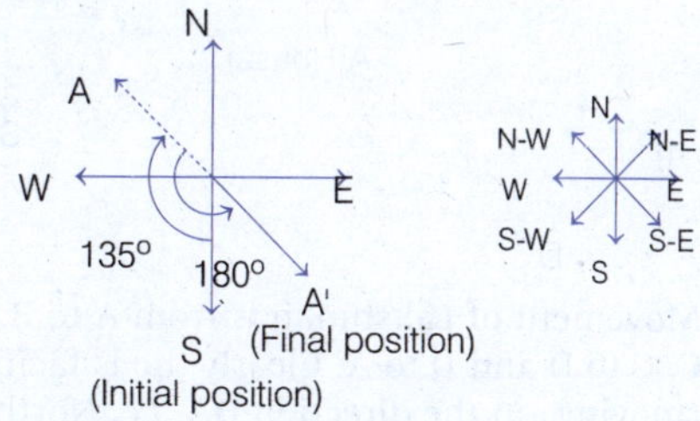

OA' is the final position at which the man is looking finally.

∴ OA' is South-East direction.

18. (d) According to the question, the direction diagram is as given below,

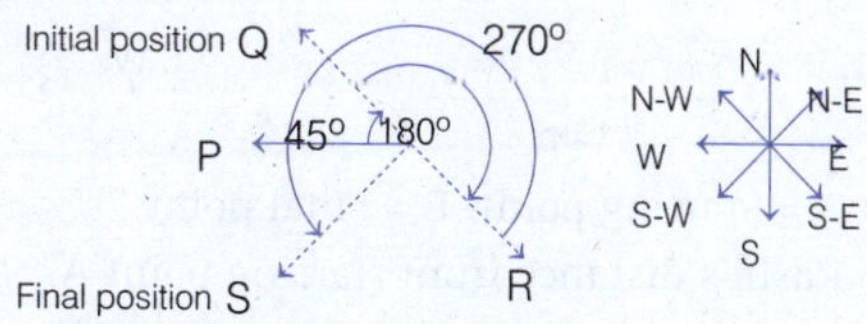

From the figure, finally he is facing in the OS direction, which is South-West.

19. (b)

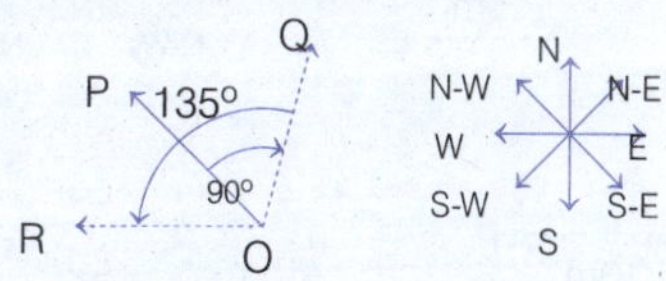

The man initially faces in the direction OP. On moving 90° clockwise, the man faces in the direction OQ. On further moving 135° anti-clockwise he faces the direction OR, which is West.

20. (d) According to the question,

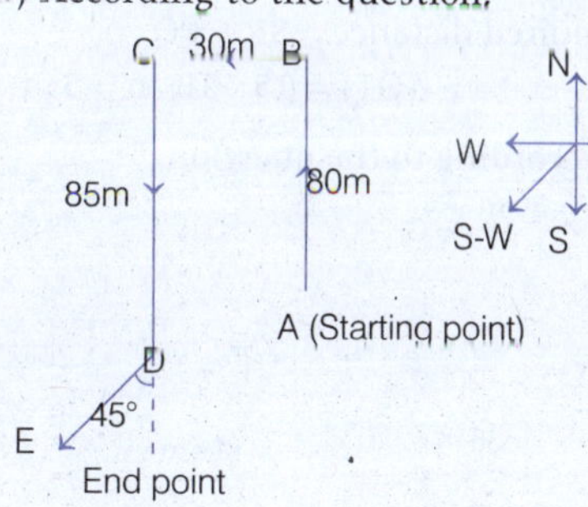

From the above diagram, it is clear that, she is finally facing South-West direction.

21. (a) According to the question,

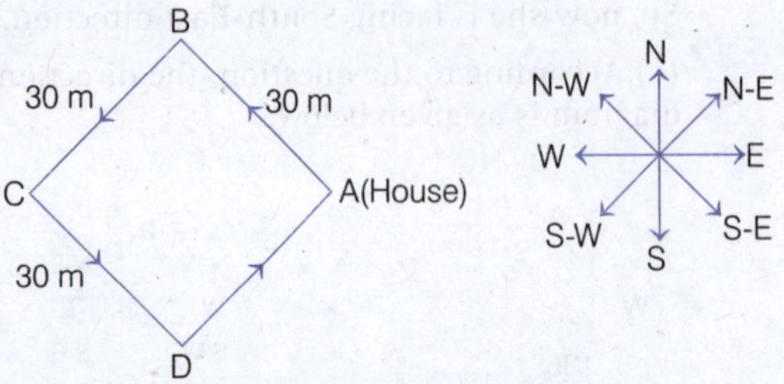

Movement of Lakshman is from A to B, B to C, C to D and D to A. Clearly, he is facing (moving) in the direction DA, i.e. North-East.

22. (c) The movement of Rashi is shown below

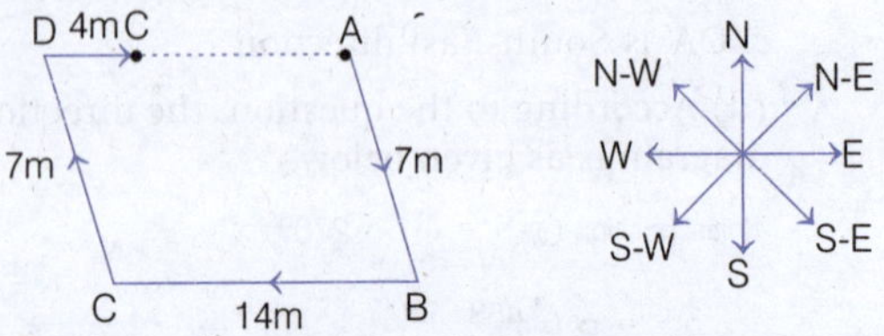

A = Starting point, E = Final point

Rashi's distance from starting point A

$= AD - DE = (14 - 4)\ m = 10\ m$

23. (a) According to the question,

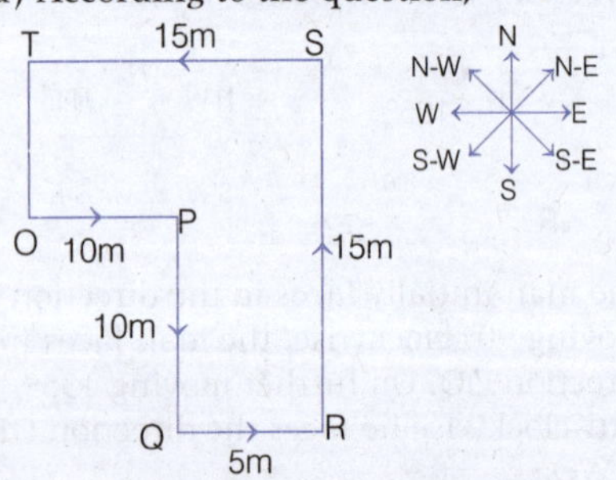

O = Starting point, T = End point.

$\therefore$ Required distance = SR – PQ

$(OT) = (15 - 10)\ m = 5\ m$

24. (d) According to the question,

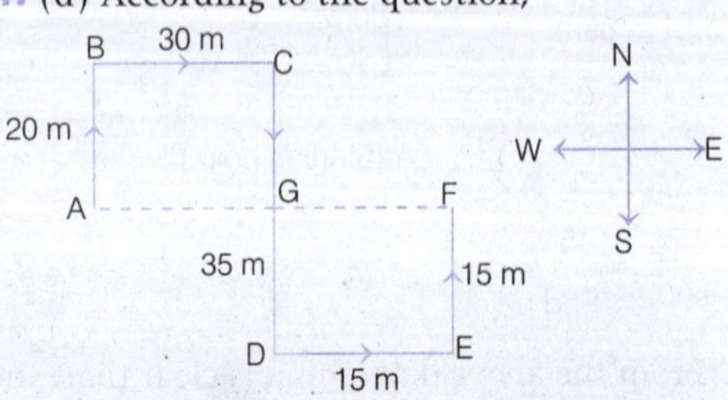

A = Starting point, F = End point.

Nayan's distance from original position A

$= AF = AG + GF = BC + DE$

$= 30 + 15 = 45\ m$

Also, F lies to the East of A.

25. (d) According to the question,

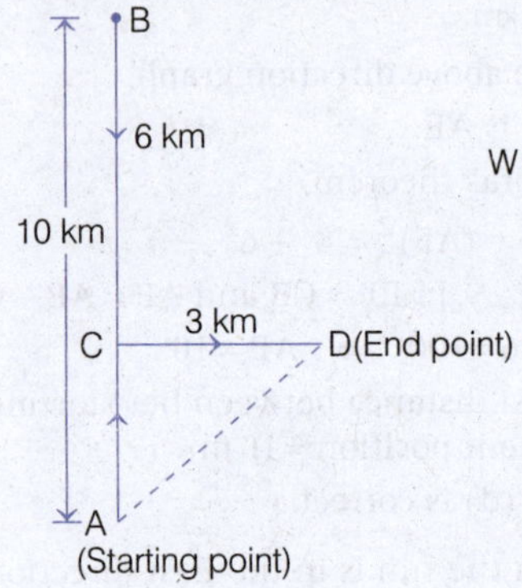

$AC = AB - BC = 10 - 6 = 4\ km$

$CD = 3\ km$

So, Ranbir's distance from starting point A,

$= AD$

$= \sqrt{AC^2 + CD^2}$

$= \sqrt{4^2 + 3^2}$

$= \sqrt{25} = 5\ km$

Also, D is to the North-East of A (starting point).

26. (d) According to the question,

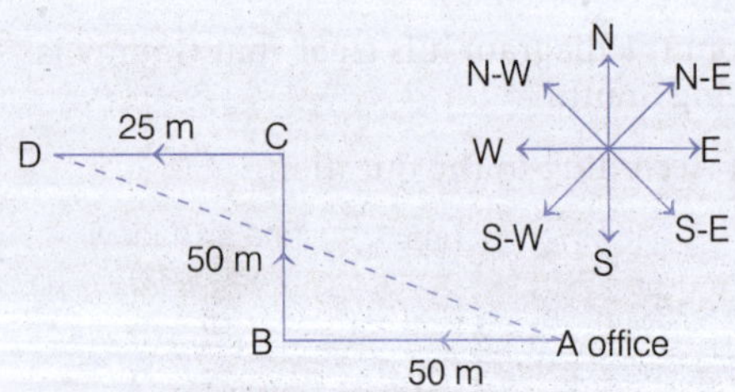

A = Starting point, D = End point

Since, Devanshu's house faces towards East and he walks from backside of his house. It means that he starts walking towards West. Hence, Devanshu's final position D is to the North-West of the starting point A.

7. Blood Relations

1. (c) The daughter of Akash's father's wife is the sister of Akash and brother of the daughter is the brother of Akash. Hence, the boy in blue shirt is the brother of Akash.

2. (a) Brother of daughter means son. Wife of my husband means herself. So, the man is son of Reena.

3. (d) The daughter of only child of Rohan's father will be the daughter of Rohan.

Thus, Rohan's wife will be the mother of this girl.

4. (c) According to the question,

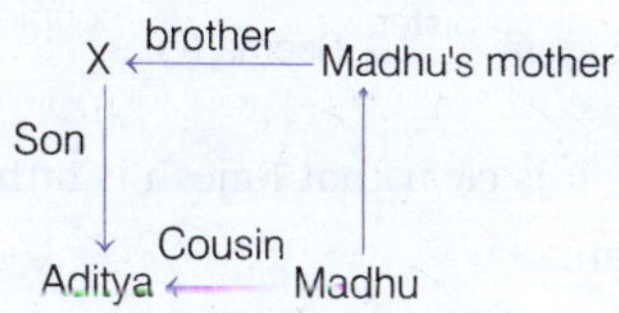

So, from above figure, Aditya is the cousin of Madhu.

5. (b) According to the question,

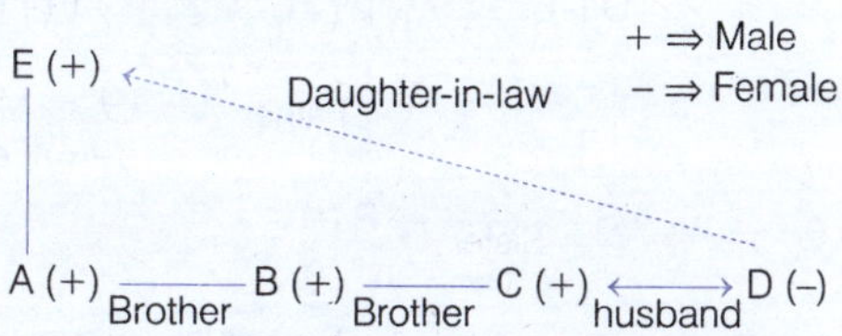

Since, E is the father of A and C is the brother of A, then D, who is wife of C, is the daughter-in-law of E.

6. (d) According to the question,

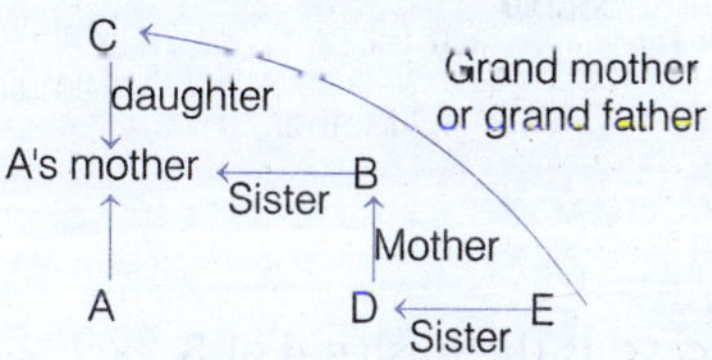

Now, it can be concluded that C is either grandmother or grandfather of E.

7. (a) According to the question,

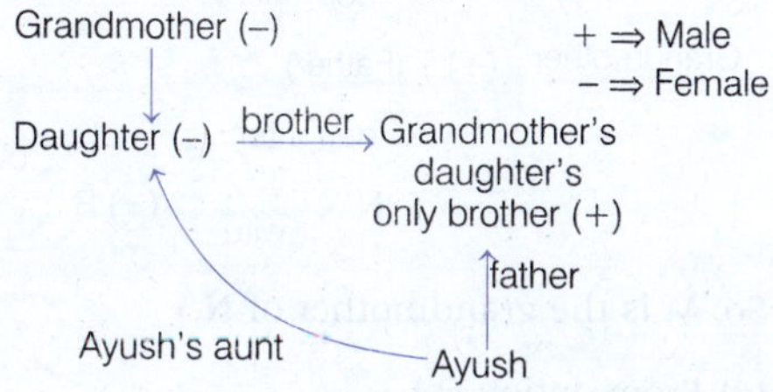

Hence, Ayush has defeated his father.

8. (d) According to the question,

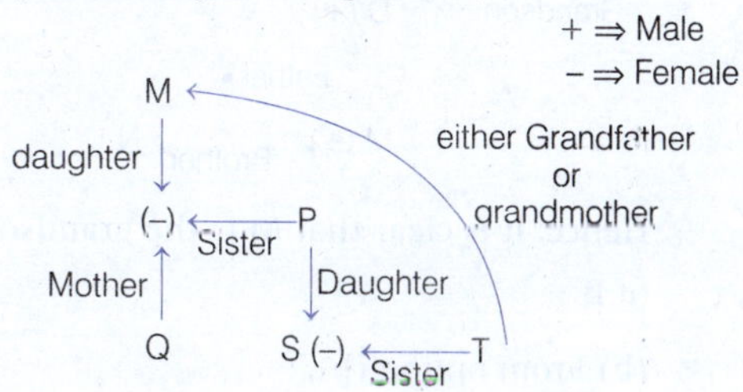

Hence, M is either the grandfather or the grandmother of T.

9. (b) According to the question,

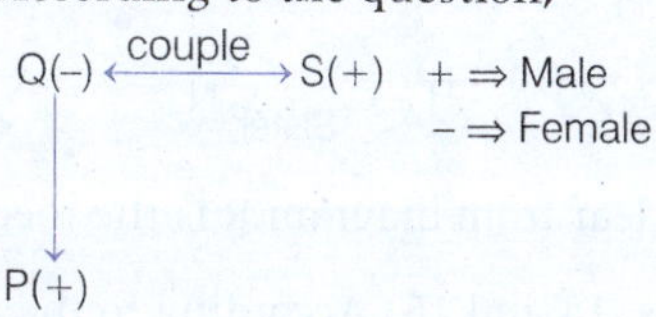

Clearly, S is the father of P.

10. (d) From option (d),

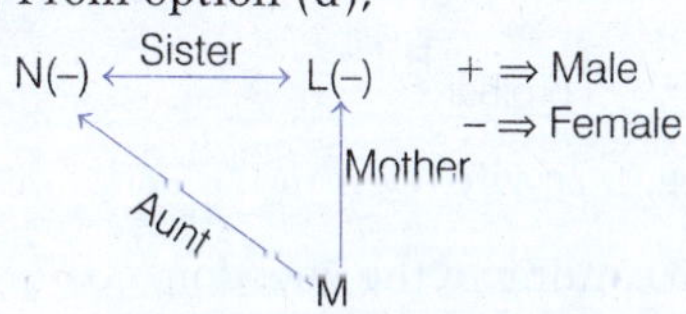

Now, it is clear that N is the aunt of M.

11. (c) From option (c),

M * T → M is the mother of T

T $ N → T is the father of N

N @ R → N is the wife of R

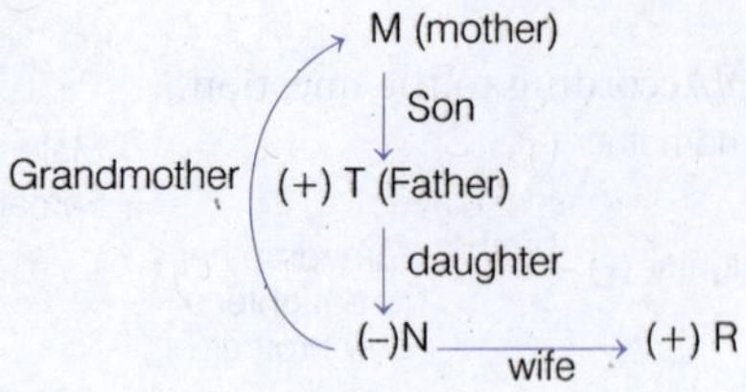

So, M is the grandmother of N.

12. (c) From option (c),

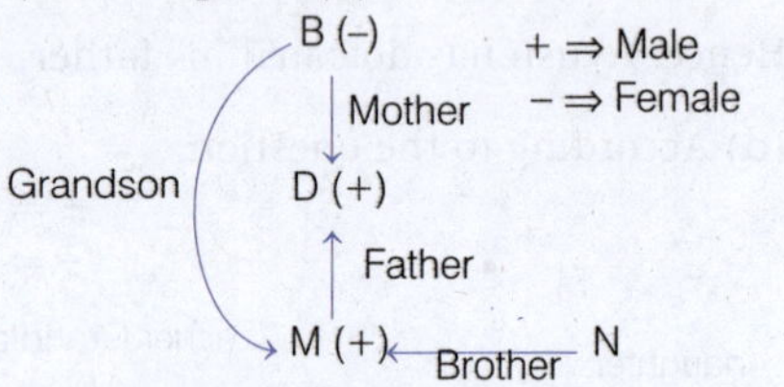

Hence, it is clear that M is the grandson of B.

13. (b) From option (b),

M – J + R – N

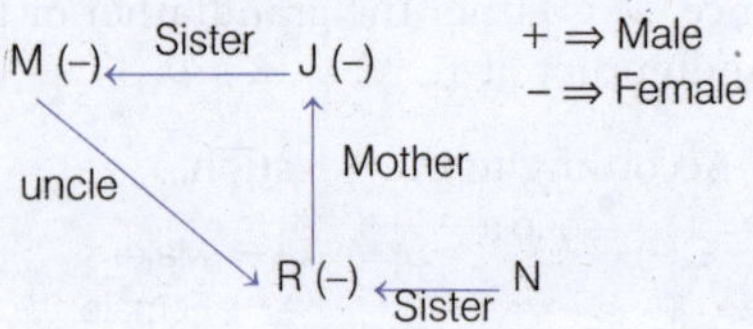

It is clear from diagram R is the niece of M.

Sol. (Q. Nos. 14 and 15) According to the question,

14. (c)

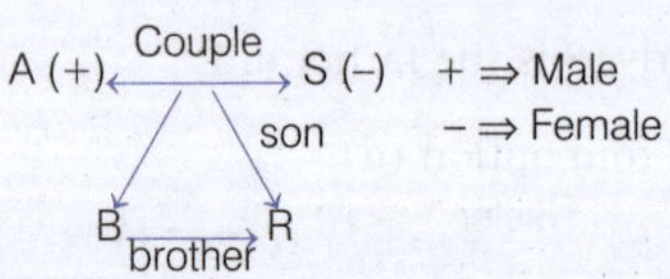

Hence, S is wife of A.

15. (a) According to the question,

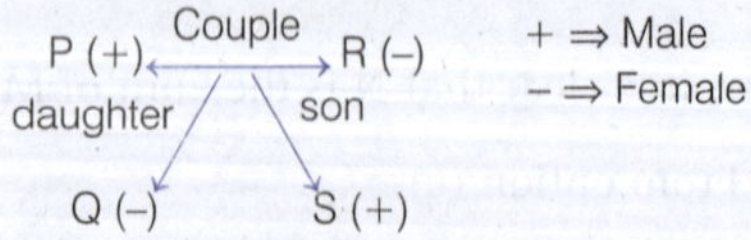

Hence, P is the father of S.

16. (d) According to the question,

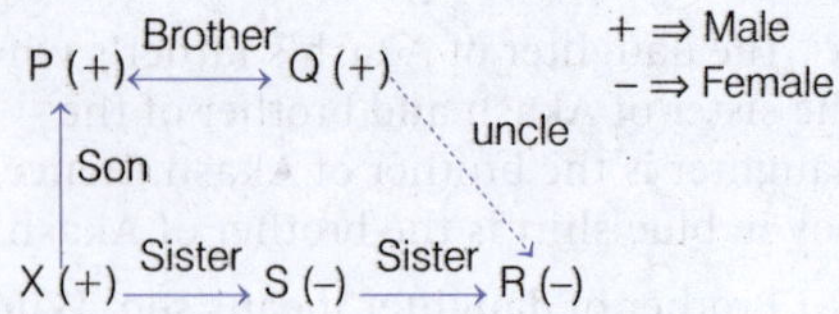

Hence, Q is the uncle of R.

17. (b) According to the question,

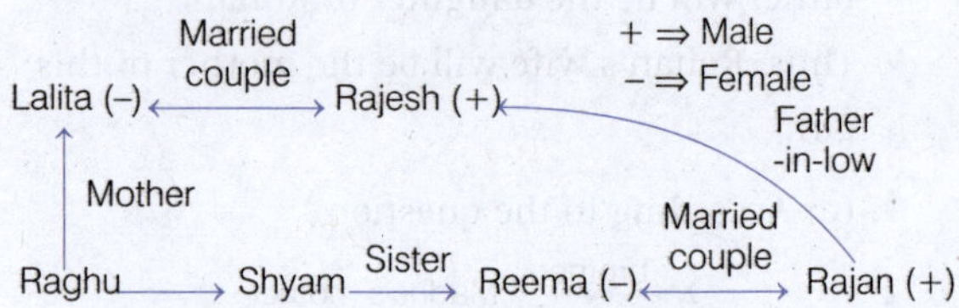

Hence, it is clear that Rajesh is father-in-law of Rajan.

18. (b) According to the question, sister-in-law

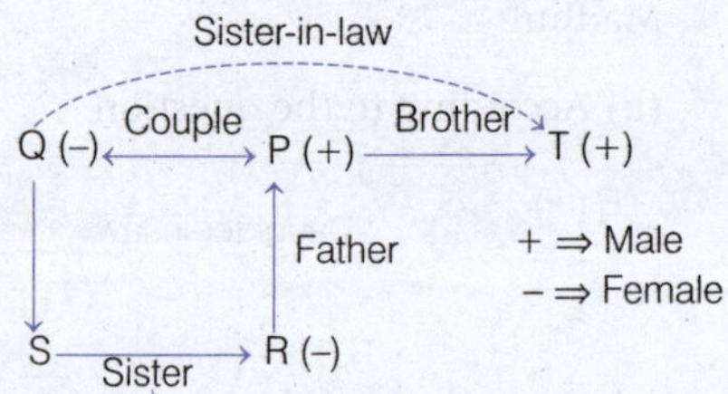

Hence, Q is sister-in-law of T.

19. (c) From option (c),

A 5 C 9 B 3 N

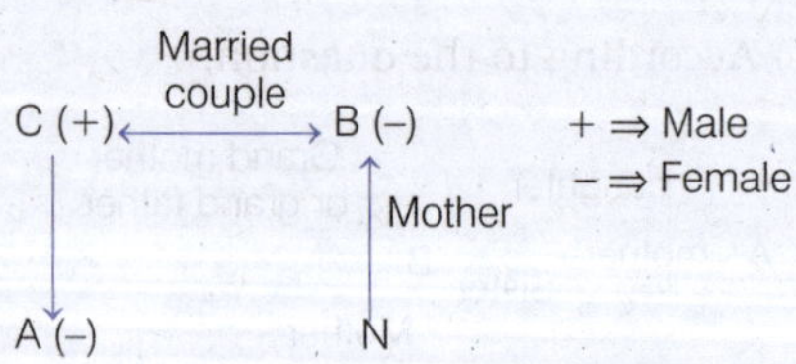

Hence, C is the husband of B.

Sol. (Q. Nos. 20 and 21)

20. (b) By drawing the family diagram, we get

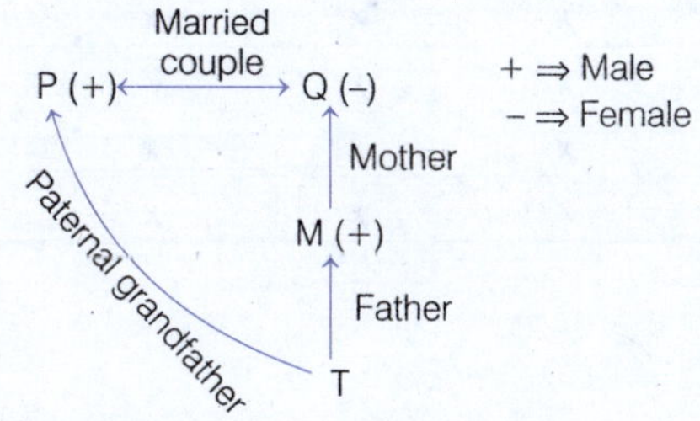

Hence, P is the paternal grandfather of T.

21. (a) By drawing the family diagram, we get

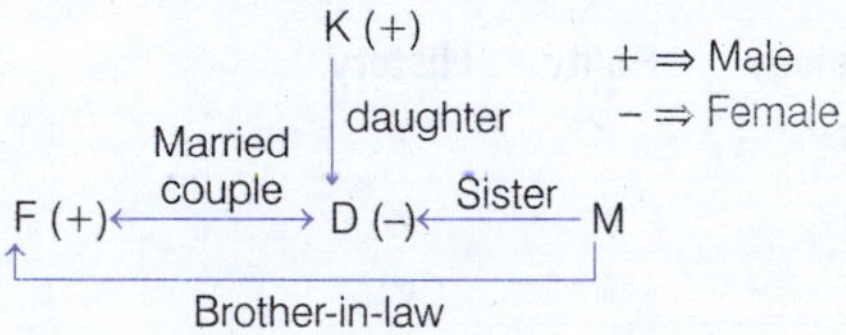

Hence, F is the brother-in-law of H.

22. (d) F × R < S ? M.

Here,

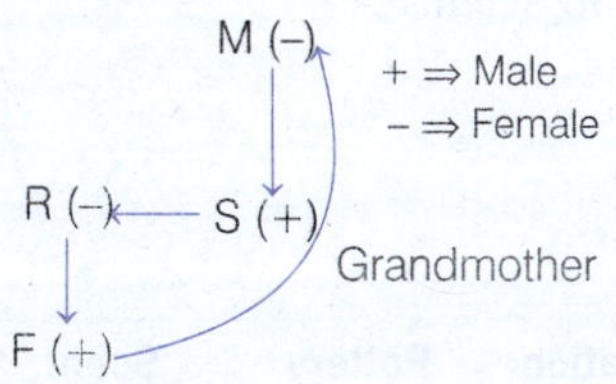

∵ S is the son of M.

∴ S × M is correct.

Hence, '×' will come in place of question mark.

8. Puzzles

1. (b) As per the given information, the final ranking of marks in the descending order is

Priya > Raj > Yash > Divya > Lucky

From the above arrangement Lucky scored lowest mark.

2. (a) On the basis of given information, the arrangement as below

Name \ Subjects	English	Mathematics	Science
Radhika	✓	✓	✓
Sonam	✓	✓	✗
Preeti	✓	✗	✓
Anita	✗	✗	✓

It is clear from the above table that, Radhika is good in all the three subjects.

Hence, option (a) is correct.

Sol. (Q. Nos. 3 and 4) Since, Chandni is standing exactly in the middle, there must be an equal number of students standing on either side of Chandni i.e. the group comprises of an odd number of girls.

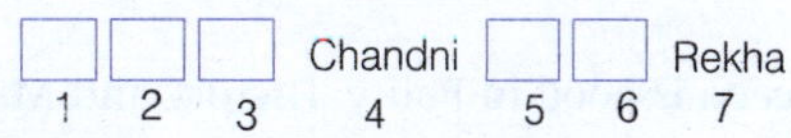

3. (c) As seen the above figure

∴ Total number of girls = 3 + 1 + 3 = 7

Hence, option (c) is correct.

4. (b) According to the given condition, Roshni is standing three positions to the left of Chandni.

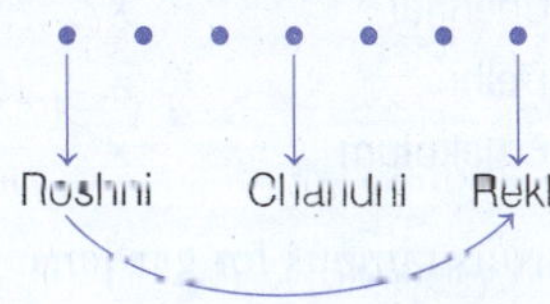

Clearly, Rekha is 6th to the right of Roshni.

Hence, option (b) is correct.

Sol. (Q. Nos. 5-7) According to the given information,

Person	Lecturer	Accountant	Clerk	Football	Swimming	Carrom	Badminton	Tennis	Cricket
A	✗	✓	✗	✗	✓	✗	✓	✗	✗
B	✗	✓	✗	✗	✓	✗	✗	✓	✗
C	✓	✗	✗	✓	✗	✗	✗	✗	✓
D	✗	✗	✓	✗	✓	✓	✗	✗	✗

5. (c) C is a lecturer.

6. (b) B plays tennis.

7. (a) A plays badminton and is an Accountant.

Sol. (Q. Nos. 8-10) According to the question,

People	Drama	Science	Mythology	Polity	History
Madhav	✓	✓	✗	✓	✗
Sheena	✓	✓	✗	✗	✓
Anju	✗	✓	✓	✓	✓
Pavitra	✓	✗	✗	✓	✓
Neena	✗	✗	✓	✓	✓

8. (c) Neena is good in Polity, History and Mythology but not in Science.

9. (a) Pavitra is good in Polity, History and Drama.

10. (d) Anju is good in History, Polity, Science and Mythology.

Sol. (Q. Nos. 11-13) According to the given information,

City	Garden	Jewellery	Education	Pottery	Scent
Agra	✗	✗	✗	✓	✗
Bengaluru	✓	✗	✗	✗	✗
Chennai	✗	✓	✗	✗	✗
Delhi	✗	✗	✗	✗	✓
Ernakulum	✗	✗	✓	✗	✗

11. (d) Bengaluru is famous for gardens.

12. (a) Pottery is available in Agra.

13. (b) Ernakulum is famous for education.

Sol. (Q. Nos. 14-16) According to the given information,

	Handball	Cricket	Painter	Singer	Dancer
Anamika	✗	✓	✗	✓	✗
Bablu	✓	✗	✓	✗	✗
Chandni	✗	✓	✓	✗	✗
Dabbu	✓	✗	✗	✗	✓

14. (c) Chandni is interested in cricket as well as painting.

15. (b) Anamika is a singer.

16. (d) Dabbu is interested in handball and dancing.

Sol. (Q. Nos. 17 and 18)
According to the given information,

17. (a) Teena's room is between Qasim and Sonu.

18. (b) The rooms of Qasim and Paras are diagonally opposite to each other.

Sol. (Q. Nos. 19 and 20)
According to the given information,

Friends	Place	Medium of travel
Payal	H	Bus
Qasim	K	Plane
Roopa	M	Car
Saloni	C	Boat
Tamas	D	Train

19. (b) Saloni travelled to city C by boat.

20. (a) Tamas travelled to city D.

9. Mathematical Reasoning

1. (b) $18 \text{ of } \frac{1}{3} + 2 - 8 \div 2(3+1)$

According to VBODMAS rule,

$= 18 \text{ of } \frac{1}{3} + 2 - 8 \div 2 \times 4$

$= 18 \times \frac{1}{3} + 2 - 8 \div 8$

$= 6 + 2 - 1$

$= 8 - 1 = 7$

2. (a) $15 \div 5 \times 3 + 6 - 2$

According to 'VBODMAS' rule,

$= \frac{15}{5} \times 3 + 6 - 2$

$= 3 \times 3 + 6 - 2$

$= 9 + 6 - 2$

$= 15 - 2 = 13$

3. (a) The operators given in option (a), satisfy the equation

$8 \div 4 \times 10 + 2 = 22$

$\Rightarrow \frac{8}{4} \times 10 + 2 = 22$

$\Rightarrow 2 \times 10 + 2 = 22$

$\Rightarrow 20 + 2 = 22$

$\Rightarrow 22 = 22$

Hence, option (a) is correct.

4. (d) The operators given in option (d), satisfy the equation

$2 \times 4 + 8 - 5 = 11$

$\Rightarrow 8 + 8 - 5 = 11$

$\Rightarrow 16 - 5 = 11$

$\Rightarrow 11 = 11$

Hence, option (d) is correct.

5. (a) On applying the interchanges, we find that the equation given in option (a) gets satisfied.

$25 \div 5 \times 2 < 20$

$\Rightarrow 5 \times 2 < 20 = 10 < 20$

Hence, option (a) is correct.

6. (b) On applying the interchanges, we find that the equation given in option (b) gets satisfied.

$8 \times 5 + 10 \div 2 - 3 = 42$

$\Rightarrow 40 + 5 - 3 = 42$

$\Rightarrow 42 = 42$

Hence, option (b) is correct.

7. (c) On applying the interchanges, we get

$1000 \div 10 \times 5 - 250 + 50$

$= 100 \times 5 - 200 = 500 - 200$

$= 300$

Hence, option (c) is correct.

8. (d) On applying the interchanges, we get

$25 \times 4 \div 2 - 10 + 35$

$= 25 \times 2 + 25$

$= 50 + 25 = 75$

Hence, option (d) is correct.

9. (b) On applying the interchanges, we find that option (b) equation will become correct.

$4 \div 2 + 6 = 8$

or $2 + 6 = 8$

i.e. $8 = 8$

Hence, option (b) is correct.

10. (c) On applying the interchanges, we find that option (c) satisfies the equation, $4 \times 2 + 6 = 14$ or $8 + 6 = 14$

i.e. $14 = 14$ which is true.

Hence, option (c) is correct.

11. (b) On applying the interchanges, we get

$50 \div 2 + 3 \times 4$

$\Rightarrow 25 + 12$

$\Rightarrow 37$

Hence, option (b) is correct.

12. (b) On finding the relation, we get

$22 \oplus = 88 = 22 \times 4$

$16 \oplus = 64 = 16 \times 4$

$9 \oplus = 36 = 9 \times 4$

So, in all terms '⊕' means '$\times 4$'.

Hence, option (b) is correct.

13. (c) On finding the relation, we get

$5 @ 9 = 45 \Rightarrow 5 \times 9 = 45$

$6 @ 12 = 72 \Rightarrow 6 \times 12 = 72$

$8 @ 6 = 48 \Rightarrow 8 \times 6 = 48$

So, '@' means '×'.

Hence, option (c) is correct.

14. (b) On finding the relation, we get

$94 \bigstar 14 = 80$

$\Rightarrow 94 - 14 = 80$

$68 \bigstar 9 = 59$

$\Rightarrow 68 - 9 = 59$

$52 \bigstar 12 = 40$

$\Rightarrow 52 - 12 = 40$

So, '★' means '–'.

Hence, option (b) is correct.

15. (d) According to the question, 'All but 8 died'. This means that 8 tigers remained alived and others died.

So, number of tigers left were 8.

16. (c) Let the number be x.

Then, $x \times x \times x = 8000$

$x^3 = 8000$

$x = \sqrt[3]{8000}$

$x = 20$

17. (b) On dividing 92 by half,

we get $= \frac{92}{\left(\frac{1}{2}\right)} = 184$

On adding $\frac{1}{4}$th of 12

$= 184 + \frac{1}{4} \times 12$

$= 184 + 3 = 187$

$\therefore$ End number $= 187$

18. (a) Given, A = 150% of B = 120% of C

$\Rightarrow$ 150% of B = 120% of C

$\Rightarrow \frac{B}{C} = \frac{120}{150}$

$\Rightarrow \frac{B}{C} = \frac{4}{5}$

$\therefore B : C = 4 : 5$

19. (a) On decoding the given expression, we get

5 ■ 3 ● 6 ▲ 3

$= 5 - 3 \times 6 \div 3$

$\Rightarrow 5 - 3 \times 6 \times \frac{1}{3} = 5 - 6 = -1$

Hence, option (a) is correct.

20. (a) On decoding the given equation, we get

8 ★ 4 ▲ ? ■ 3 = 9

$\Rightarrow 8 + 4 \div ? - 3 = 9$

$\Rightarrow 8 + 4 \times \frac{1}{?} - 3 = 9$

$\Rightarrow 8 + \frac{4}{?} - 3 = 9$

$\Rightarrow \frac{4}{?} = 9 + 3 - 8$

$\Rightarrow \frac{4}{?} = 4 \Rightarrow ? = 1$

Hence, option (a) is correct.

21. (a) On decoding the given equation, we get

5 ? 3 ● 12 ▲ 6 = 11

$\Rightarrow 5 ? 3 \times 12 \div 6 = 11$

By hit and trial, put ? = '+'

Then, LHS $= 5 + 3 \times 12 \times \frac{1}{6}$

$= 5 + 3 \times 2$

$= 5 + 6 = 11 =$ RHS

So, '+' or '★' will come in place of '?' mark.

Hence, option (a) is correct.

22. (a) Let the present ages of Ayush and Amit be $3x$ and $4x$ respectively.

According to the question,

$3x + 20 = 62$

$\Rightarrow 3x = 62 - 20$

$3x = 42$

$x = 14$

$\therefore$ Present age of Amit

$= 4x = 4 \times 14$

$= 56$ yr

23. (b) On applying given interchanges, we find that option (b) satisfies the equation.

$6 \div 3 \times 2 + 1 = 5$

or $2 \times 2 + 1 = 5$

i.e. $5 = 5$ which is true.

Hence, option (b) is correct.

10. Venn-Diagram

1.(c)

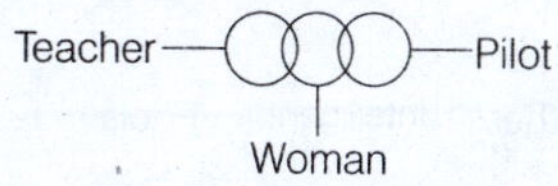

Woman can both be pilot and teacher.

2.(a)

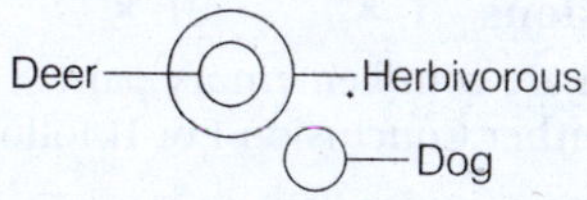

Deer is a herbivorous animal, whereas dog is a omnivorous animal and therefore it is different.

3.(a)

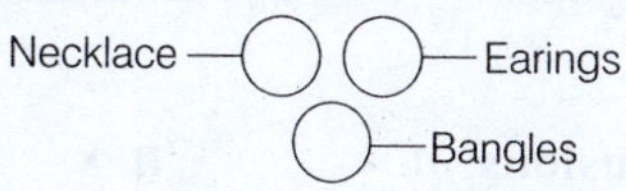

Necklace, earings and bangles are the types of ornaments but all three are different.

4.(b)

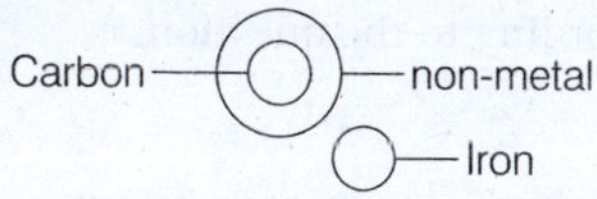

Carbon is a non-metal but iron is a metal, hence it is different.

5.(c)

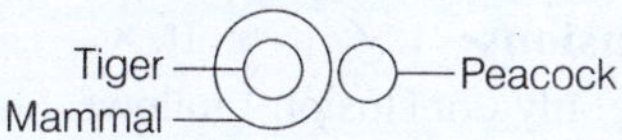

Tiger is a mammal, whereas peacock is a bird.

6.(a)

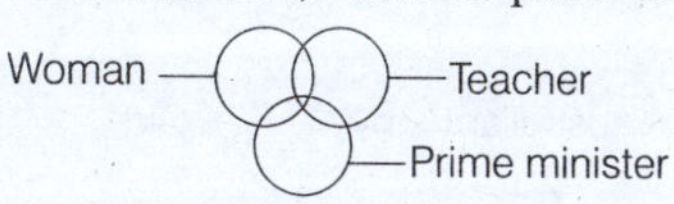

A woman can be teacher or a prime minister

A teacher can be a woman and prime minister.

A prime minister can be a woman as well as a teacher.

7.(a)

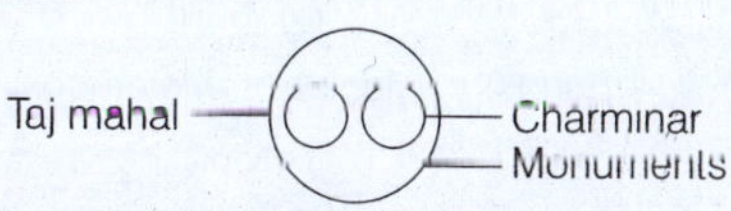

Tajmahal and Charminar both are monuments.

8.(a)

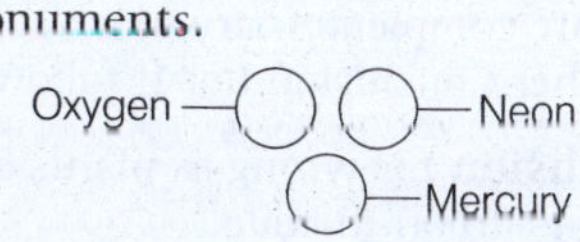

Oxygen and Neon are two different gases, whereas mercury is a metal.

9.(a) G is that part which is common to all three circles, it means that G represents those people who like all the three things.

10.(a)

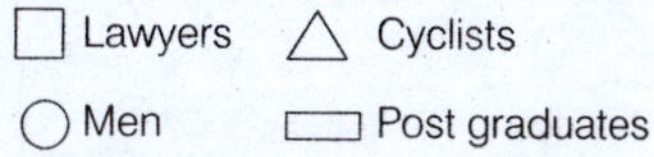

∴Letters which represent men who are not cyclist = B, C, D.

11.(c) A, E, F represents Americans who are not policeman.

12.(b) Letters A, D represents Australian who are rangers.

13.(b) Number of people studying only 2 subjects = 6 + 12 + 5 = 23

14.(a) Total number of women who are scientist = 19 + 4 = 23

15.(d) 'T' represents the students who study both Physics and Chemistry but not Mathematics.

16.(d) People who are only social scientists is represented by letter 'V'.

17.(c) 'O' shows the persons who are lawyers, engineers and doctors but not social scientist.

18.(d) 'K' represents people who are not social scientist and doctor but are lawyer and engineer both.

19.(b) Graduate men who are in private jobs are represented by number '3' as it occupies the space common to circle, square and triangle.

20.(d) Number '9' represents non-graduate men who have private jobs as well as are old.

11. Analytical Reasoning

1.(b) According to the question,

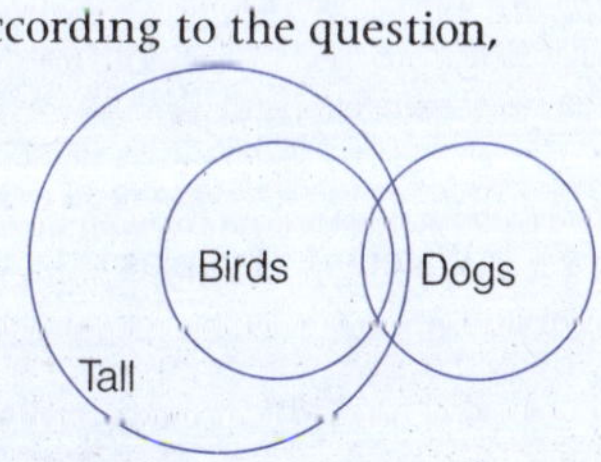

Conclusions I. × II. ✓

Hence, only Conclusions II follows.

2. (a) According to the question,

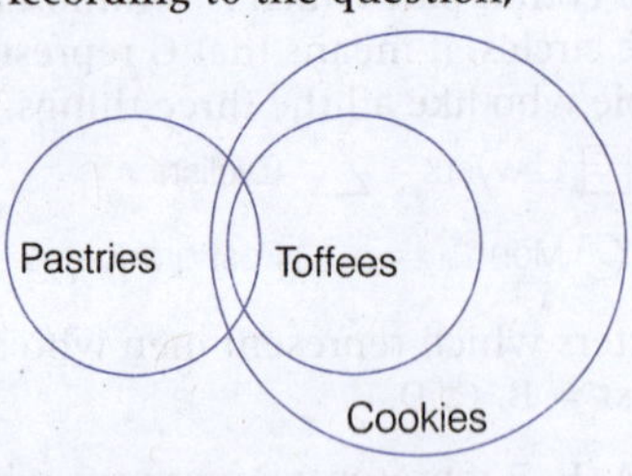

Conclusions I. ✓ II. ×

Hence, only Conclusion I follows.

3. (a) According to the question,

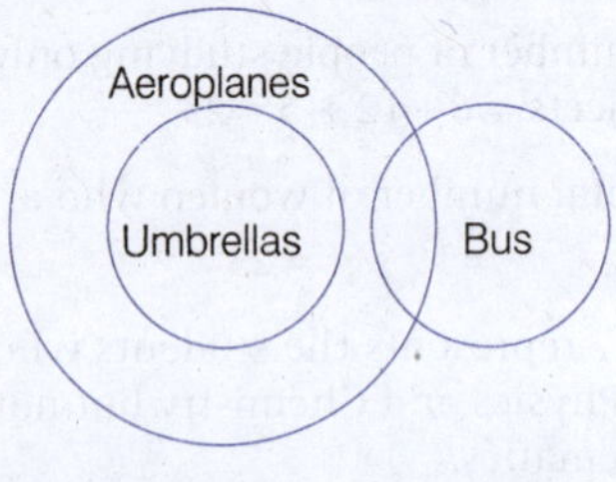

Conclusions I. ✓ II. ×

Hence, only Conclusion I follows.

4. (a) According to the question,

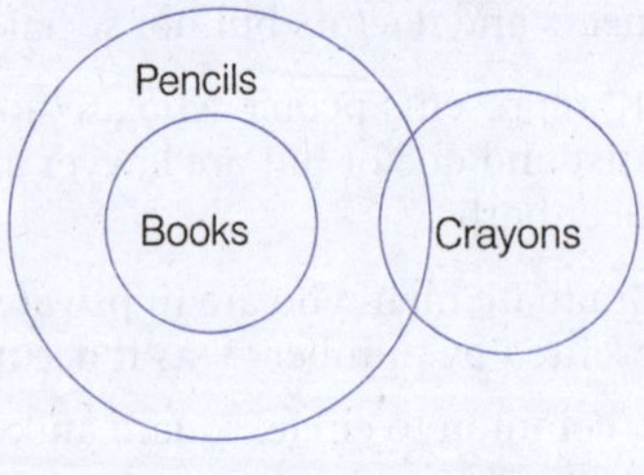

Conclusions I. ✓ II. ×

Hence, only Conclusion I follows.

5. (d) According to the question,

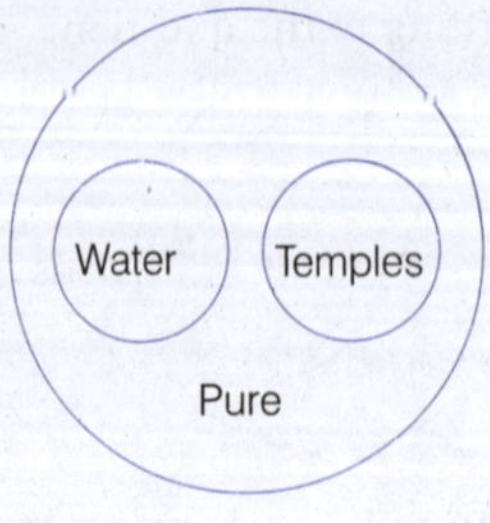

Conclusions I. × II. ×

Hence, neither conclusion I nor II follows.

6. (c) According to the question,

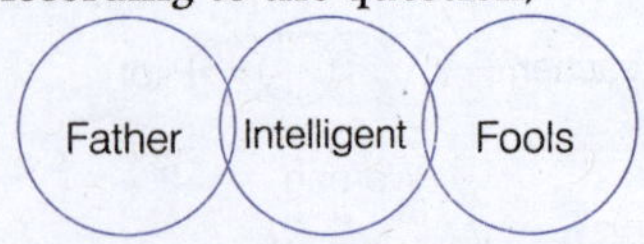

Conclusions I. × II. ×

But both are complementary pair.

Hence, either Conclusion I or II follows.

7. (c) According to the question,

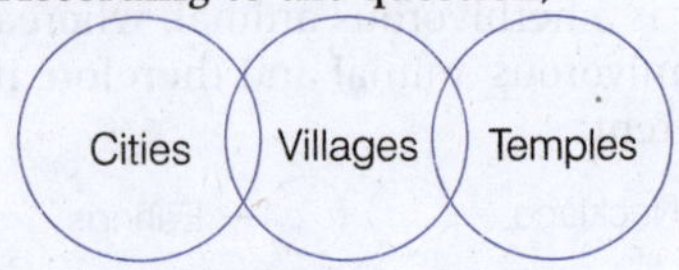

Conclusions I. × II. ×

But both are complementary pair.

Hence, either Conclusion I or II follows.

8. (a) According to the question,

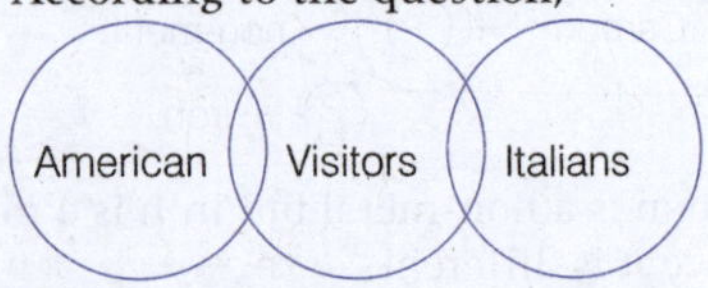

Conclusions I. ✓ II. ×

Hence, only Conclusion I follows.

9. (d) According to the question,

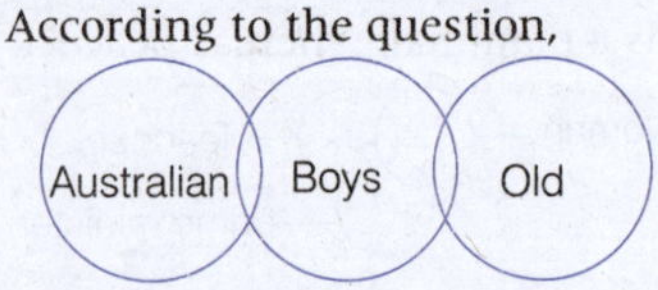

Conclusions I. × II. ×

Hence, neither Conclusion I nor II follows.

10. (c) According to the question,

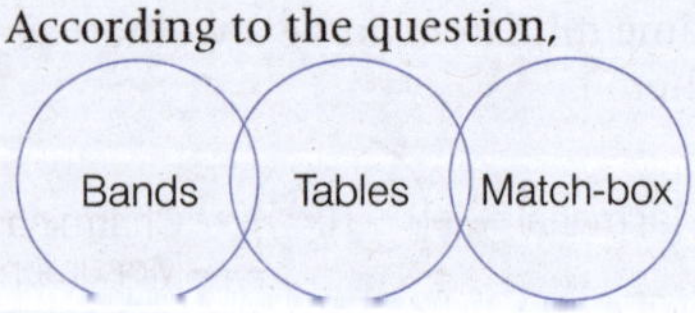

Conclusions I. × II. ×

But both are complementary pair.

Hence, either Conclusion I or II follows.

11. (d) **Conclusion I** is wrong as plants also breathe out carbon-dioxide.

Conclusion II is wrong as not only animals but plants also breathe out carbon-dioxide. Various other processes on earth also exhale carbon dioxide.

12. (b) **Conclusion I** is wrong as sun is not the only source of light, there are many other sources of light as well.

Conclusion II is true as sun is a star.

13. (a) **Conclusion** I follows but it doesn't mean that woman are not good.

Hence, Conclusion I follows.

14. (d) **Conclusion I** doesn't follow, as maintenance of law and order can not be the only reason for progress of a nation. There can be various other reasons also like economic development.

Conclusion II also doesn't follow as nothing is mentioned about China in the statement.

15. (c) Both Conclusions I and II follows because, it is true that Indian zoos are national property and it is the responsibility of government to take care of it.

16. (a) **Conclusion I** directly follows from the statement.

17. (a) According to the question,

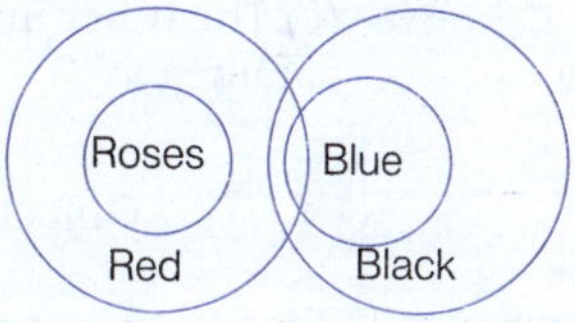

Conclusions I. ✓ II. ×

Hence, only Conclusion I follows.

18. (d) According to the question,

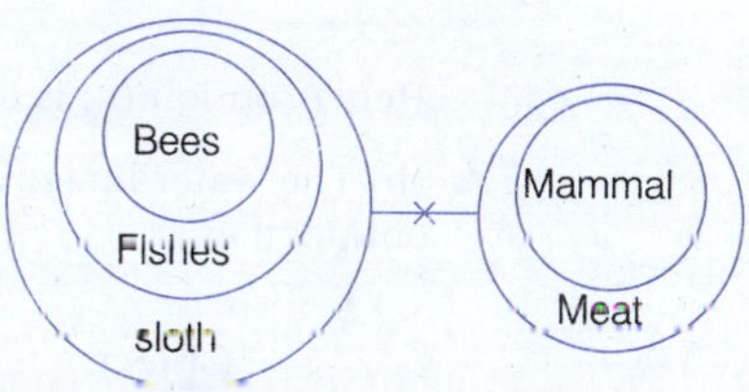

Conclusions I. × II. ×

But both are complementary pair.
Hence, either Conclusion I or II follows.

19. (b) According to the question,

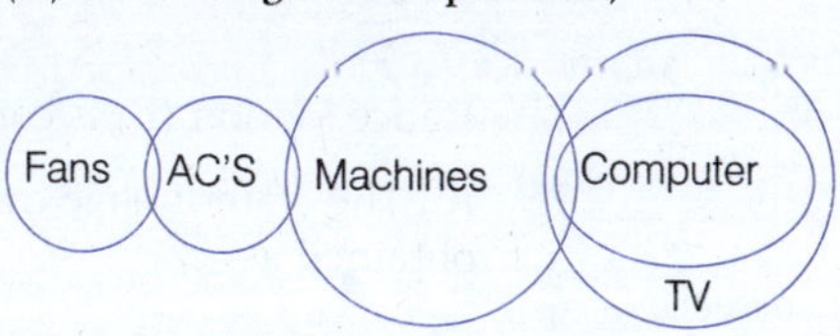

Conclusions I. × II. ✓

Hence, only Conclusion II follows.

20. (a)

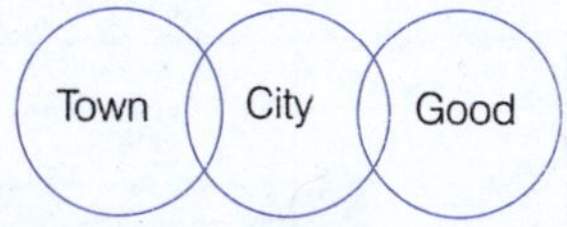

Conclusions I. ✓ II. ×

Hence, only Conclusion I follows.

21. (d) It is clearly mentioned in the statement that meditation provides eternal peace, it doesn't means that meditation ensures prosperous life or it eradicate poverty.

Hence, neither Conclusion I nor II follows.

22. (c) Here the statement is only talking about the singing and dancing not about the other arts and cultural activities so we can not conclude that all artists are singer.

Hence, Conclusion I is false.

Here Conclusion II is also false because statement is not talking about the popularity of the dancer so, we cannot conclude that all artists are well known dancers.

Hence, neither Conclusion I nor II follows.

23. (b) Only Conclusion II shows above statement.

12. Mirror and Water Image

1. (c) Here, the mirror is kept diagonally to the left corner of the object so its mirror image will appear on the top left as shown below

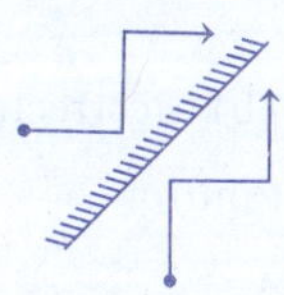

So, the correct mirror image in given by option (c).

Hence, option (c) is correct.

2. (c) The mirror image of the given object is

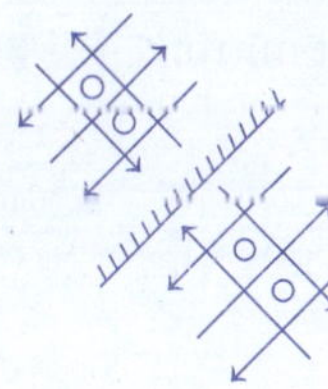

Hence, option (c) is correct.

3. (c) The mirror image of the given object is

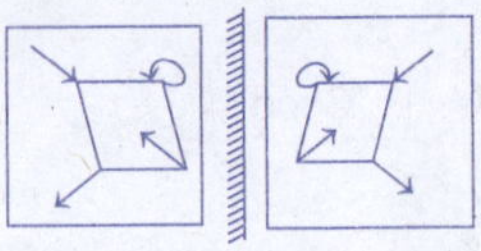

Hence, option (c) is correct.

4. (b) The mirror image of the given object is

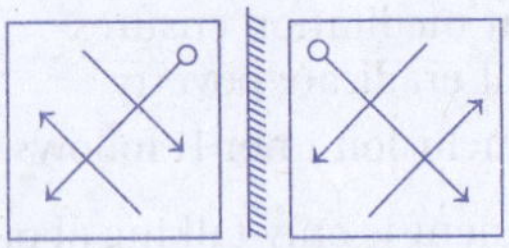

Hence, option (b) is correct.

5. (a) The mirror image of the given object is

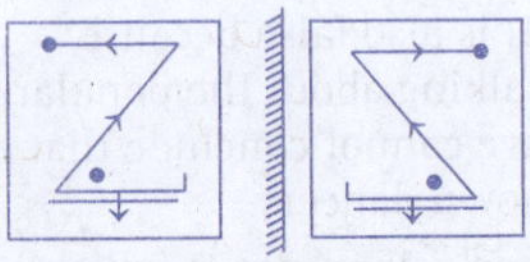

Hence, option (a) is correct.

6. (b) The correct mirror image is

Hence, option (b) is correct.

7. (b) The correct mirror image is

Hence, option (b) is correct.

8. (b) The correct mirror image is

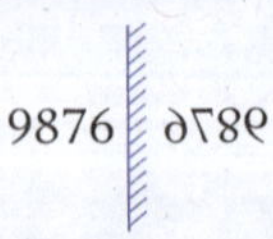

Hence, option (b) is correct.

9. (c) The correct mirror image is

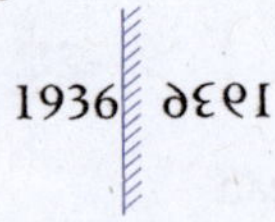

Hence, option (c) is correct.

10. (c) The correct mirror image is

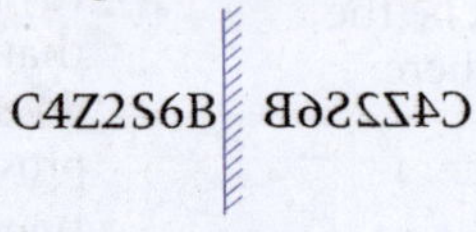

Hence, option (c) is correct.

11. (d) The mirror image of the given object is

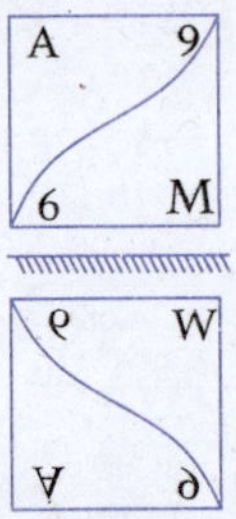

Hence, option (d) is correct.

12. (d) The water image can be obtained as

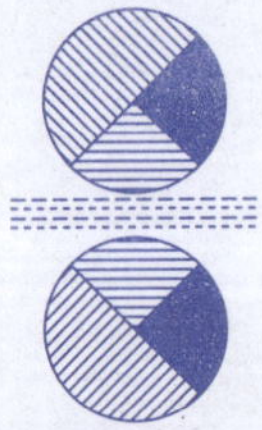

Hence, option (d) is correct.

13. (d) The water image can be obtained as

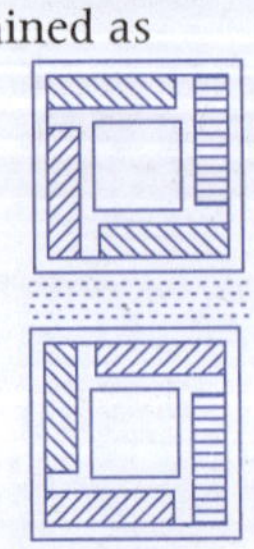

Hence, option (d) is correct.

14. (d) The water image can be obtained as

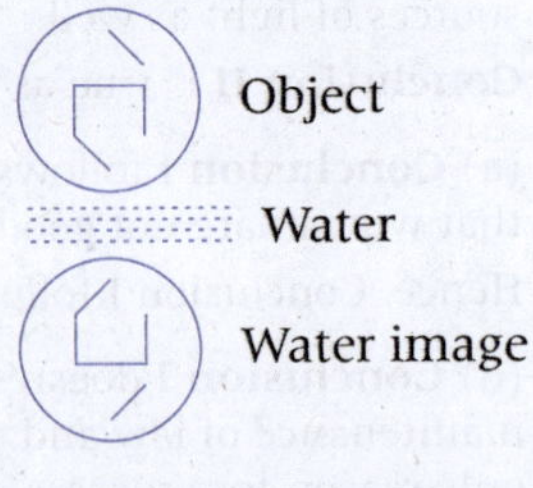

Hence, option (d) is correct.

15. (b) The water image can be obtained as

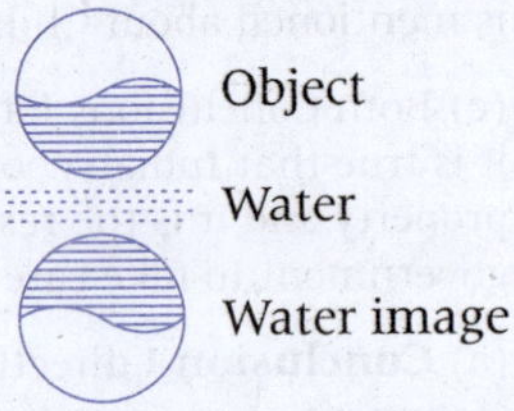

Hence, option (b) is correct.

16. (c) The water image can be obtained as

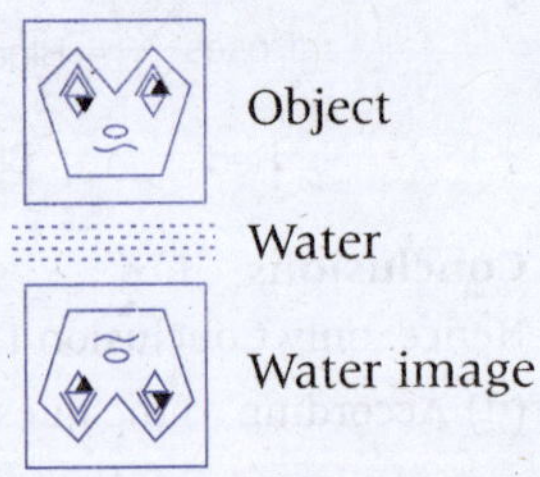

Hence, option (c) is correct.

17. (b) The water image can be obtained as

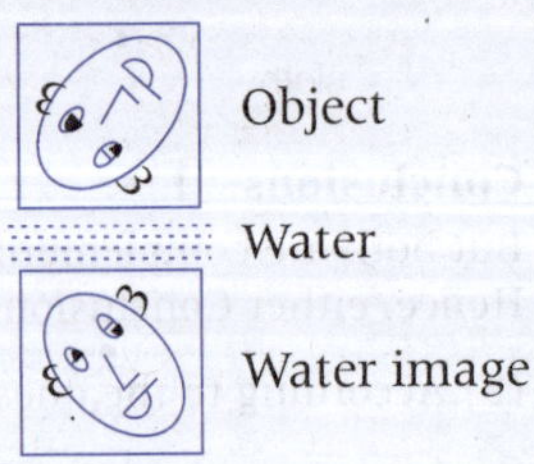

Hence, option (b) is correct.

18. (c) The water image can be obtained as

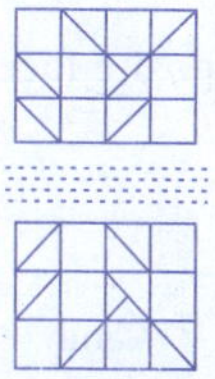

Object

Water

Water image

Hence, option (c) is correct.

19. (d) The water image can be obtained as

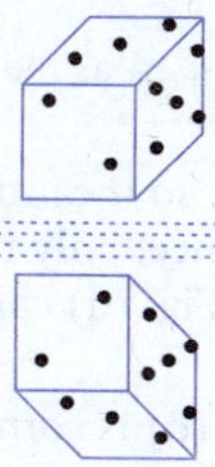

Object

Water

Water image

Hence, option (d) is correct.

20. (c) The water image can be obtained as

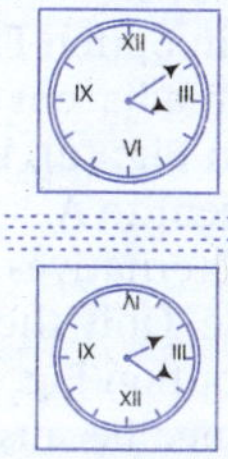

Object

Water

Water image

Hence, option (c) is correct.

21. (c) The water image can be obtained as

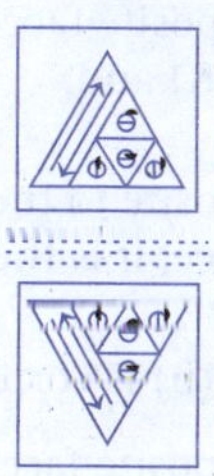

Object

Water

Water image

Hence, option (c) is correct.

22. (c) The water image can be obtained as

QUESTIONS

Water

ΌUESTIONƧ

Hence, option (c) is correct.

23. (d) Here, to get the correct water image of the image word, we should find out the water image of each letter.

image

Water

ıɯɐƃǝ

So, the required water image is ıɯɐƃǝ.

Hence, option (d) is correct.

24. (b) The water image can be obtained as

8324

Water

832ᔭ

Hence, option (b) is correct.

25. (c) The water image can be obtained as

K 9 J 6 F 0

Water

K ∂ Ꮭ ዖ Ⅎ 0

Hence, option (c) is correct.

26. (b) The mirror image of the given object is

Hence, option (b) is correct.

27. (a) The mirror image of the given object is

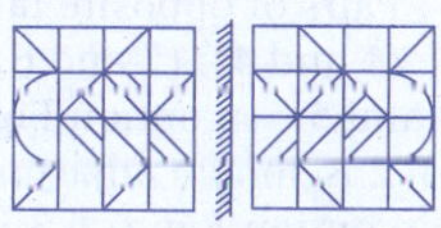

Hence, option (a) is correct.

28. (c) The correct mirror image is

12#3C%8BA | AB8%Ɔ3#21

Hence, option (c) is correct.

29. (b) The water image can be obtained as

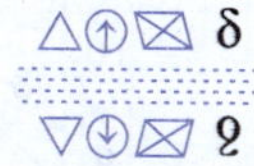

Hence, option (b) is correct.

30. (a) The mirror image of the given object is

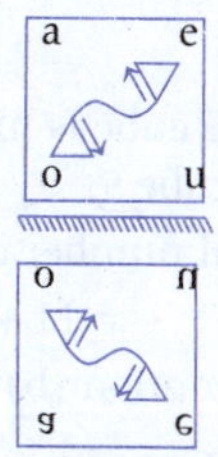

Hence, option (a) is correct.

13. Cubes and Dice

1. (b) The given figure is a perfect cube having 4 small cubes on each side.

∴ Total number of cubes

$= 4 \times 4 \times 4$

$= 64$ cubes

Hence, option (b) is correct.

2. (a) In the given figure, there are 12 visible cubes as shown

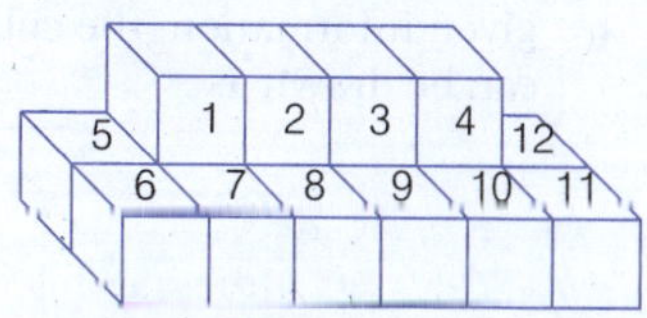

and 1 cube is hidden below each of the cubes 1, 2, 3 and 4.

∴ Total number of cubes

$= 12 + 4 = 16$

Hence, option (a) is correct.

3. (b) In the given figure, there are 11 visible cubes as shown

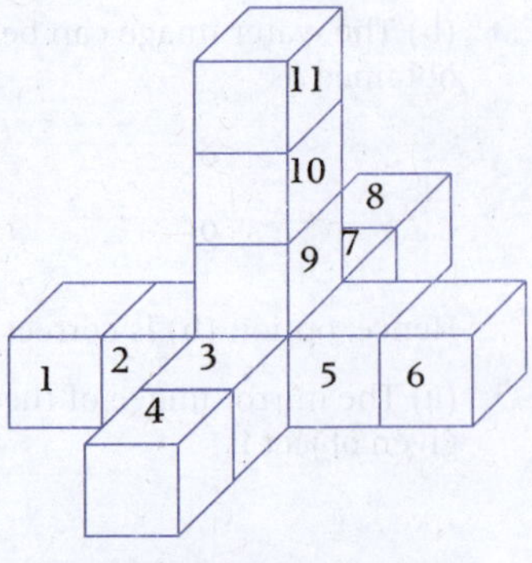

and one cube is hidden below cube 9.

$\therefore$ Total number of cubes
$= 11 + 1 = 12$

Hence, option (b) is correct.

4. (a) In the given figure, there are 6 layers of 4 cubes each as shown

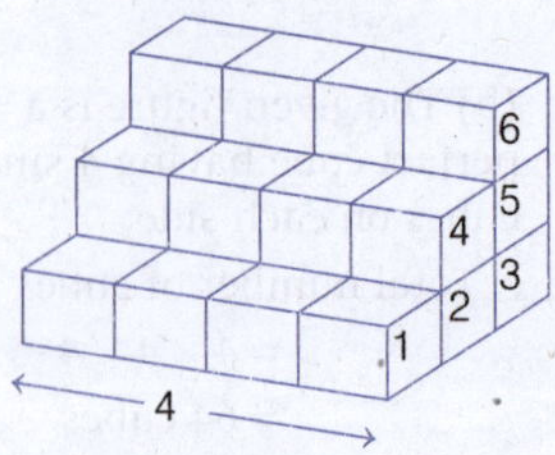

$\therefore$ Total number of cubes
$= 6 \times 4 = 24$

Hence, option (a) is correct.

Sol. (Q. Nos. 5-8) Based on the given information, the cube can be drawn as

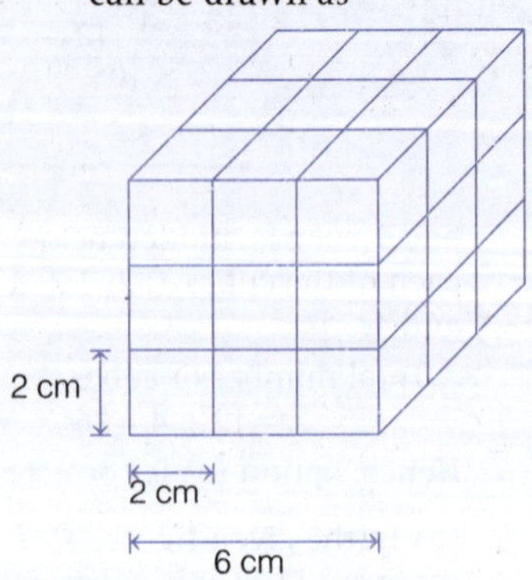

5. (a) There are $3 \times 3 \times 3 = 27$ smaller cubes in the solid cube.

Hence, option (a) is correct.

6. (b) The cube which is surrounded by other cubes on all its faces will not be painted and in a $3 \times 3 \times 3$ arrangement, there is only one such cube, which is present in the centre of all other cubes.

So, only 1 cube has no face painted.

Hence, option (b) is correct.

7. (c) On each of the faces of the original solid cube, there is only 6 small cube whose only one face is painted. As there are 6 faces in a cube,

$\therefore$ Number of small cubes having one face painted = 6

Hence, option (c) is correct.

8. (c) At each corner of the original solid cube, there is a small cube having three faces painted. As there are 8 corners in a cube.

$\therefore$ Number of small cubes having three faces painted = 8

Hence, option (c) is correct.

9. (b) Pairs of opposite faces are (1 and 4), (2 and 6) and (3 and 5). In option Fig. (a), 2 is shown adjacent to 6, in option Fig. (c), 3 is shown adjacent to 5 and in option Fig. (d), 1 is shown adjacent to 4. Hence, these alternatives are not possible. Only the cube given in option Fig. (b) can be formed because 6, 5 and 4 can be on adjacent faces.

Hence, option (b) is correct.

10. (d) Pairs of opposite faces are

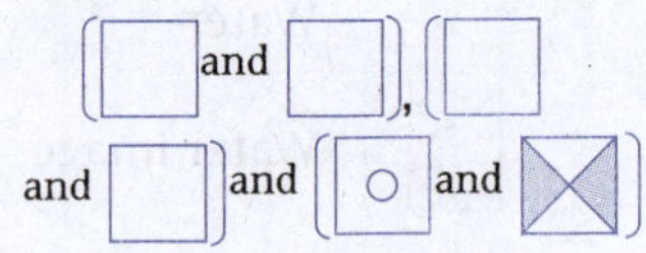

Fig. (a) and (b) can be eliminated straight away. The cube given in Figure (c) shows 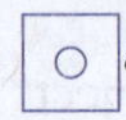 and 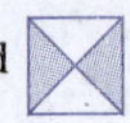 as the two adjacent faces, so it cannot be formed. Hence, only the cube given in Fig. (d) can be formed.

Hence, option (d) is correct.

11. (d) Pairs of opposite faces are (F and B), (E and C) and (D and A). In option Fig. (a), E is shown adjacent to C, in option Fig. (b), F is shown adjacent to B and in option Fig. (c), D is shown adjacent to A. Hence, these alternatives are not possible. Only the cube given in option Fig. (d) can be formed because F, E and D can be on adjacent faces.

Hence, option (d) is correct.

12. (b) Pairs of opposite faces are (Q, S), (P, R) and (Top, T).

Since, T is opposite to the 'Top' face, hence, it is the base of the cube.

Hence, option (b) is correct.

13. (d) Pairs of opposite faces are (1, 2), (4, 5) and (3, 6). Hence, the face having six dots is opposite to the face having three dots when the given figure is folded to form a cube.

Hence, option (d) is correct.

14. (a) The face having 2 dots appears in both the positions. Clearly, the faces having 1, 3, 5 and 6 dots are adjacent to the face having 2 dots. So, the face having 4 dots is opposite to the face having 2 dots. So, the face with 2 dots will be on the top when the face with 4 dots is at the bottom.

Hence, option (a) is correct.

15. (b) Since, total number of dots on opposite faces is always 7, therefore the pairs of opposite faces are (1, 6), (2, 5) and (3, 4). But option Fig. (a) shows 1 dot adjacent to 6 dots, option Fig. (c) shows 3 dots adjacent to 4 dots and option Fig. (d) shows 2 dots adjacent to 5 dots.

So, only Fig. (b) can be formed.

Hence, option (b) is correct.

16. (a) From the three figures, it is clear that the numbers 1, 3, 4 and 5 are adjacent to the number 6. The only number left is 2 which lies opposite to 6.

Hence, option (a) is correct.

17. (a) From figures I and II, it is clear that the letters B, C, D and F appear adjacent to the alphabet E. The only letter left is A which appears opposite to E. So, the letter opposite to A is E.

Hence, option (a) is correct.

18. (d) From figures I, II and III, it is clear that 1, 3, 5 and 6 dots lie adjacent to the face having 2 dots. The only face left is the one having 4 dots which lies opposite to the face having 2 dots.

Now, from figures I and II, we find that 2, 3 and 5 dots lie adjacent to 1 dot. Therefore, either the face having 4 dots or the face having 6 dots will lie opposite to 1 dot. But since 4 dots lie opposite to 2 dots, so 6 dots will be there on the face opposite to the face with 1 dot.

Hence, option (d) is correct.

19. (a) Length of the longest visible edge of cube

= 3 units

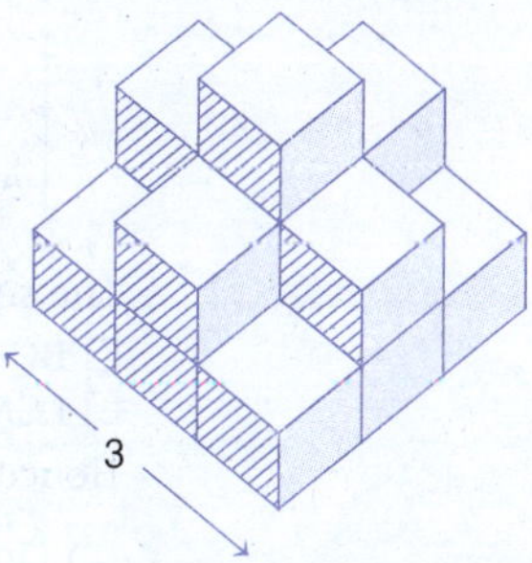

∴ Total number of cubes required to build complete cube

$= 3 \times 3 \times 3$
$= 27$ cubes

Number of cubes given in figure = 15

Now, cubes required to complete the given figure

$= 27 - 15$
$= 12$ cubes

Hence, option (a) is correct.

20. (b) Length of the longest visible edge of cube

= 4 units

∴ Total number of cubes required to build complete cube

$= 4 \times 4 \times 4 = 64$

Number of cubes given in figure = 40

Now, cubes required to complete the given figure

$= 64 - 40 = 24$

Hence, option (b) is correct.

21. (d) Pairs of opposite faces are

( and ), ( and ) and ( and )

Upon folding the sheet (X), only the cube given in Figure (d) can be formed.

Hence, option (d) is correct.

22. (c) From figures I and II, we find that the

faces adjacent to 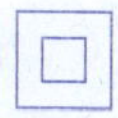 are , 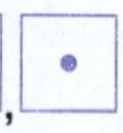, 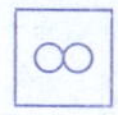 and 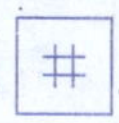. The only face left is  which obviously is opposite to the face 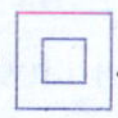.

Hence, the symbol opposite the cross

(×) is square 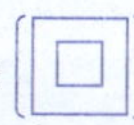

Hence, option (c) is correct.

23. (b) From figures I and III, it is clear that the

faces adjacent to  are 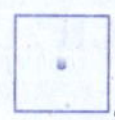, 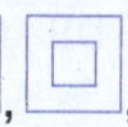,  and 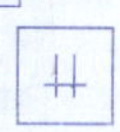

The face left is 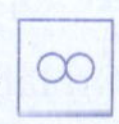 which lies opposite to the face .

Thus, the symbol at the bottom of figure II is

.

Hence, option (b) is correct.

14. Counting of Figures

1. (b) On labelling the given figure, we get

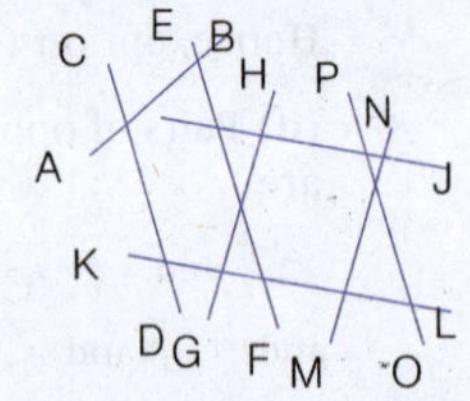

From the above figure, we get lines namely AB, CD, EF, GH, IJ, KL, MN and OP = 8 lines

Hence, option (b) is correct.

2. (a) On labelling the given figure, we get

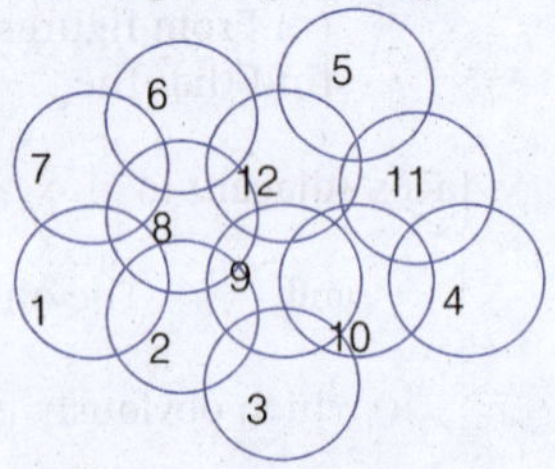

So, there are 12 circles.

Hence, option (a) is correct.

3. (a) On labelling the given figure, we get

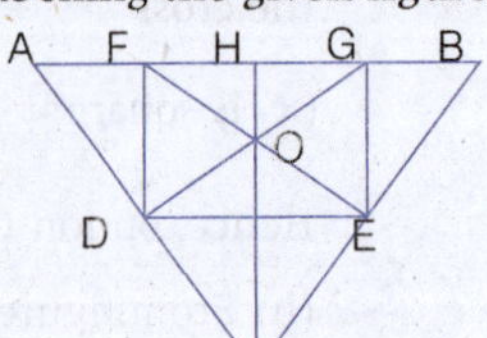

From the figure, the straight lines are

AB , BC , AC , DE , CH , DG , EF, GE and DF = 9 straight lines

Hence, option (a) is correct.

4. (c) On labelling the given figure, we get

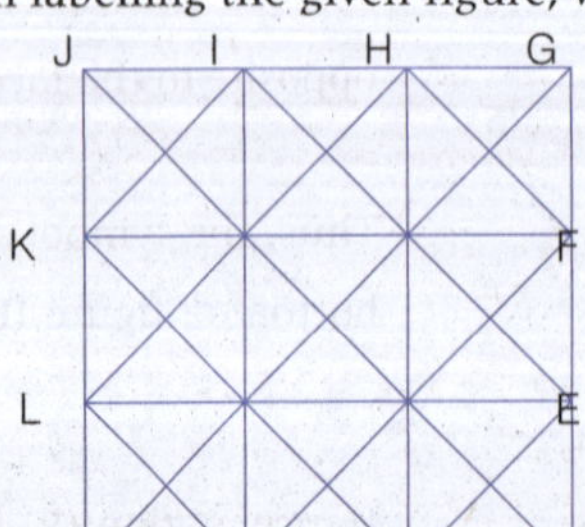

From figure, the straight lines are

= AD, DG, GJ, AJ, BI, CH, EL, FK, KI, LH, AG, BF, CE, BL, CK, DJ, EI and FH = 18 straight lines

Hence, option (c) is correct.

5. (d)

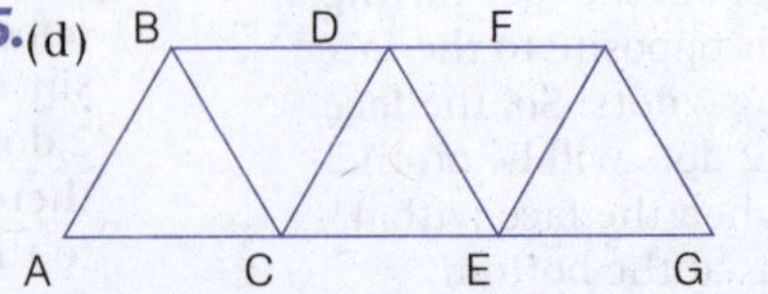

The above figure has six parallelograms, ABDC, ABFE, BCED, BCGF, CDFE, DEGF

6. (b) The given figure can be labelled as

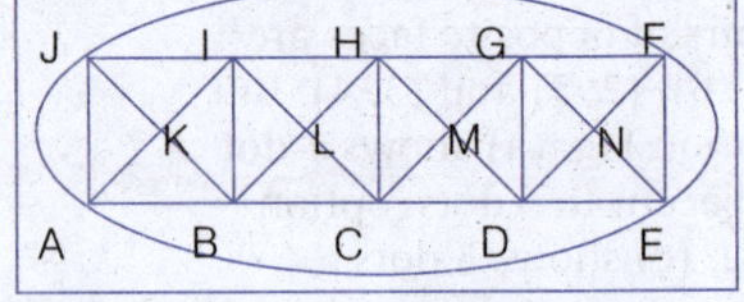

The squares are namely ☐ ABIJ, ☐ BCHI, ☐ CDGH, ☐ DEFG, ☐ KBLI, ☐ LCMH and ☐ MDNG = 7 squares

Hence, option (b) is correct.

7. (c) On labelling the given figure, we get

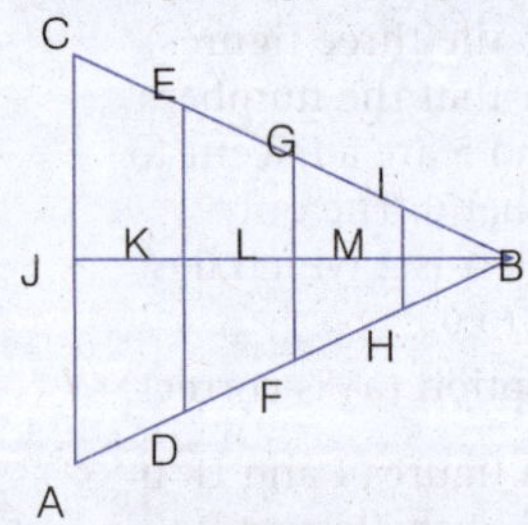

Number of triangles formed from single unit

= ΔBIM, ΔBMH = 2

Number of triangles formed from two units

= ΔBGL, ΔBLF and ΔBIH = 3

Number of triangles formed from 3 units

= ΔBEK, ΔBDK = 2

Number of triangles formed from 4 units

= ΔBCJ, ΔABJ and ΔBGF = 3

Number of triangle formed from 6 units

= ΔBDE = 1

Number of triangles from 8 units = ΔABC = 1

$\therefore$ Total number of triangles

= 2 + 3 + 2 + 3 + 1 + 1

= 12 triangles

Hence, option (c) is correct.

8. (c) On labelling the given figure, we get

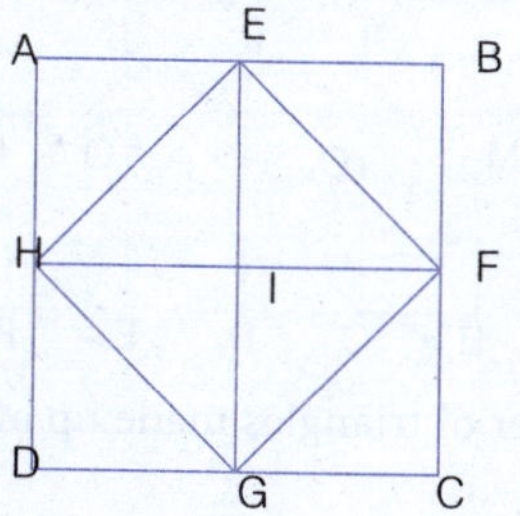

From figure,
Triangles formed from 1 unit
= ΔAEH, ΔEHI, ΔEBF, ΔEFI, ΔFGC, ΔIFG, ΔDGH and ΔHIG = 8
Triangles formed from two triangles
= ΔHEF, ΔEFG, ΔHFG and ΔGHE = 4
∴ Total number of triangles = 8 + 4 = 12
Hence, option (c) is correct.

9. (a) On labelling the given figure, we get

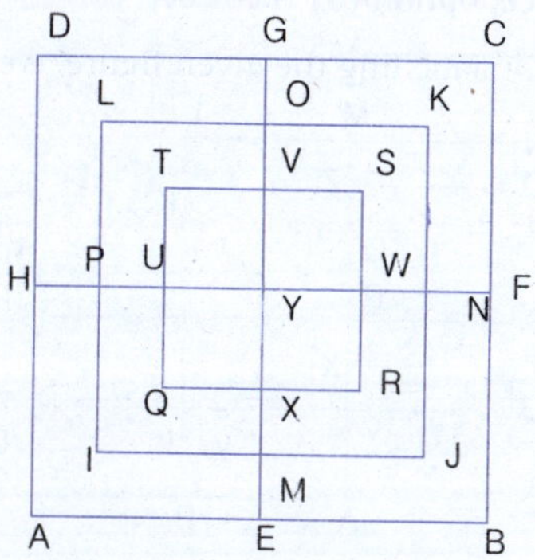

Squares are namely as □ TVYU, □ VSWY, □ YWRX, □ XYUQ, □ QRST, □ YPLO, □ YNKO, □ YNJM, □ YMIP, □ IJKL, □ GYFC, □ GYHD, □ YEAH, □ YFBE and □ ABCD
= 15 squares
Hence, option (a) is correct.

10. (d) On labelling the given figure, we get

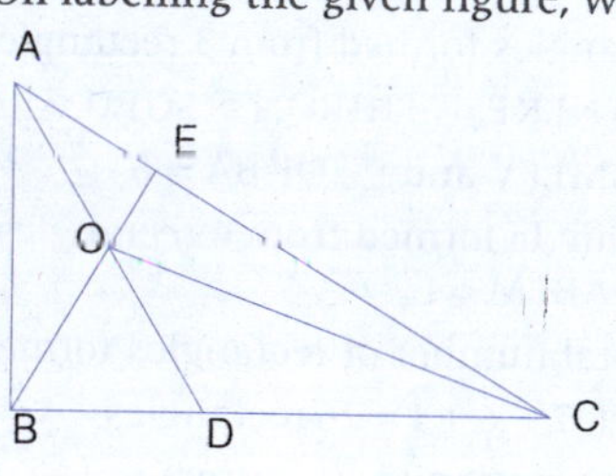

Triangles formed from 1 unit = ΔAOE, ΔEOC, ΔOCD, ΔODB and Δ AOB = 5
Triangle formed from 2 triangles
= ΔAOC, ΔBOC, ΔABD and ΔAEB = 4
Triangles formed from 3 triangles
= ΔBEC and ΔADC = 2
Triangle formed from 5 triangles = ΔABC
∴Total number of triangles
$= 5 + 4 + 2 + 1 = 12$
Hence, option (d) is correct.

11. (c) On labelling the given figure, we get

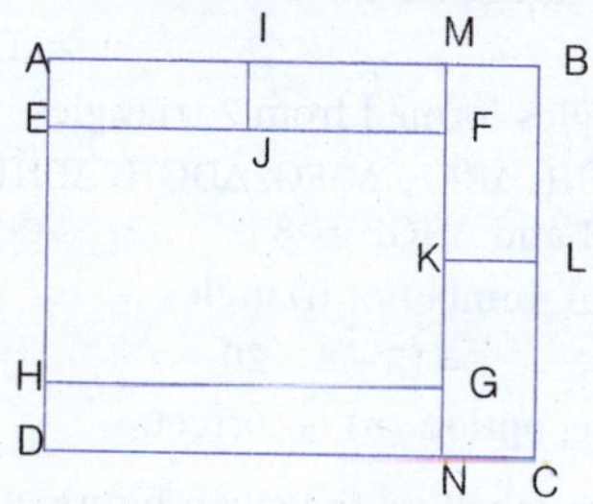

∴ Total number of rectangles
= ▭AIJE, ▭IMFJ, ▭MBKL, ▭ KLNC, ▭HGND, ▭EFGH, ▭AMFE, ▭MBCN, ▭ABCD, ▭AMGH, ▭EFND and ▭AMND = 12
Hence, option (c) is correct.

12. (a) On labelling the given figure, we get

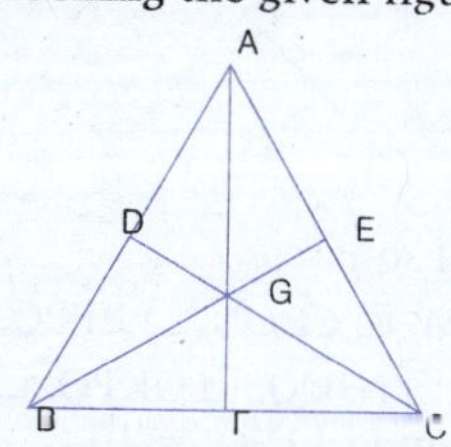

Triangles formed from 1 unit = ΔADG, ΔAEG, ΔEGC, ΔCFG, ΔFBG and ΔBGD = 6
Triangles formed from 2 triangles
= ΔAGB, ΔAGC and ΔBGC = 3
Triangles formed from 3 triangles
= ΔABF, ΔACF, ΔDCB, ΔEBC, ΔDCA and ΔAEB = 6
Triangles formed from 6 triangles = ΔABC = 1
∴Total number of triangles
$= 6 + 3 + 6 + 1 = 16$
Hence, option (a) is correct.

13. (b) On labelling the given figure, we get

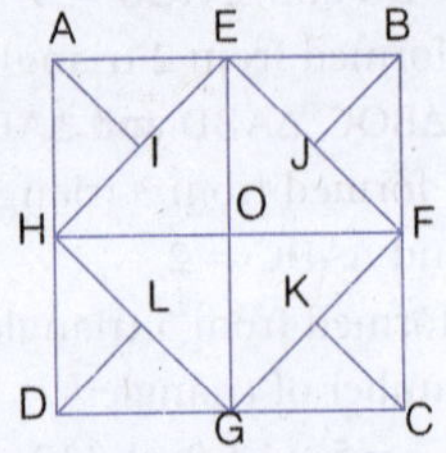

Triangles formed from 1 unit
= ΔAIE, ΔAIH, ΔBJE, Δ BJF, ΔCKF, ΔCKG, Δ DLG, ΔDLH, ΔHOE, ΔEOF, ΔFOG and ΔGOH
= 12

Triangles formed from 2 triangles
= ΔAEH, ΔBEF, ΔCFG, ΔDGH, ΔEHF, ΔFEG, ΔGFH and ΔHGE = 8

∴ Total number of triangles
= 12 + 8 = 20

Hence, option (b) is correct.

14. (a) On labelling the given figure, we get

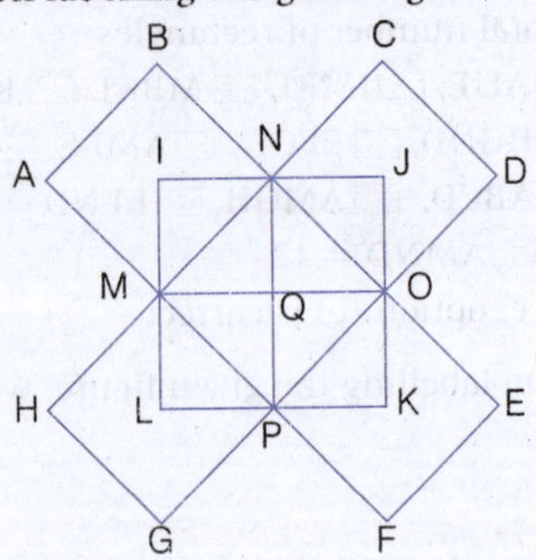

Number of squares
= □ABNM, □ CDON, □ EFPO, □ GHMP, □ INQM, □ NJOQ, □ OKPQ, □ PLMQ, □ NOPM and □ IJKL = 10

Hence, option (a) is correct.

15. (b) On labelling the given figure, we get

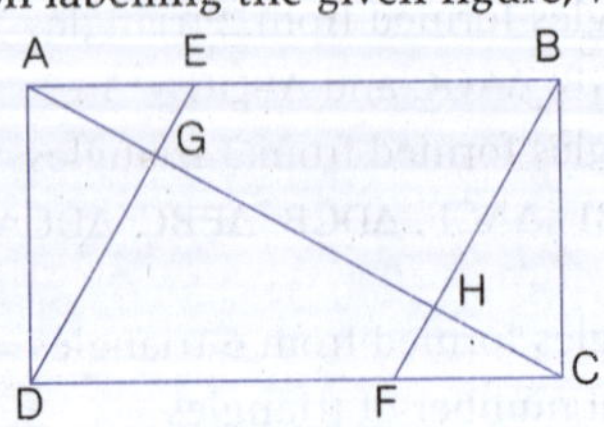

Number of quadrilaterals = ABCD, EBFD, ABFD, CDEB, AHFD, CGEB, DGHF and EGBH = 8

Hence, option (b) is correct.

16. (d) On labelling the given figure, we get

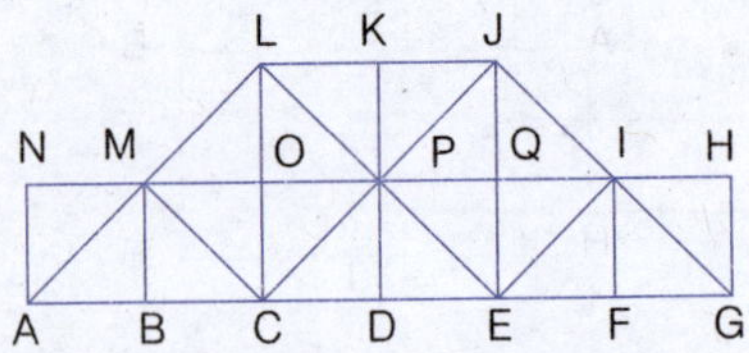

Number of triangles made up of single unit = 18

Triangles formed from 2 small triangles
= ΔAMC, ΔCPE, ΔEIG, ΔMLP, ΔPJI, ΔMCP, ΔPEI, ΔLPJ, ΔLMC, ΔLPC, ΔJPE and Δ JIE = 12

Triangles formed from 4 small triangles
= ΔACL, ΔCJL, ΔCEL, ΔCEJ, ΔEJL and ΔJEG = 6

Triangles formed from 8 small triangles = Δ ALE and ΔCJG = 2

∴ Total number of triangles
= 18 + 12 + 6 + 2 = 38

Hence, option (d) is correct.

17. (a) On labelling the given figure, we get

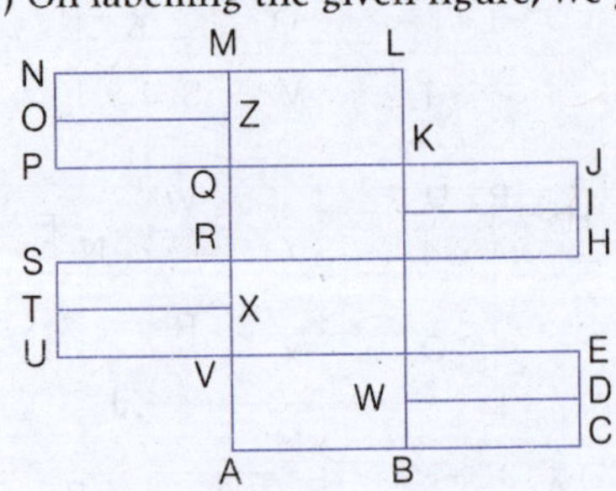

Rectangles made up of 1 unit
= □ NMZO, □ PQZO, □ MQKL, □ JKYI, □ YIHG, □ QKGR, □ STXR, □ RGFV, □ TXVU, □ AVFB, □ EFWD and □ BCDW = 12

Rectangles formed from 2 rectangles
= □ MNPQ, □ SRVU, □ GHJK, □ BCEF, □ MLGR, □ QKFV and □ ABGR = 7

Rectangles formed from 3 rectangles
= □ NLKP, □ JHRQ, □ SGFU, □ ACEV, □ MLFV and □ QKBA = 6

Rectangle formed from 4 rectangles
= □ ABLM = 1

∴ Total number of rectangles formed
= 12 + 7 + 6 + 1 = 26 rectangles

Hence, option (a) is correct.

18. (d) On labelling the given figure, we get

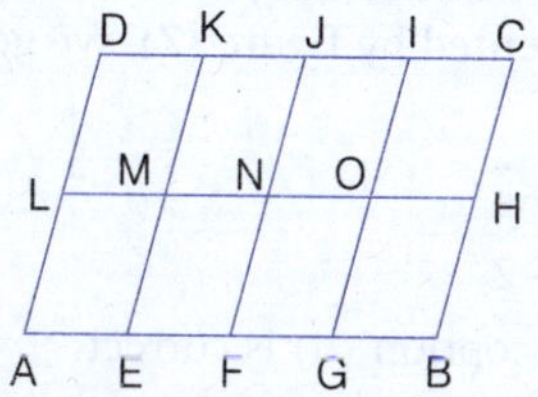

Number of parallelograms formed from single unit

= ▱ AEML, ▱ EFNM, ▱ FGON, ▱ GBHO, ▱ HCIO, ▱ IONJ, ▱ JNMK and ▱ KMLD = 8

Number of parallelograms formed from 2 small parallelograms

= ▱ LNJD, ▱ MOIK, ▱ NHCJ, ▱ AFNL, ▱ EGOM, ▱ FBHN, ▱ AEKD, ▱ EFJK, ▱ FGIJ and ▱ GBCI = 10

Number of parallelograms formed from 3 small parallelograms = ▱ LOID, ▱ MHCK, ▱ AGOL and ▱ EBHM = 4

Number of parallelograms formed from 4 small parallelograms

= ▱ AFJD, ▱ EGIK, ▱ FBCJ, ▱ LHCD and ▱ ABHL = 5

Number of parallelograms formed from 6 small parallelograms = ▱ AGID and ▱ EBCK = 2

Number of parallelograms formed from 8 small parallelograms = ▱ ABCD = 1

∴ Total number of parallelograms formed

$= 8 + 10 + 4 + 5 + 2 + 1 = 30$

Hence, option (d) is correct.

19. (d) On labelling the given figure, we get

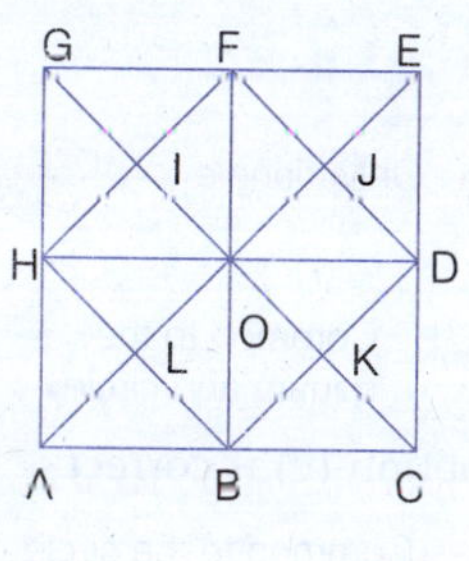

For counting triangles,

Total number of triangles formed of 1 unit = 16

Total number of triangles formed from 2 small triangles = 16

Total number of triangles formed from 4 small triangles = 8

Total number of triangles formed from 8 small triangles = 4

∴ Total number of triangles

$= 16 + 16 + 8 + 4$

$= 44$ triangles

Now, the squares are namely

□ABOH, □BCDO, □ ODEF, □ FOHG, □BKOL, □KDJO, □ OJFI, □IOLH, □BDFH and □ACEG = 10 squares

Hence, option (d) is correct.

20. (c) On labelling the given figure, we get

For triangles,

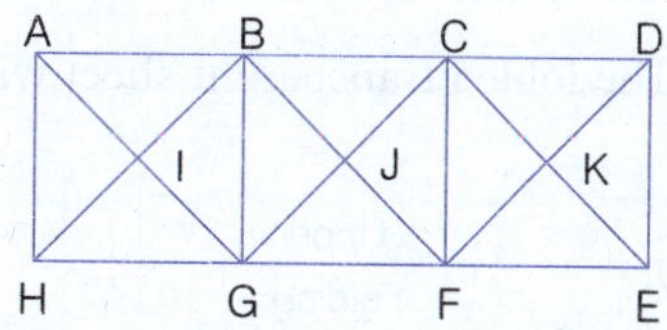

Triangles formed from 1 unit

= ΔABI, ΔBGI, ΔGHI, ΔHAI, ΔBCJ, ΔCFJ, ΔFGJ, ΔGBJ, ΔCDK, ΔDEK, ΔCFK and ΔFCK = 12

Triangles formed from 2 triangles

= ΔABH, ΔABG, ΔBGH, ΔGHA, ΔBCG, ΔBCF, ΔCFG, ΔFGB, ΔCDF, ΔCDE, ΔDEF and ΔEFC = 12

Triangles formed from 4 triangles

= ΔHBF, ΔGCE, ΔAGC and ΔBFD = 4

∴Total number of triangles

$= 12 + 12 + 4$

$= 28$

For squares,

Total number of squares

= □ ABGH, □BCFG, □CDEF, □ IBJG and □ JCKF = 5

Hence, option (c) is correct.

15. Paper Folding and Paper Cutting

1. (b) The folded transparent sheet will appear as

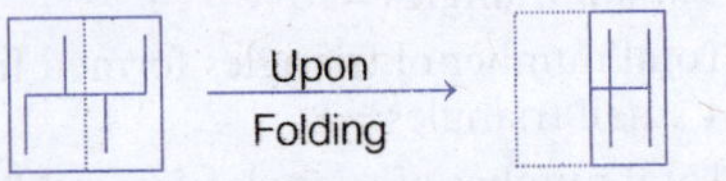

Hence, option (b) is correct.

2. (c) The folded transparent sheet will appear as

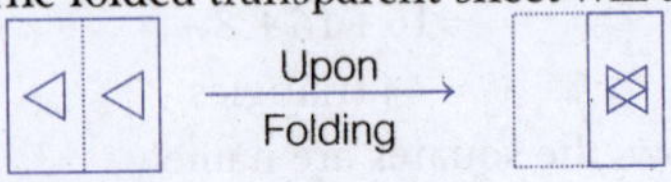

Hence, option (c) is correct.

3. (a) The folded transparent sheet will appear as

Hence, option (a) is correct.

4. (c) The folded transparent sheet will appear as

Hence, option (c) is correct.

5. (c) The folded transparent sheet will appear as

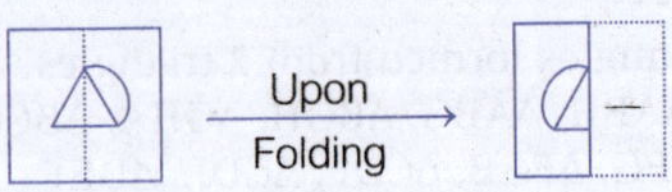

Hence, option (c) is correct.

6. (b) Upon unfolding the folded paper, represented by figure (Z), we get

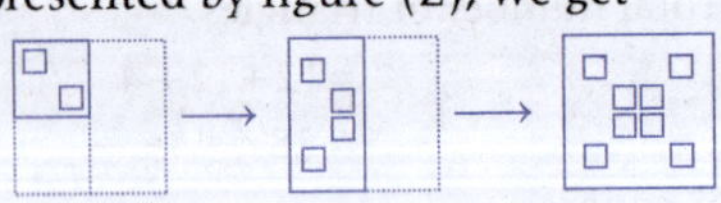

Z

Hence, option (b) is correct.

7. (a) Upon unfolding the folded paper, represented by figure (Z), we get

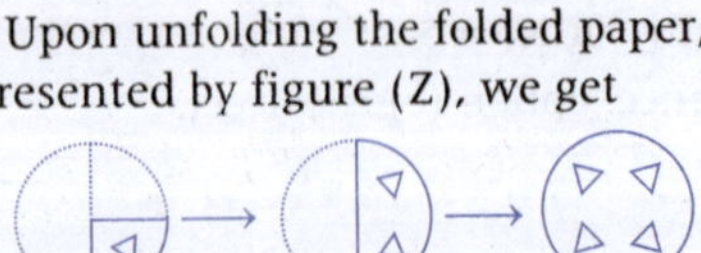

Z

Hence, option (a) is correct.

8. (d) Upon unfolding the folded paper, represented by figure (Z), we get

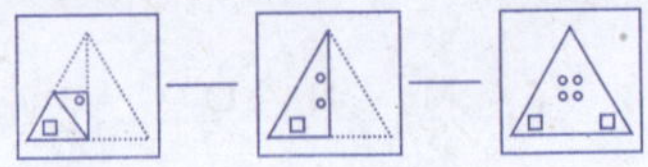

Z

Hence, option (d) is correct.

9. (d) Figure given in option (d) will show the unfolded pattern of the question figure.

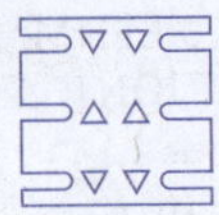

10. (b) Figure (b) will show the unfolded pattern of the question figure.

11. (a) Answer figure (a) follows the manner in which the paper is folded and punch is made.

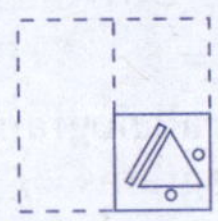

12. (a) Answer figure (a) follows the manner in which the paper is folded and punch is made.

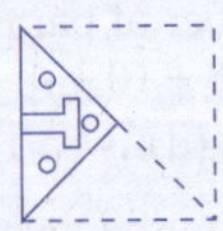

16. Dot Situation

1. (c)

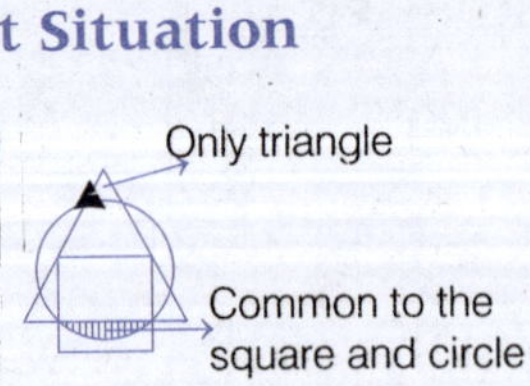

Hence, option (c) is correct.

2. (c)

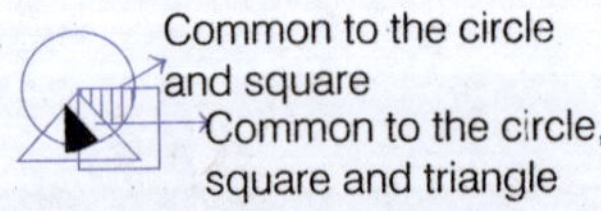

Hence, option (c) is correct.

3. (b)

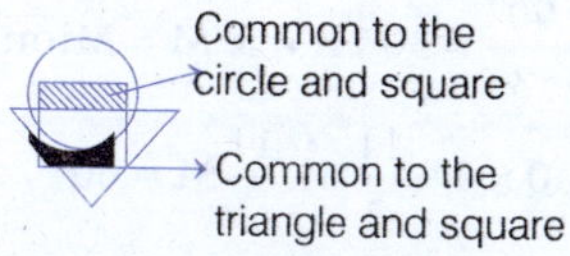

Hence, option (b) is correct.

4. (b)

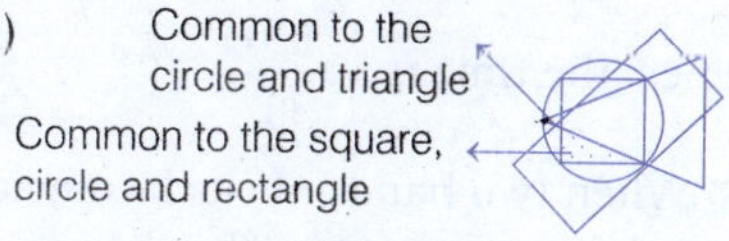

Hence, option (b) is correct.

5. (a)

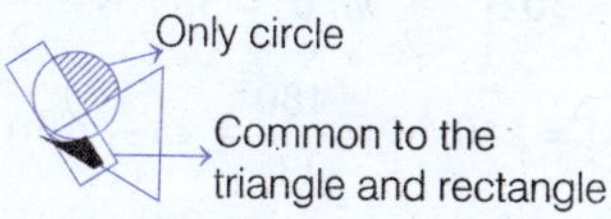

Hence, option (a) is correct.

6. (a)

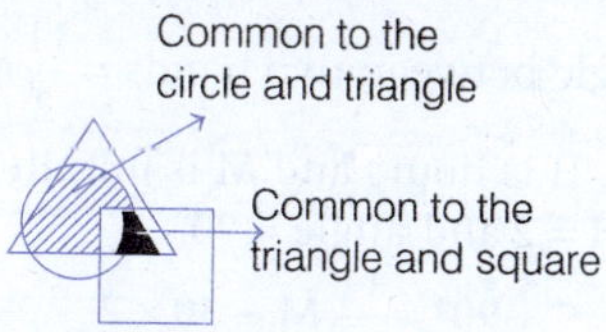

Hence, option (a) is correct.

7. (c)

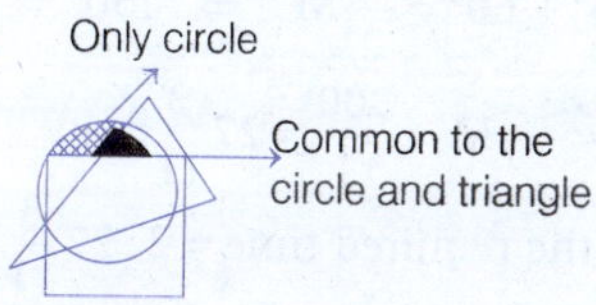

Hence, option (c) is correct.

8. (d)

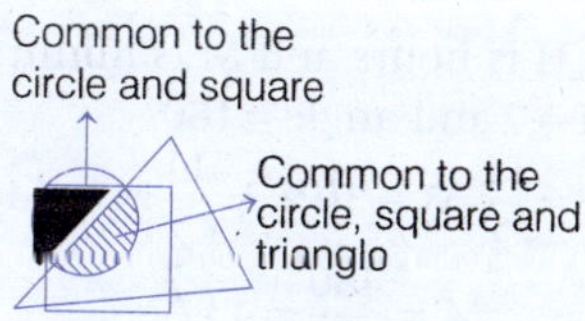

Hence, option (d) is correct.

9. (a)

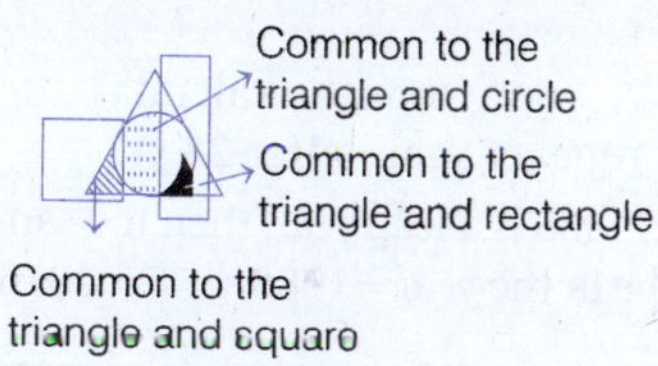

10. (a)

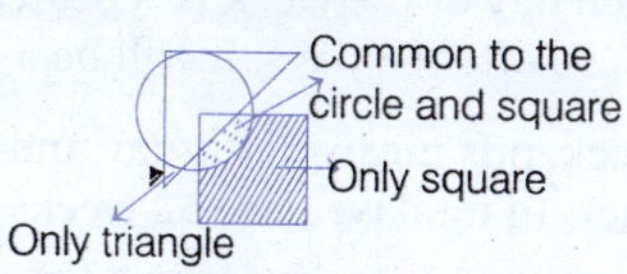

11. (c)

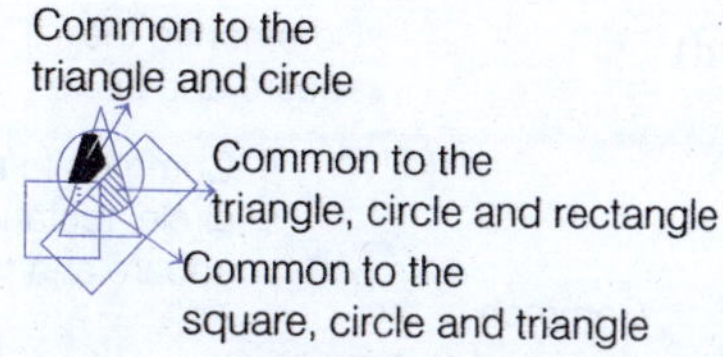

12. (d)

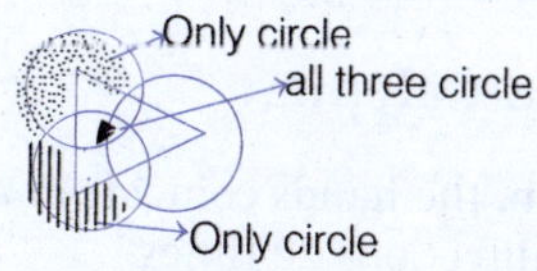

13. (d)

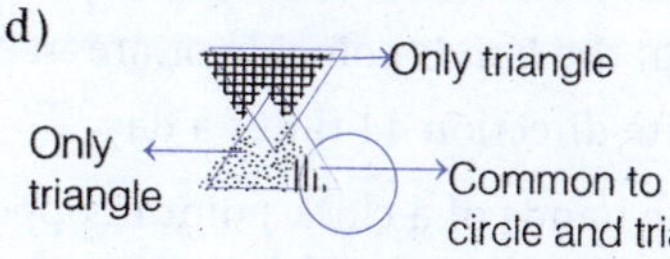

14. (c)

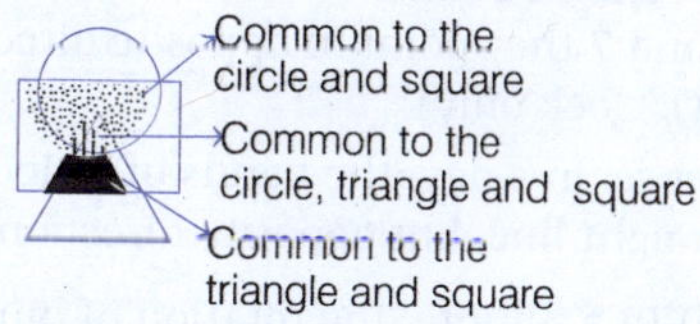

15. (a)

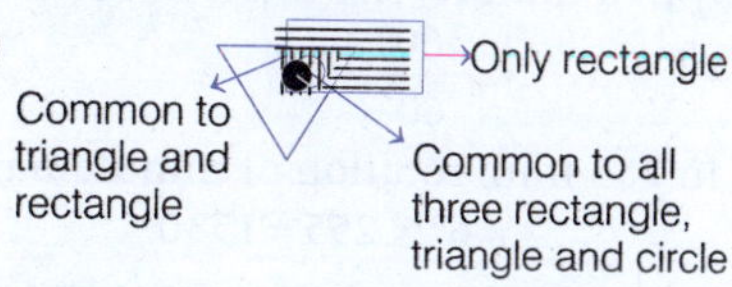

16. (a)

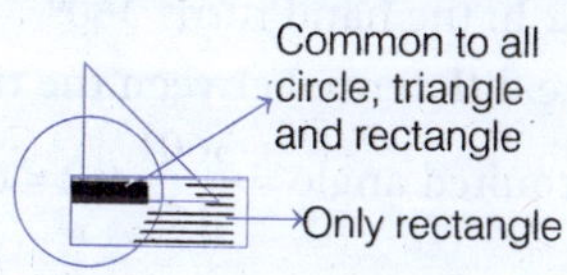

17. (c)

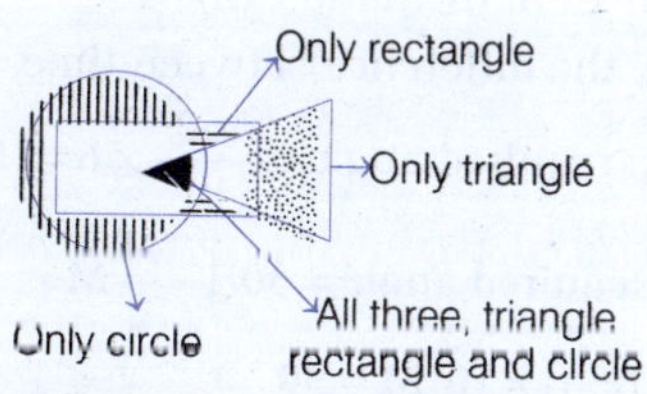

18. (b)

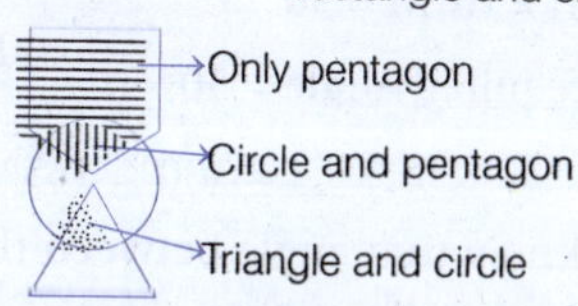

19. (d)

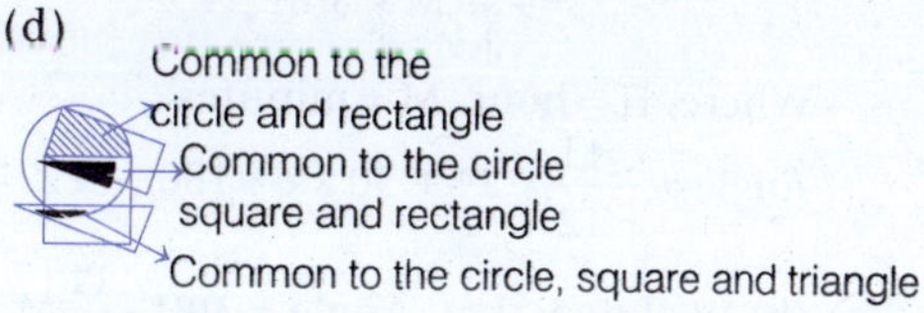

20. (d)

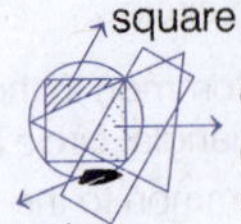

17. Clock and Calendar

1. (c) In 12 h, the hands coincide or are in opposite directions 22 times.
In 24 h, the hands coincide or are in opposite direction 44 times a day.

2. (b) The hands of a clock point in opposite direction 11 times in 12 h (because between 5 and 7 they point in opposite directions at 6 O, clock only).
Hence, in a day, the hands of a clock are in straight line, but opposite direction 22 times.

3. (b) In a minute, the rotation of minute hand $\pm\frac{360^o}{60}=6^o$
$\therefore$In 255 min, rotation of minute hand $=6^o\times 255=1530^o$

4. (b) In 12 h, the hand turns 360º.
Here, the difference between the time = 2 h
Then, required angle $=\frac{360^o}{12}\times 2=60^o$

5. (c) In 12 h, the hand turns 360º.
Here, the difference between time = 6 h
Thus, required angle $=\frac{360^o}{12}\times 6=180^o$

6. (d) Required angle $=30H-\frac{11}{2}M$
Where, H = 10, M = 30
Hence, required angle $=30\times 10-\frac{11}{2}\times 30$
$=300^o-165^o=135^o$

7. (d) We know that angle between the hands
$=-\frac{11}{12}M+30H$
Where, H = hour, M = minutes
Angle $=-\frac{11}{12}\times 24+30\times 6=180^o-22^o=158^o$

8. (b) We know that, Angle $=30H-\frac{11}{2}M$,
Angle $=\frac{90^o}{3}=30^o$, H = 3, M = Minutes
$30^o=30\times 3-\frac{11}{2}M,\ \frac{11}{2}M=60^o$
$M=\frac{120}{11}=1\frac{10}{11}$ min
Hence, the time is $3:\frac{120}{11}$.

9. (a) When two hands of clock coincide, the angle between them is 0º.
Angle $=30H-\frac{11}{2}M,\ 0^o=30\times 8-\frac{11}{2}\times M$
$\frac{11}{2}M=240,\ M=\frac{480}{11}=43\frac{7}{11}$ min
Hence, the time is $8:43\frac{7}{11}$.

10. (c) Angle between two hands $=\frac{11}{2}M-30H$
Where, H is hours and M is minutes.
Here, H = 2 and angle = 90º
$90^o=\frac{11}{2}M-30\times 2$
$90^\circ+60^\circ=\frac{11}{2}M \Rightarrow 150^\circ=\frac{11}{2}M$
$M=\frac{300}{11}=27\frac{3}{11}$
Hence, the required time $=2:27\frac{3}{11}$

11. (c) Angle between two hands $=\frac{11}{2}M-30H$
Where, H is hours and M is minutes.
Here, H = 2 and angle = 180º
$180^o=\frac{11}{2}M-30\times 2,\ \frac{11}{2}M=240$
$M=\frac{480}{11}=43\frac{7}{11}$
Hence, the required time $=02:43\frac{7}{11}$.

12. (c) We know that the calendar after a leap year repeats again after 28 yr.
Here, 1988 is a leap year, then the same calendar will be in the year = 1988 + 28 = 2016

13. (b) Each day of the week is repeated after 7 days, so after 63 days, it will be a Monday.

14. (a) Weekends means Saturday and Sunday together. In total we have 52 weeks in a year. So, there are 52 weekends in a year.

15. (a) Given year is divided by 4 and the quotient gives the number of leap years.

Here, $\frac{100}{4} = 25$

As, 100 is not a leap year

$\Rightarrow \quad 25 - 1 = 24$ leap year.

16. (a) 350 days $= \frac{350}{7} = 50$, weeks = no odd days

So, it will be a Saturday.

17. (b) On 31st December, 2005, it was Saturday. Number of odd days from 2006 to 2009

$= 1 + 1 + 2 + 1 = 5$ days

On 31st December 2009, it was Thursday. Thus, on 1st Jan 2010 it is Friday.

18. (b) The year 2006 is an ordinary year. So, it has 1 odd day. So, the day on 8th Dec 2007 will be 1 day beyond the day on 8th Dec 2006.

But 8th Dec 2007 is Saturday.

So, 8th Dec 2006 is Friday.

19. (d) The year 2004 is a leap year. It has 2 odd days. The day on 8th Feb, 2004 is 2 days before the day on 8th Feb, 2005.

Hence, this day is Sunday.

20. (b) The year 2007 is an ordinary year. So, it has 1 odd day. 1st day of 2007 was Monday.

1st day of year 2008 will be 1 day beyond Monday. Hence, it will be a Tuesday.

21. (b) Varun's birthday = 6 th Dec, 1989

Then, after 5 years 8 months and 22 days.

= 28 days 8 months and 1995

($\because$ 12 months = 1 year)

= 28.08.1995

22. (b) As month begins on Saturday. So 2nd, 9th, 16th, 23rd, 30th will be Sundays, while 8th and 22nd days are second and fourth Saturday.

Thus, there are 7 holidays in all.

Hence, number of working days $= 30 - 7$

$= 23$

23. (b) We shall find the day on 1st April 2001.

1st April 2001 = (2000 yr + Period from 1.1.2001 to 1.4.2001)

Odd days in 1600 yr = 0

Odd days in 400 yr = 0

Jan Feb March April

$31 + 28 + 31 + 1 = 91$ days 0 odd days

Total number of odd days $= 0 + 0 + 0 = 0$

On 1st April, 2001 it was Sunday.

In April, 2001, Wednesday falls on 4th, 11th, 18th and 25th.

24. (a) 15th August 2010 = (2009 yr + Period 1.1.2010 to 15.8.2010)

Odd days in 1600 yr = 0

Odd days in 400 yr = 0

9 yr = (2 leap years + 7 ordinary years)

$= (2 \times 2 + 7 \times 1) = 11 = 4$ odd days.

Jan Feb March April May Jun Jul Aug

$31 + 28 + 31 + 30 + 31 + 30 + 31 + 15$

$= 227$ days

$= 32$ weeks + 3 days

$= 3$ odd days

Total number of odd days

$= (0 + 0 + 4 + 3) = 7 = 0$ odd days.

Given day is Sunday.

25. (d) We know that hour hand moves $\frac{1^\circ}{2}$ in One minute, i.e. $6^\circ = 1$ min

So, $20^\circ = \frac{1}{1/2} \times 20 = 40$min

Hour hand cover 20° in 40 min.

Therefore, in 40 min, the minute hand covers $= 6^\circ \times 40^\circ = 240^\circ$